CITY OF NEW YORK

REPORT

OF

Colonel WILLIAM M. BLACK

Corps of Engineers, U. S. A.

AND

Professor EARLE B. PHELPS

CONCERNING THE

Location of Sewer Outlets

AND THE

Discharge of Sewage into New York Harbor

SUBMITTED TO THE

BOARD OF ESTIMATE AND APPORTIONMENT

MARCH 23, 1911

M. B. BROWN PRINTING & BINDING CO.,
49-57 PARK PLACE, NEW YORK.

1381–11–500

TABLE OF CONTENTS.

BOARD OF ESTIMATE AND APPORTIONMENT,
CITY OF NEW YORK,
March 14, 1911.

Hon. WILLIAM J. GAYNOR, *Mayor,*
Chairman of the Board of Estimate and Apportionment:

SIR—I beg to submit herewith the final report of Colonel William M. Black and Professor Earle B. Phelps, giving the result of their investigation as to the location of sewer outlets and the discharge of sewage into the waters about New York, which was authorized by resolution adopted by the Board of Estimate and Apportionment on November 12, 1909.

Five preliminary reports have already been submitted to the Board, as follows:

1. Drainage of Flushing District, April 22, 1910.
2. Drainage of Corona District, June 17, 1910.
3. Oxygen content as a standard, July 1, 1910.
4. Drainage of Jamaica District, January 12, 1911.
5. Drainage of Richmond District, March 9, 1911.

The present report gives the general result of their study of the circulation of the waters in the harbor and the capacity of these waters to receive sewage without undue pollution, with recommendations as to the standard of purity which should be maintained in the different portions of the harbor. These studies are based upon the constitution of the water in the different portions of the harbor as the result of the tidal movements and the mixture of sewage bearing waters with clean sea water entering the harbor from the sea at Sandy Hook and from Long Island Sound at Throgs Neck, and the water from the Hudson River, which is already more or less polluted. For the purpose of this investigation and the computations, they have divided the harbor into seven different areas, namely, the Lower and Upper Bays, the Hudson River, below and above Ninety-sixth street, the East River, below and above Hell Gate, and the Harlem River.

The degree of pollution and the capacity of the harbor waters to care for additional sewage is expressed in terms of the dissolved oxygen remaining in the water, and the recommendation in this final report is that 70 per cent. of the saturation value of dissolved oxygen would be a proper standard of purity to be maintained if possible.

The report contains a discussion of the renewal of the oxygen content of water by absorption from the atmosphere and by aeration through disturbances caused by wind, by passing vessels, and by tidal currents. It appears to be conclusively shown that the extent of the renewal of the normal oxygen content by these agencies has been greatly overestimated, and that their effect is so slight as to be almost negligible. The belief is expressed that were all the sewage of the City discharged at Throgs Neck or at the Narrows, that is, at the points of entrance of unpolluted sea water into the harbor, a safe limit of pollution could be maintained without treatment of the sewage until the population shall have reached more than 7,000,000. It is also believed that crude sewage can safely be discharged in the vicinity of Riker's Island or the Narrows for some years to come, but that at other points partial purification will soon be necessary, at least during the summer months, while even with such partial purification a proper system of discharge and dispersion will be necessary.

The report gives the results of a series of experiments to determine the practicability of a system of forced aeration following a short period of septic treatment, the estimated cost of which is given at $2.00 per million gallons of sewage treated, with the probability of a material reduction as the result of further experiment. The suggestions in this and previous reports as to the details of the sewerage plans for different parts of the City must not be considered as anything more than suggestions, but they appear so reasonable that it is believed that they will be found in their general features to be logical and practicable and along lines which will commend themselves to the several Borough Presidents in the completion of their drainage plans.

The amount of work which has been done within the limits of time and funds which were available is quite remarkable, and these results could not have been obtained except for the fact that the investigations of the United States Coast and Geodetic Survey and of the United States Engineer Corps were fully availed of. In discussing the question of the pollution of the waters of the harbor and the necessity for treating sewage discharging into them, the absence of any accepted standard by which the degree of pollution and the necessity for treatment could be judged, has been a serious handicap. It may be that the use of the percentage of the saturation value of dissolved oxygen will furnish a standard which can be generally accepted. Colonel Black and Professor Phelps have suggested that 70 per cent. of this value would be a proper standard of purity which the City should endeavor to maintain, but they admit that this whole matter is one upon which there is at present much difference of opinion, and I believe that if this question could be submitted to a committee of especially qualified engineers for a report as to a proper standard for the harbor waters, the conclusion of such a committee would be accepted not only by the City of New York, but by other cities similarly situated, and that a valuable contribution would be made to the vexed subject of the protection of navigable waters from undue pollution by the sewage of great seacoast cities.

The experiments already referred to may, if continued, produce results of considerable economic value. They were started at the Twenty-sixth Ward sewage disposal plant, in the Borough of Brooklyn, and they could be continued at this plant under the supervision of the President of the Borough of Brooklyn at an expense which would be small in comparison with the value of the results which may be attained. An enlargement of this plant will probably be necessary in the near future, and in planning such enlargement provision could well be made for experimental work on the lines suggested.

I would recommend that the Board appoint a commission of five engineers, to consist of Colonel William M. Black, a representative to be designated by the Metropolitan Sewerage Commission, and three others who are generally recognized as authorities in this particular field of engineering work, and that such commission be instructed to advise the Board of Estimate and Apportionment at as early a date as possible of their conclusions as to the percentage of the saturation value of dissolved oxygen which the City should strive to maintain in the waters of the harbor of New York.

I would also recommend that the President of the Borough of Brooklyn be requested to continue the investigations inaugurated by Colonel Black and Professor Phelps to determine the feasibility of an economic application of the treatment of sewage by forced aeration, and to advise the Board of the result of such investigations and experiments.

It is further recommended that the Secretary be authorized and directed to have five hundred (500) copies of this report printed as a pamphlet, together with the five preliminary reports as appendices.

Respectfully,

NELSON P. LEWIS,
Chief Engineer.

New York, February 16, 1911.

Mr. Nelson P. Lewis,
Chief Engineer,
Board of Estimate and Apportionment,
277 Broadway, New York City:

Sir—We have the honor to submit the following final report of the work done under the directions contained in your letters of October 11 and November 18 and 20, 1909, and the terms of acceptance named in the letter of Colonel Black, dated December 21, 1909.

In brief, the problems laid before us were to determine the most advantageous points for sewage discharge for the areas draining into the East River from the districts of Greater New York on Long Island to the east of Newtown Creek; for the portion of the Borough of The Bronx draining into the same waterway; for the drainage areas tributary to Jamaica Bay, including Far Rockaway and Coney Island, and for the Borough of Richmond; and further, to determine the degree of purification, if any, to which the sewage would have to be subjected before discharge in order that the waters in question should not be polluted unduly thereby.

The solution of the problems involves:

1. The determination of a standard of purity for the harbor waters.

2. A study of the circulation of these waters through the various parts of the harbor, with a view to determining for each part the general constitution of the waters in that part during any one tidal period, what proportion of the total volume had come direct from the unpolluted waters of the sea or Sound and what proportion from other parts of the harbor, where, for a greater or less period, they had been receiving sewage.

3. A study of the capacity of the waters of each part to receive sewage without undue pollution, including in this a study of the sources of supply of oxygen.

4. A study of an economical method of partial purification, applicable to the conditions of New York.

5. A study of the terrain of the various districts, of present and expected population, of the drainage areas from which sewage can be collected, of the lines along which it can be moved for disposal, of the volumes of sewage to be provided for, of the available points for discharge, and finally for each district, of the degree of purification demanded by the capacity of the portion of the harbor in question to care for the sewage without undue pollution.

For this work one year's time and $10,000 were available. It was found that under these conditions the field work had to be limited to the determination of the dissolved oxygen in the waters at the harbor entrances and to the experimental work required to develop the method of partial purification. In the studies, existing maps had to be used for the terrain and existing data for the circulation of the waters in the harbor.

The results of our investigations may be briefly summarized as follows:

(1) The amount of dissolved oxygen in the harbor waters furnishes the most satisfactory criterion of the purity of these waters. We believe that this natural purifying agent should not be drawn upon to an extent which

will reduce it below 70 per cent. of the full saturation value. This standard of purity refers not only to average conditions throughout the harbor and its tributaries, but also to the average condition within any of the sub-areas into which for the purposes of this study we have divided these waters.

(2) We have shown that the circulation of water through these various sub-areas makes the condition of each dependent to a large extent upon the conditions in one or more of the others. We have determined these complex relationships with a reasonable degree of accuracy and in this way have been able to determine the most suitable points for sewage discharge and the probable effect of such discharge not only upon the area immediately adjacent, but upon the entire body of water under consideration. If the sewage of the entire drainage area tributary to these waters could be concentrated at the two entrances, namely, at the Narrows and at Throgs Neck, we estimate that the standard of purity laid down could be maintained, for the present at least, and for the immediate future until such a time that the population of this entire district has reached 7.4 millions. Such an arrangement would develop the fullest use of the natural purifying agencies. Any other system of discharge will result, even under present conditions of population, in the production of local conditions below our proposed standard. That standard can be maintained at present by purifying the sewage which enters these waters at other points than those indicated to a degree which will reduce its oxygen requirements to one-third their present value.

(3) The partial purification proposed in the last sentence will maintain our proposed standard of purity also in each of the several sub-areas considered, providing a proper system of discharge and dispersion be employed in each case. Under the present unsatisfactory method of discharge local nuisances are created and would continue to exist even after the purification which we have indicated had been established. These are due not to insufficient volumes of water as compared with the volume of sewage discharged, but to the fact that the fullest use of this water cannot be attained under existing conditions. In studying the sources of oxygen available for purification we have found that a serious misconception exists of the importance of reaeration by partially de-aerated waters. We have determined that this reaeration factor is one that is without material significance in the case of the waters of New York Harbor.

(4) We have determined by experiments upon a practical scale made both at Brooklyn and at Boston, that a degree of purification which will reduce the oxygen requirements of the sewage to one-third their present value during the summer months, can be obtained by a short period of septic treatment followed by forced aeration. The cost of such treatment will not exceed all told two dollars per million gallons, and further studies will doubtless make it possible to reduce this cost materially.

(5) Our studies of main drainage schemes are included in four appendices to this report and summarized in Chapter IV. herein. Separate schemes are submitted for the four drainage areas designated, Flushing, Corona, Jamaica and Richmond Drainage Areas, respectively.

These studies were necessary in order that feasible points of discharge might be located and they have been worked out only in detail sufficient to determine the feasibility of our proposed discharge points. While they have been made to conform as far as possible with existing and proposed works, they are in no sense offered as complete or final drainage plans. We have shown the most advantageous point of final discharge in each case and the feasibility of concentrating the drainage of the district at these points. If better lines and grades exist they can undoubtedly be found by a proper and thorough study of the situation.

The problems involved are of great magnitude and the importance to New York of their correct solution can hardly be exaggerated. In presenting this, their final report, the writers realize its incompleteness as regards some of the questions involved. They feel, however, that the lines they have followed are correct and that their studies will at least make more plain the path for further investigation.

We recommend that further investigations be directed along the following lines:

(1) The establishment of a standard of purity upon a firmer basis of fact than that which now exists. We realize fully that this standard is the foundation stone of our work; we also realize that this whole matter is one upon which there are differences of opinion and that these opinions have but a slight satisfactory basis of observed facts. This is a matter which should be made the subject of the most thorough investigation possible, the results of which should be submitted to the impartial judgment of a commission of engineers for final settlement.

(2) We further recommend, in view of the favorable results of our experimental work, that the Twenty-sixth Ward Disposal Plant be equipped for the purification of the sewage now flowing through it by the process of aeration which we have developed in order that the merits and economy of this process may be more fully and finally determined. This project should in no sense be regarded as an experiment, since the process has already been carried through the experimental stage, and since, as we have shown, some purification of the sewage from this district will be required in the near future. At the same time the results obtained at this plant and the improvements in the process which will necessarily result from a careful study of the proposed plant, will be of immediate value in the solution of the final problem of disposal at other points throughout the Greater City.

(3) Finally, we recommend a careful study of the whole matter of sewage discharge with reference to the proper dispersion of the sewage stream in the body of water into which it flows. Neglect of this matter is bound to result in serious local nuisances and will render it impossible to utilize to the point of fullest economy the natural purifying agencies which exist.

Very respectfully,

W. M. Black,
Earle B. Phelps.

Capacity of New York Harbor to Receive and Reduce Sewage

BY

W. M. BLACK
Colonel, Corps of Engineers, U. S. A.
Member, American Society of Civil Engineers

AND

EARLE B. PHELPS
Professor of Chemical Biology, Massachusetts Institute of Technology
Consulting Sanitary Engineer, Assoc. American Society of Civil Engineers

---

FEBRUARY 16, 1911

CONTENTS OF FINAL REPORT.

CONTENTS—Continued.

TABLES.

PLATES AND DIAGRAMS.

CONTENTS—Continued.

CHAPTER I.

1. Standard of Purity for the Harbor Waters.

It is only within recent years that well-founded complaints have been made about the foulness of the harbor waters. As yet, to the superficial observer, only small portions of these waters are manifestly in a condition to be regarded as a nuisance. The condition has come gradually and with the increase of population. The increase continues, and it is certain that unless remedial measures are taken greater and greater portions of the harbor will be reduced to the conditions of the Gowanus Canal, for example. For years the capacity of the harbor waters was sufficient to receive and digest without injury the sewage of the population of the harbor drainage area. Gradually the volume of sewage poured into them and into the rivers tributary to them has increased until to-day the higher classes of fish have disappeared, bathing in them has become unpleasant, if not dangerous, and portions of them in appearance and smell have more the characteristics of drains than of living waters. From a technical standpoint the most simple measure of the pollution of any waterway is found in the proportion of dissolved oxygen contained therein. Pure, living water contains dissolved oxygen to its saturation value, in an amount which is different for fresh water and for sea water and which varies with the temperature. The amount of oxygen found at saturation in fresh water is 6.38 grains per cubic foot at 32 degrees Fahrenheit and 4.04 grains per cubic foot at 68 degrees. For sea water the corresponding figures are 5.10 grains and 3.29 grains. Sewage as delivered at the sewer mouth is in a highly putrescible condition, and the putrefaction is continued after diffusion in a waterway, robbing the water of its oxygen on the one hand, but on the other reducing the organic materials of the sewage into stable and innocuous forms. The effect on the water is practically harmless when not used for domestic purposes, until this diminution of its oxygen has continued through a considerable percentage of the saturation volume. For example, probably the first indication of pollution is the disappearance of major fish life, for the existence of which 70 per cent. of the saturation volume of oxygen is necessary. Other forms of fish life can exist until the limit of 30 per cent. has been reached. When the remaining volume of dissolved oxygen in a stream falls below 50 per cent., the stream may at times become turbid and noisome during hot weather, as is illustrated in the Passaic River, in which in the neighborhood of the Pennsylvania Railroad bridge on January 19, 1911, the dissolved oxygen was found to have about 38 per cent. of the saturation value. When reduced below 30 per cent., the condition of the water is such as to constitute a nuisance during the summer season. When any standard is fixed, the amount of sewage which can be poured into the waters without purification is also fixed, though this amount will be greater in winter than in summer on account of the slower rate of putrefaction in cold weather and the greater amount of dissolved oxygen found in the water. Therefore, a higher standard entails greater expense for sewage purification maintenance than a lower. On the other hand, it is practically impossible to obtain or maintain an even diffusion of sewage through the waters of any large waterway. The adoption of a high standard affords greater certainty that no portion of the waterway shall be polluted to a known degree.

After a careful consideration of the whole question, the writers recommend that for New York 70 per cent. of the saturation value be adopted as the standard below which the dissolved oxygen in its harbor waters be not permitted to fall—a standard of which the maintenance can be made evident by the existence of the major fish life formerly so abundant here. The calculations of the capacity of the harbor to receive sewage given hereafter are based on this standard.

2. Circulation of the Waters in the Harbor.

The sources of the harbor waters are the discharge of the streams tributary to them, the direct drainage from the shores and the tidal influx of sea water through the Sandy Hook and Throgs Neck entrances. Originally all of these sources were unpolluted. To-day the streams are polluted by the drainage from the population along their shores. The Passaic is polluted to a degree which has caused an expensive project to be proposed by the State of New Jersey, under which all of the sewage from the district draining into it is to be collected and after partial purification, as required by the United States authorities, is to be discharged into the Upper Bay near Robbins Reef. This project when carried out will better the existing conditions under which these polluted waters are now emptied through Newark Bay and the Kill von Kull, purified only by the comparatively small amount of reaeration and sedimentation they receive in the passage through Newark Bay. Recent observations made by the United States in a section of the Hudson just above the northern limit of Greater New York show that during the low water period, that stream has been polluted to beyond a safe limit before it reaches the harbor. The direct drainage from the shores is also now a source of pollution. The only unpolluted source of supply is then the sea. Observations made in Ambrose Channel in February, 1910, show that the waters brought in by the flood tide there contain 98 per cent. of the saturation amount of the dissolved oxygen. Other observations at Throgs Neck entrance from the Sound made in January, 1910, show that the ebb (westerly) waters there contain oxygen to 90 per cent. of the saturation value.

Careful observations and analyses of the circulation of the waters in New York Harbor were made by the U. S. Coast and Geodetic Survey through a series of years ending in 1886. Subsequent observations and measurements of the currents in the Harlem have been made by the Engineer Department, U. S. Army. From the record of these observations the following studies have been made:

Plate No. 1 shows a map of the harbor of New York. The circulation of the waters therein is the result of harbor currents caused by two tidal waves, the crest of one of which reaches Sandy Hook at 7½ hours after the time of lunar culmination, while that of the other arrives at the Throgs Neck entrance from the Sound three hours later. The induced waves meet and interfere over two routes between these points; one via the East River direct and the other via the Hudson, Harlem and East Rivers. The currents are the result of the slopes produced by these waves. A full descrip-

PLATE 1

NEW YORK HARBOR
NEW JERSEY
Long Island Sound
Bronx.
East R.
Queens.
Area F
Area G
Area D
Manhattan
Area C
Area E
Upper Bay
Newark Bay
Kill Van Kull
Brooklyn
Area B
Jamaica Bay
Richmond
ARTHUR KILL
Coney Is.
Rockaway
Area A
Lower Bay
Sandy Hook.
ATLANTIC OCEAN.
NOTE: Figures show channel distances
in miles from bar at Sandy Hook

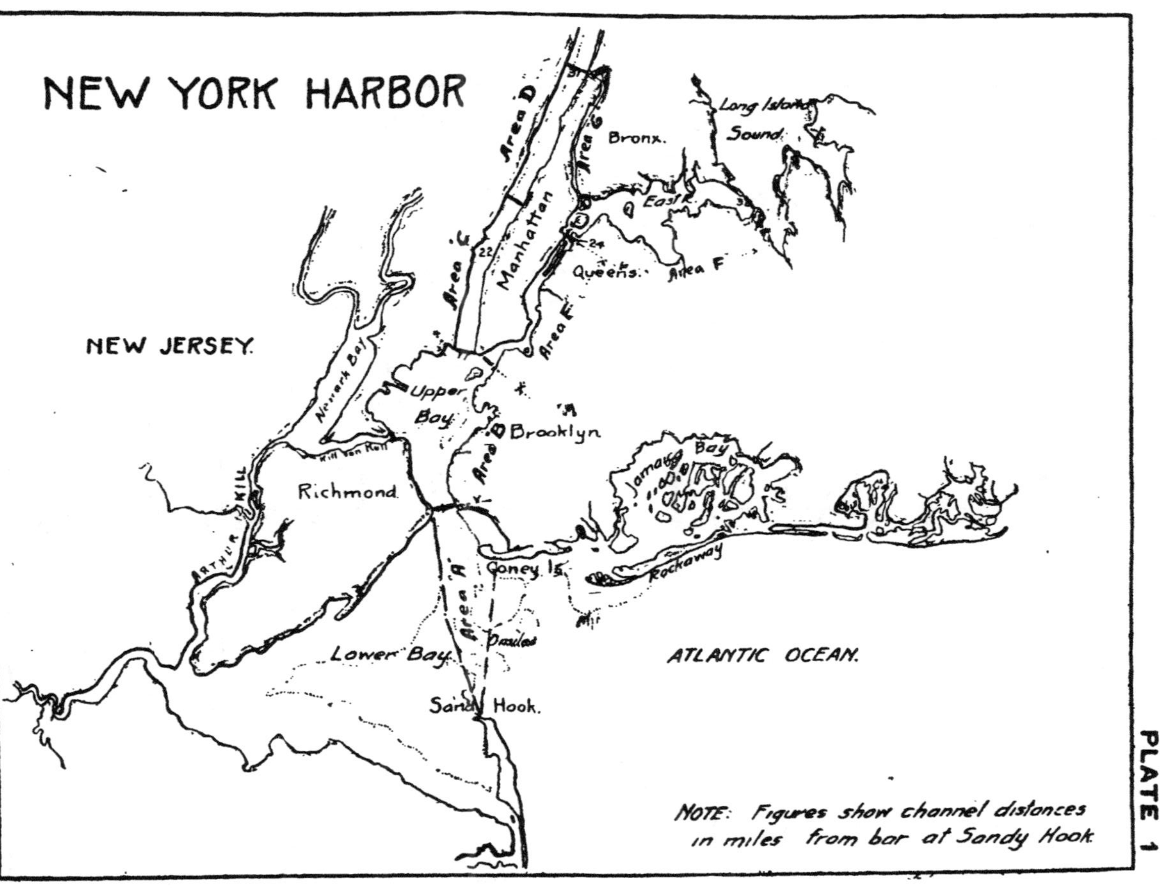

PLATE 2

MEAN TIDAL AND VELOCITY CURVES.
The Narrows, N.Y. Harbor.
Velocities, feet per second.
Flood
Ebb
Tide.
Velocity.
M.S.L. Sandy Hook
Fine dotted lines show stages of tide at which current directions change.
Lunar Hours after Moon's Transit
Tidal Heights, feet.

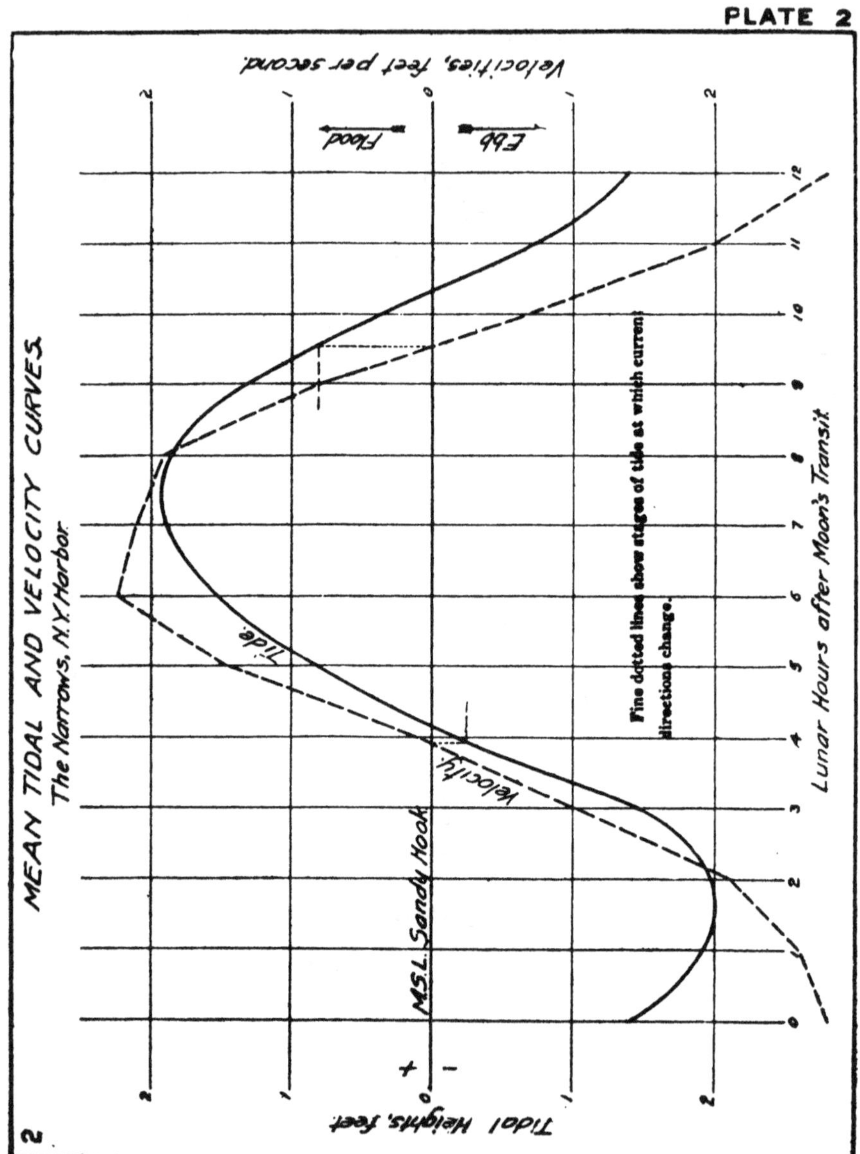

PLATE 3

3
MEAN TIDAL AND VELOCITY CURVES.
42nd St., Hudson River.
M.S.L., Sandy Hook.
Velocity.
Tide.
Tidal Heights, Feet.
Velocities, feet per second.
North.
South.
Fine dotted lines show stages of tide at which current directions change.
Lunar Hours after Moon's Transit.

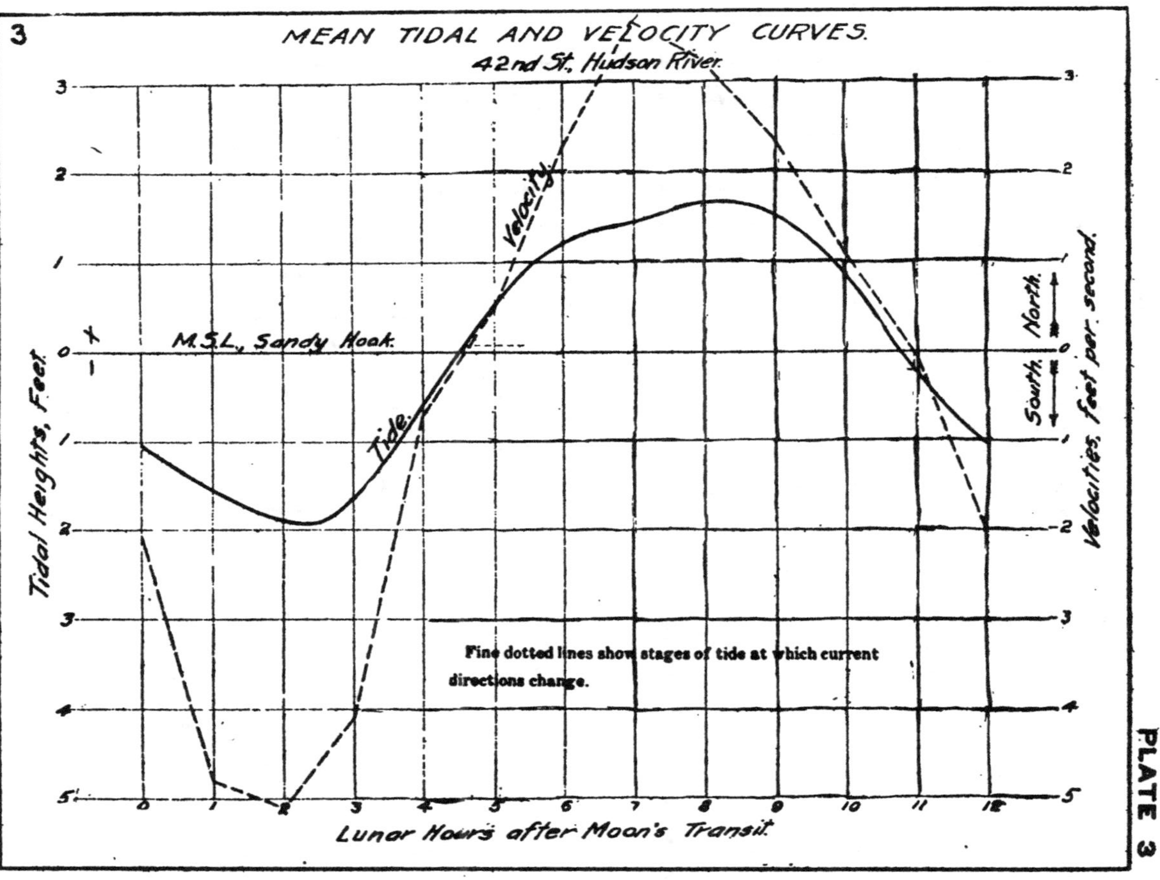

PLATE 4

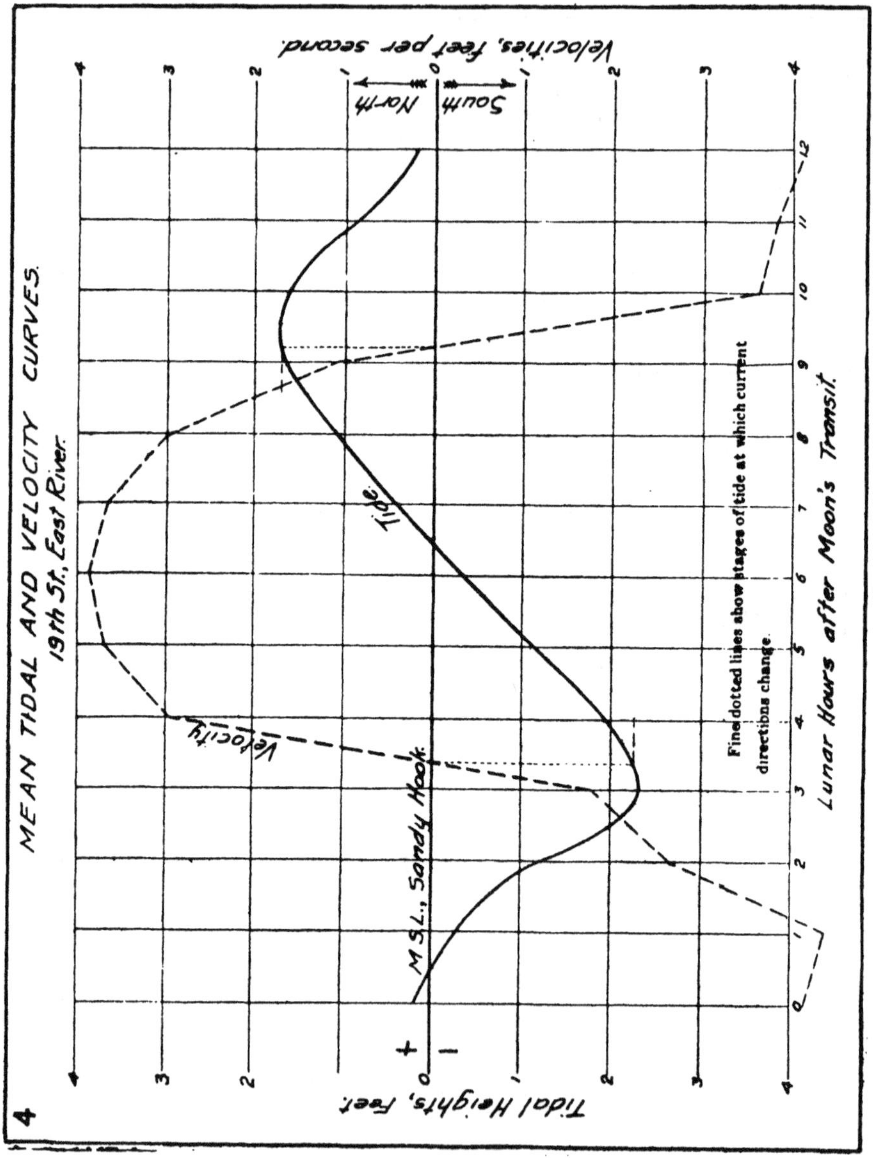

MEAN TIDAL AND VELOCITY CURVES.

19th St., East River.

Velocities, feet per second.

North

South

Tidal Heights, Feet.

M.S.L., Sandy Hook.

Tide.

Velocity

Fine dotted lines show stages of tide at which current directions change.

Lunar Hours after Moon's Transit.

4

PLATE 5

5
MEAN TIDAL AND VELOCITY CURVES.
Throgs Neck, East River.
Fine dotted lines show stages of tide at which current directions change.
Tidal Heights, Feet.
M.S.L., Sandy Hook.
Tide.
Velocity
West
East
Velocities, feet per second.
Lunar Hours after Moon's Transit.

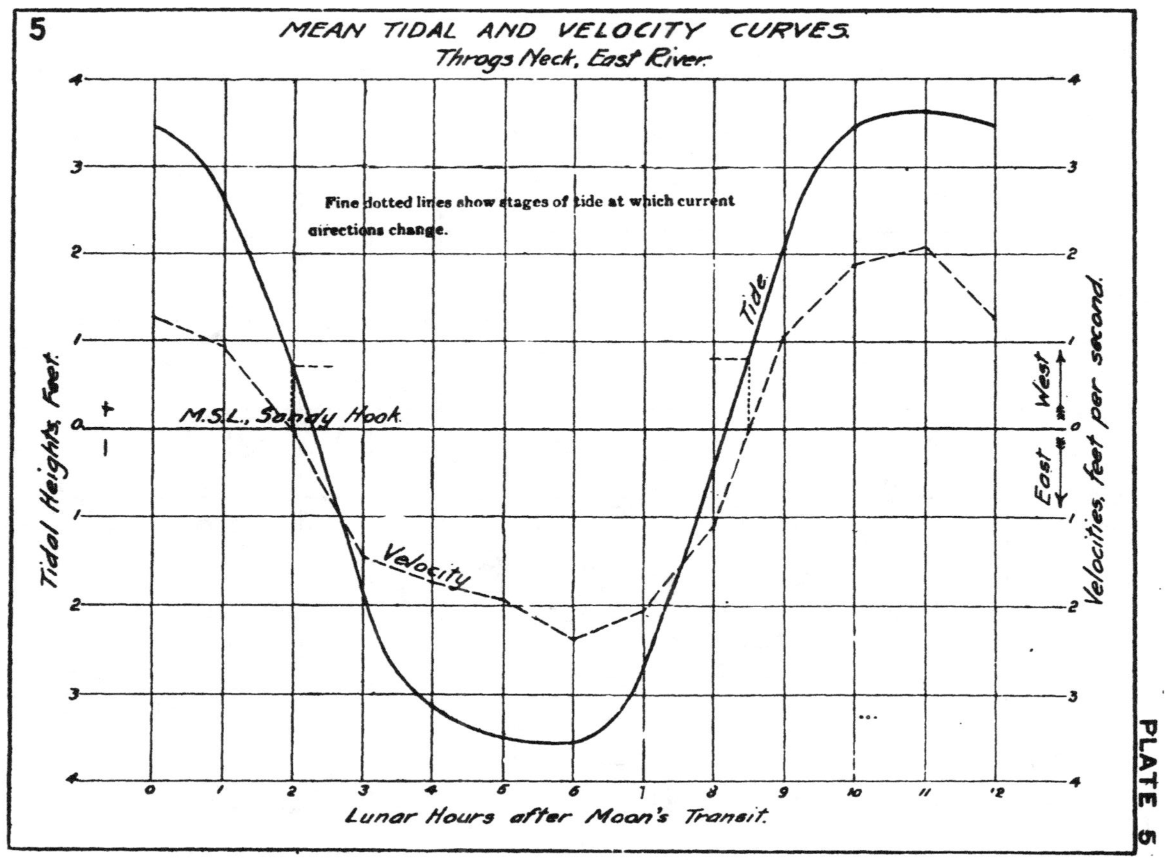

PLATE 6

MEAN TIDAL CURVES.
New York Harbor.
Tidal Heights, feet.
Lunar Hours after Moon's Transit
Throgs Neck
Hell Gate
E. 19th St.
W. 42nd St.
Narrows
Sandy Hook
M.S.L. Sandy Hook.
Tidal Heights, Feet.
6

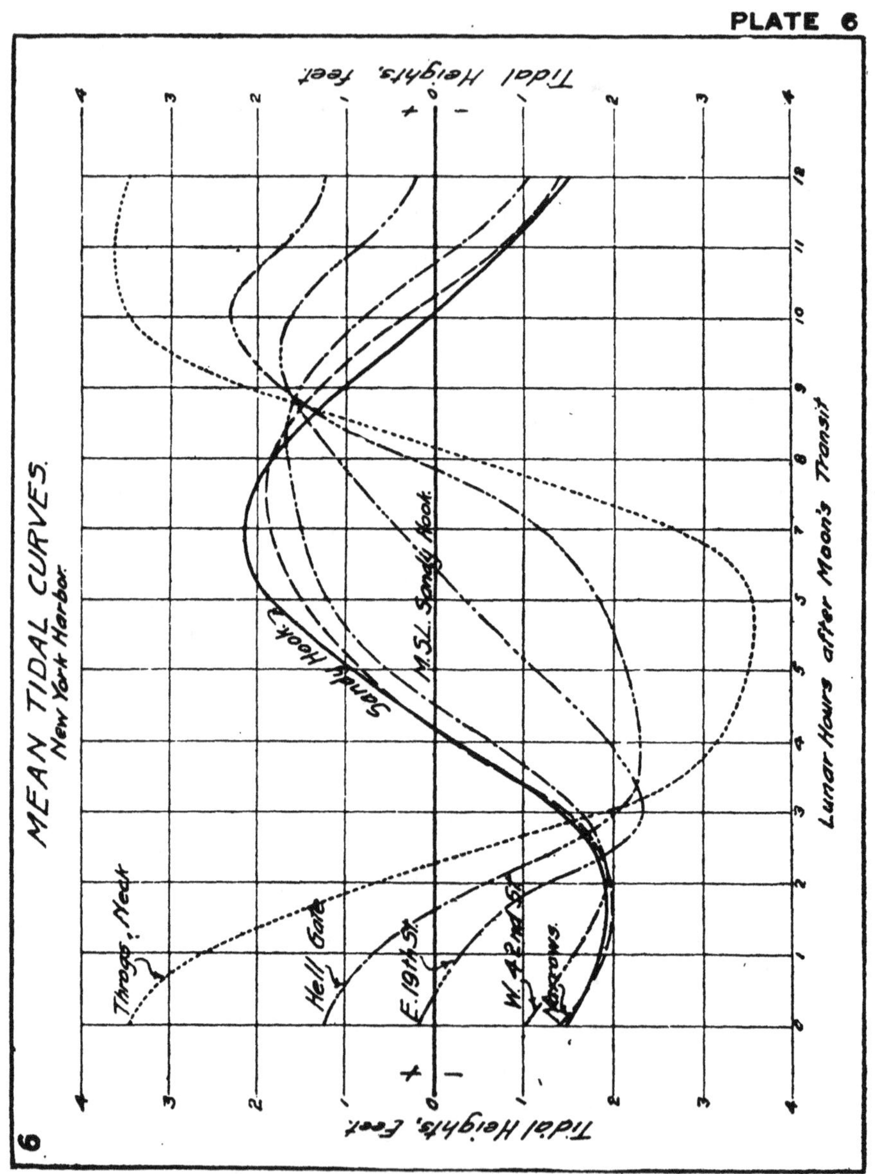

PLATE 7

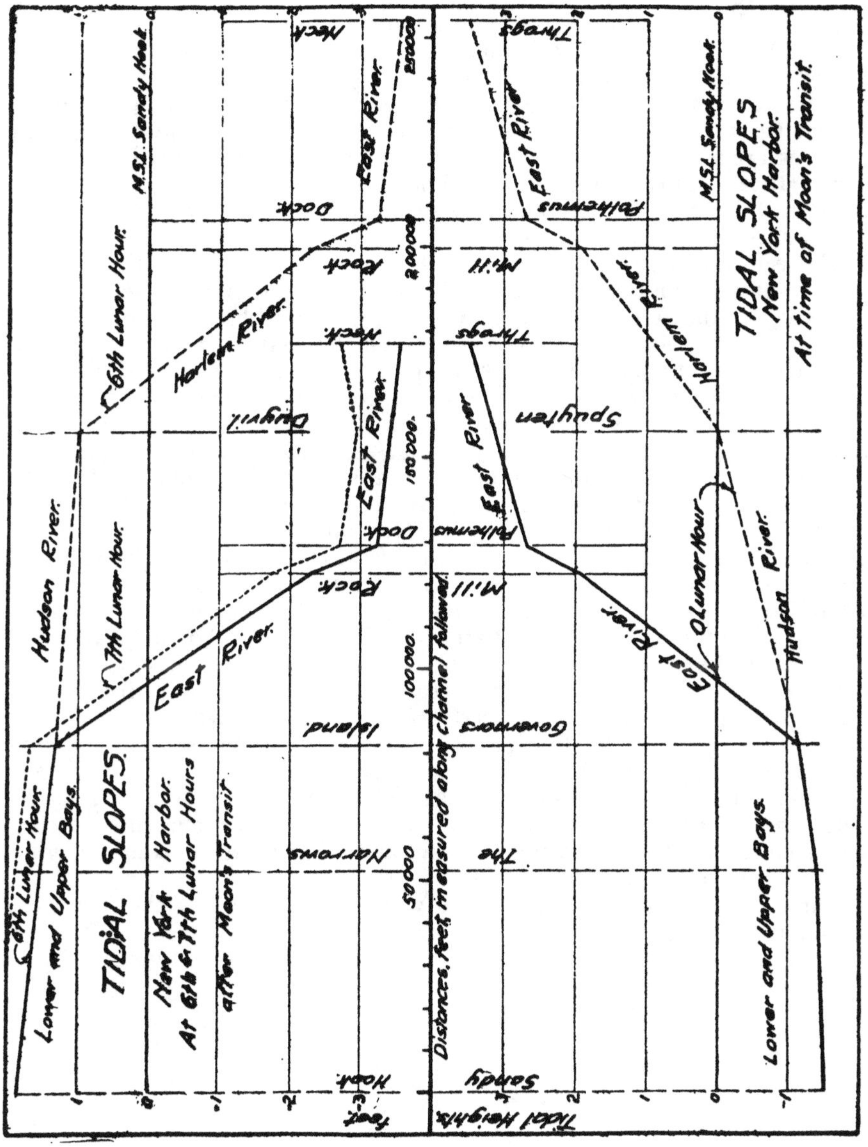

TIDAL SLOPES
New York Harbor.
At 6th & 7th Lunar Hours
after Moon's Transit

TIDAL SLOPES
New York Harbor.
At time of Moon's Transit.

Distances, feet, measured along channel followed.

Tidal Heights.

Feet

Sandy Hook — The Narrows — Governors Island — Mill Rock — Polhemus Dock — Spuyten Duyvil — Throgs Neck — Mill Rock — Polhemus Dock — Throgs Neck

Lower and Upper Bays. — Hudson River. — East River. — Harlem River. — M.S.L. Sandy Hook.

6th Lunar Hour. — 7th Lunar Hour. — 0 Lunar Hour.

50000 — 100000. — 150000. — 200000 — 250000

tion of these currents for each lunar hour is printed in Appendix No. 9 of the Report for 1888 of the U. S. Coast and Geodetic Survey, reproduced on pages 158-171 of the Report of the Metropolitan Sewerage Commission of New York for 1910.

Plates Nos. 2, 3, 4 and 5 show the changes in level of the water surface and the velocities and directions of the currents induced in the Narrows, in the Hudson River at Forty-second street, in the East River at Nineteenth street and at Throgs Neck, respectively.

Plate No. 6 shows these tidal curves superposed. In general it may be said that the current directions at any hour between the points for which the curves are given may be determined from the relative elevations of the water surface at those points at that time.

Plate No. 7 shows tidal slopes in the harbor at the time of lunar culmination and six hours later.

The velocities of the currents and the volumes of water will vary with the range of tides on different days. In the Hudson they are also modified by the stage of the river. The shallow and obstructed channels of the Little Hell Gate and Bronx Kills passages between the Harlem and East Rivers cause marked variations in the flow through the Harlem for tides of different ranges, and consequently a difference in the relative volumes passing by the two routes between the Sandy Hook and Throgs Neck entrances to the harbor.

The measurement of the volumes of tidal flow in any channel is difficult, due to the constant variation of velocity through all parts of the section measured and also due to the fact that frequently the currents at the top and bottom of the section are flowing in different directions. The volumes given hereafter for the flow at Sandy Hook and the Narrows and in the East and Hudson Rivers are taken from the reports of the Coast and Geodetic Survey and are the results of calculations by Prof. Henry Mitchell, who was in charge of the observations. To avoid confusion, the currents will be denoted as " ebb " and "flood," respectively, as shown by the direction of the flow with relation to the Sandy Hook entrance. It will be noted then that the term " ebb " at the Throggs Neck entrance will be used for currents from the Sound into the East River, and that the term " flood " at Throgs Neck will denote currents from the East River into the Sound. Similarly, in the Harlem River the term " ebb " will be used for currents flowing north from the East River to the Hudson, and " flood " for currents flowing south from the Hudson into the East River.

The following table will show the volumes assumed for the flow past the sections named, during flood and ebb:

TABLE I.

Sandy Hook—		
Flood	23,322,888,000	cubic feet.
Ebb	24,658,449,000	" "
Narrows—		
Flood	12,703,616,480	" "
Ebb	13,819,895,144	" "
East River at Nineteenth street—		
Flood	4,007,175,676	" "
Ebb	4,454,937,257	" "
East River at Throgs Neck—		
Flood	4,257,000,000	" "
Ebb	4,689,000,000	" "
Hudson River at Thirty-ninth street—		
Flood	6,225,985,545	" "
Ebb	6,996,678,413	" "
Harlem River at Two Hundred and Sixteenth street—		
Flood	227,531,520	" "
Ebb	231,840,200	" "
Kill von Kull—		
Flood	1,712,415,362	" "
Ebb	1,790,103,372	" "

For convenience in the following discussion the waters of the harbor have been divided as follows:

A—Lower Bay, east of a line drawn from Sandy Hook through West Bank Light to Fort Wadsworth Light.
B—Upper Bay.
C—Hudson River, from Battery to West Ninety-sixth street.
D—Hudson River, from West Ninety-sixth street to Spuyten Duyvil.
E—East River, from Battery to Hell Gate.
F—East River, from Hell Gate to Throgs Neck.
G—Harlem River.

As exemplified in Plates 2 to 6, the change of current direction from flood to ebb or from ebb to flood does not in all cases coincide with the change in direction of the tidal rise or fall; in other words, does not come at either high or low water. In determining the amount of water flowing into or from any one of these areas during any tidal period it is necessary to compute the volumes with reference to the elevation of the surface plane at the beginning of the period and the change of elevation during the period.

TABLE 2.

Showing Changes in Elevation of Water Surface During Flood and Ebb Current Periods Referred to Plane of Mean Low Water.

Area.	Current.	Elevation at Beginning of Tidal Period.	Maximum or Minimum Elevation; Mean Range of Tide.	Elevation at End of Tidal Period.
A—Lower bay	Flood	0.4	4.0	3.4
	Ebb	3.4	0.0	0.4
B—Upper bay	Flood	1.7	3.9	2.8
	Ebb	2.8	0.0	1.7
C—Hudson River, from Battery to Ninety-sixth street	Flood	2.0	3.6	2.0
	Ebb	2.0	0.0	2.0
D—Hudson River, from Ninety-sixth street to Spuyten Duyvil	Flood	2.0	3.6	2.0
	Ebb	2.0	0.0	2.0
E—East River, Battery to Hell Gate	Flood	0.0	4.1	4.1
	Ebb	4.1	0.0	0.0
F—East River, Hell Gate to Throgs Neck	Flood	4.7	7.2	4.5
	Ebb	4.5	0.0	4.7
G—Harlem River	Flood	0.2	4.4	4.2
	Ebb	4.2	0.0	0.2

An inspection of the map will show that of the areas named, the Hudson River, the East River from the Battery to Hell Gate, and the Harlem River are channels of comparatively regular cross-section in which the current velocity and direction are comparatively uniform from bank to bank; while the areas of the Lower Bay, the Upper Bay and the East River from Hell Gate to Throgs Neck comprise channels with bays or basins filled and emptied from the channels.

The modification which this difference causes in the circulation of the waters is exemplified as follows: When the flood (easterly) current begins in the East River, opposite Old Ferry Point, the water level is at 4.26 feet above the mean low water plane and falling. The mean velocity is given for each lunar hour. While this flood flow continues, the water surface falls from 4.26 feet above mean low water to mean low water and then rises to 4.47 feet above mean low water. The probable effects to the east of Old Ferry Point are that at the end of the flood flow, the entire body of water in the channel east to Stepping Stones Light plus the tidal prism of the bays at the side, to the elevation 4.47, is composed of water, more or less polluted, which had flowed out past Old Ferry Point.

When the ebb current sets in, the water surface is rising, the flow is through the channel and into the bays. As the surface rises, the tidal prism of the bays is completed from the channel and the volume of water flowing back past Old Ferry Point consists of the water which had flowed out, admixed with a volume of normal sound water equal to the amount used in filling the tidal prisms of the side bays plus the preponderance of ebb flows in the East and Harlem Rivers. The volume of this normal sound water thus entering (about 1,496,222,000 cubic feet), gives the measure of the new supply of oxygen provided by one tide through this entrance. Before the tide turns again this water has been divided between the East and Harlem Rivers and has entered into its work in the harbor.

For the Narrows, when the flow to the south, or the ebb, begins, the water level is at 2.8 feet above the mean low water plane and falling. While the ebb flow continues the surface falls from 2.8 feet above mean low water to mean low water and then rises to 1.7 feet above mean low water.

At the end of this tidal period, the entire body of water in the channel from the Narrows south to the entrance of the Ambrose Channel and on the shoals at either side to the elevation of 1.7 is of that derived from other parts of the harbor.

When the flood current sets in, a circulation similar to that at Throgs Neck takes place. It is estimated that the volume of normal sea water passing through the Narrows during each flood equals 2,398,800,000 cubic feet.

The estimated volumes of water in the various areas are as follows:

TABLE 3.

Locality.	Channel Volume, Cu. Ft.	Tidal Area, Sq. Ft.	Volume of Tidal Prism Cu. Ft. at End of		Total Volume Cu. Ft. at End of	
			Ebb.	Flood.	Ebb.	Flood.
Lower Bay	10,084.399.200	550,988,700	220,395,480	1,873,361,580	10,304,794,700	11,957,760,800
Upper Bay	11,079.890,000	530,579,340	901,985,000	1,485,622,000	11,981,875.000	12,565,512,000
Hudson River, to Ninety-sixth street	5,109,763,600	140.533,330	281,066,660	281,066,660	5,390,830,300	5.390,830,300
Hudson River, Ninety-sixth street to Spuyten Duyvil	4,546.328,950	148,088,891	296,177,782	296,177,782	4.842,506,700	4,842,506,700
East River, to Hell Gate	3,116,265,700	97,400,500	....	399.342,050	3,116,265,700	3,515,607,800
East River, Hell Gate to Throgs Neck	6,027,461,580	327.965,179	1,541.436 340	1,475,843,300	7.568.897.900	7.503,304,900
Harlem River	198,752,000	24.674,600	4.934,920	103,633,320	203.686,900	302,385,300

An exact determination of the amount of water in any one of the areas at any tidal period derived from the various tributary areas is manifestly impracticable, but it is possible to make an analysis based on reasonable assumptions of flow as shown hereafter; and the reliability of the analysis is susceptible of indirect proof should the determination of pollution obtained thereby agree with the chemical analysis of the waters.

Tests for dissolved oxygen in the harbor waters have been made by the Metropolitan Sewerage Commission at various points, but it does not appear that any series of tests were made through an entire cross-section of any of the channels during an entire tidal period. The results published in the Commission's report are interesting and instructive, but they do not give a certain measure of the average condition of the waters. In September, 1910, under the direction of the United States authorities, Prof. Earle B. Phelps made a series of determinations of dissolved oxygen through a cross-section of the Hudson, opposite Mount St. Vincent, close to the northern city limit and covering nearly an entire 12-hour period. The total number of samples taken was 42. The percentage of sea water varied from 40.5 per cent. to 55.5 per cent., with an average of 42.2 per cent. Dissolved oxygen was found in quantities varying from 39.6 per cent. to 66.8 per cent. of the saturation values, with an average of 51.2 per cent. The effect of this pollution on the harbor capacity for receiving sewage is very apparent in the figures given later for the capacity of the "Upper Hudson" at ebb, and "Harlem" at flood periods.

From the figures given in Table No. 3 for the flow and volume of water in the various areas of the harbor, together with the Coast and Geodetic Survey determinations of velocities, a study was made of the probable sources of the waters in each area at the end of the flood and ebb.*

As an example, the Upper Bay at the end of the ebb is taken.

The ebb flow through the Narrows is known. This water is drawn from the Upper Bay and the waters tributary to it, and these again are replaced by those drawn from sources still further up. The volume in the Upper Bay (channel plus tidal prism volume), at the beginning of the ebb is 12,565,512,000 cubic feet. The ebb flow through the Narrows is 13,819,-895,144 cubic feet, giving a remainder of 1,254,383,144 cubic feet, drawn from the Kill von Kull and the Hudson and East Rivers. This was proportioned arbitrarily among the three as seemed just. The volume in the Upper Bay at the end of the ebb is 11,981,875,000 cubic feet. This water is composed entirely of that received from the Kill von Kull, East and Hudson Rivers. Considering the current velocities, it was found that the portion received from the East River comprised all of the water from the Battery to Hell Gate plus a portion of that in the area from Hell Gate to Throgs Neck. Also, that the portion received from the Hudson River was equal to all of that in the area from the Battery to Ninety-sixth street, plus a portion of that in the area from Ninety-sixth street to Spuyten Duyvil. The same method was followed for the other areas. For convenience, these volumes were reduced to percentages and the various volumes were given a characteristic letter.

Let A and A′ represent the water in the Lower Bay east of line joining Sandy Hook, West Bank Light and Fort Wadsworth Light at the end of the flood and ebb, respectively.

*The writers are indebted to Mr. W. L. Kuehnle for valuable assistance in this study.

B and B′ represent the waters in the Upper Bay.

C and C′ represent the waters in the Hudson River from the Batttery to Ninety-sixth street.

D and D′ represent the waters in the Hudson River from Ninety-sixth street to Spuyten Duyvil.

E and E′ represent the waters in the East River from the Battery to Hell Gate.

F and F′ represent the waters in the East River from Hell Gate to Throgs Neck.

G and G′ represent the waters in the Harlem River.

Let K denote the waters received from the Kill von Kull.

L the waters received from the Hudson River above Spuyten Duyvil.

M the clean waters received from the Sound at one end and the sea at the other.

Let n denote the tide under consideration, either ebb or flood.

Let n-1 denote the previous tide either flood or ebb.

Let n-2 denote the second previous tide, either ebb or flood.

Table 4.

Then for the end of the flood

$A_n = 11{,}957{,}760{,}800$ cu. ft. (M)
$B_n = .9868\ A'_{n-1} + 2{,}398{,}821{,}800$ cu. ft. (M)
$C_n = .0132\ A'_{n-1} + .4384\ B'_{n-1}$
$D_n = .0697\ B'_{n-1} + .7435\ C'_{n-1}$
$E_n = .2934\ B'_{n-1}$
$F_n = .0410\ B'_{n-1} + E'_{n-1} + .4976\ F'_{n-1} + .6325\ G'_{n-1}$
$G_n = .0094\ C'_{n-1} + .0365\ D'_{n-1} + .3675\ G'_{n-1}$

For the end of the ebb

$A'_n = .6880\ B_{n-1} + .1420\ C_{n-1} + .2220\ E_{n-1} + 113{,}303{,}400$ cu. ft. (K)
$B'_n = .8580\ C_{n-1} + .3316\ D_{n-1} + .7780\ E_{n-1} + .1760\ F_{n-1} + 1{,}676{,}800{,}000$ cu. ft. (K)
$C'_n = .2473\ C'_{n-2} + .1549\ D'_{n-2} + .6684\ D_{n-1} + .2462\ G_{n-1}$
$D'_n = .8088\ D'_{n-2} + .5305\ G_{n-1} + 766{,}383{,}700$ cu. ft. (L)
$E'_n = .4129\ F_{n-1}$
$F'_n = .4085\ F'_{n-2} + .3945\ F_{n-1} + 1{,}496{,}222{,}000$ cu. ft. (M)
$G'_n = .0176\ F_{n-1} + .2333\ G_{n-1}$

Table 5.

For the end of the flood, obtained by substituting the actual volumes for the percentages of Table 4.

$A_n = 11{,}957.7$ million cu. ft. (M)
$B_n = 10{,}166.7$ million cu. ft. $(A'_{n-1}) + 2{,}398.8$ million cu. ft. (M)
$C_n = 138.1$ million cu. ft. $(A_{n-1}) + 5{,}252.7$ million cu. ft. (B'_{n-1})
$D_n = 835.2$ million cu. ft. $(B'_{n-1}) + 4{,}007.3$ million cu. ft. (C'_{n-1})
$E_n = 3{,}515.6$ million cu. ft. (B'_{n-1})
$F_n = 491.6$ million cu. ft. $(B'_{n-1}) + 3{,}116.3$ million cu. ft. $(E'_{n-1}) + 3{,}766.6$ million cu. ft. $(F'_{n-1}) + 128.8$ million cu. ft. (G'_{n-1})
$G_n = 50.6$ million cu. ft. $(C'_{n-1}) + 177.0$ million cu. ft. $(D'_{n-1}) + 74.8$ million cu. ft. (G'_{n-1})

For the end of the ebb

A'_n =8,644.8 million cu. ft. (B_{n-1}) + 766.2 million cu. ft. (C_{n-1}) + 780.5 million cu. ft. (E_{n-1}) + 113.3 million cu. ft. (K)
B'_n =4,624.7 million cu. ft. (C_{n-1}) + 1,605.9 million cu. ft. (D_{n-1}) + 2,735.1 million cu. ft. (E_{n-1}) + 1,338.8 million cu. ft. (F_{n-1}) + 1,676.9 million cu. ft. (K)
C'_n =1,332.9 million cu. ft. (C'_{n-2}) + 749.8 million cu. ft. (D'_{n-2}) + 3,236.7 million cu. ft. (D_{n-1}) + 71.4 million cu. ft. (G_{n-1})
D'_n =3,915.7 million cu. ft. (D'_{n-2}) + 160.4 million cu. ft. (G_{n-1}) + 766.4 million cu. ft. (L)
E'_n =3,116.3 million cu. ft (F_{n-1})
F'_n =3,091.9 million cu. ft. (F'_{n-2}) + 2,980.8 million cu. ft. (F_{n-1}) + 1,496.2 million cu. ft. (M)
G'_n =133.1 million cu. ft. (F_{n-1}) + 70.5 million cu. ft. (G_{n-1})

Table 6.

In percentages of the volume in each area in question the formulae become:

For the end of the flood

A_n =100% (M)
B_n =80.91% (A'_{n-1}) + 19.11% (M)
C_n =2.57% (A'_{n-1}) + 97.43% (B'_{n-1})
D_n =17.24% (B'_{n-1}) + 82.76% (C'_{n-1})
E_n =100% (B'_{n-1})
F_n =6.55% (B'_{n-1}) + 41.53% (E'_{n-1}) + 50.20% (F'_{n-1}) + 1.72% (G'_{n-1})
G_n =24.75% (G'_{n-1}) + 16.71% (C'_{n-1}) + 58.54% (D'_{n-1})

For the end of the ebb

A'_n =83.89% (B_{n-1}) + 7.45% (C_{n-1}) + 7.56% (E_{n-1}) + 1.10% (K)
B'_n =38.60% (C_{n-1}) + 13.40% (D_{n-1}) + 22.83% (E_{n-1}) + 11.17% (F_{n-1}) + 14.40% (K)
C'_n =24.72% (C'_{n-2}) + 13.92% (D'_{n-2}) + 60.04% (D_{n-1}) + 1.32% (G_{n-1})
D'_n =80.86% (D'_{n-2}) + 3.31% (G_{n-1}) + 15.83% (L)
E'_n =100% (F_{n-1})
F'_n =40.85% (F'_{n-2}) + 39.38% (F_{n-1}) + 19.77% (M)
G'_n =65.38% (F_{n-1}) + 34.62% (G_{n-1})

Capacity of the Harbor Waters to Receive Sewage Without Undue Pollution.

From the equations given above the composition of the waters of each of the parts of the harbor can be calculated for any tidal period. Jamaica Bay is entirely independent, and its capacity is discussed separately in the special report submitted on the drainage area tributary to it. The Lower Bay to the west of the channel leading to the Narrows is also independent. Its waters are changed with each tide, and the circulation between the Kill von Kull and the Arthur Kill is but slight.

It may be assumed with safety that the west part of the Lower Bay has sufficient capacity to receive and care for all of the sewage from its drainage area. Our data is insufficient to show with certainty the conditions in the Arthur Kill, but from the tidal conditions it is evident that its capacity is not large and it is now receiving over 16,000,000 gallons per day from the New Jersey sewer systems discharging into it. Further discussion of this capacity will be found in Chapter IV., in the report on the Borough of Richmond.

Returning to the other portions of the harbor discussed in the preceding pages it may be stated that their only source of supply of unpolluted water is from the sea and Sound—and that the oxygen of this supply is augmented to any appreciable degree only through reaeration while in the harbor.

Much misapprehension exists as to the extent to which the harbor waters renew their oxygen from this source and it is, therefore, deemed advisable to go into this subject somewhat extensively. The subject has been under investigation for some years by Prof. Phelps, and his conclusions are embodied in the following chapters. For present purposes it is sufficient to state that under the most favorable assumptions the absorption of oxygen from the air (reaeration) in the waters of New York Harbor will give an increase of 1.9 per cent. of the saturation value in 24 hours or of 0.475 per cent. in a six-hour period.

Our studies have shown that the volume of pure sea water which enters the harbor limits between the Narrows and Throgs Neck each twelve hours is 29,135 million gallons, which contain under summer conditions about 1,946,218 pounds of dissolved oxygen. If this oxygen were to be reduced to 70 per cent. of the saturation value by sewage reduction, 583,865 pounds would be so used in the twelve hours. The total volume of water in New York Harbor within the limits named is 251,418 million gallons; if this is reduced to 70 per cent. it will in itself absorb in twelve hours 0.95 per cent. of its saturation value or 159,550 pounds. This with the amount available from the pure sea water entering gives a total of 743,415 pounds of oxygen. This assuming a sewerage production of 100 gallons per capita per day would care for a population of 7.4 millions.

The above figures show great possibilities could all of the sewage discharge be concentrated at the two entrances, and there thoroughly diffused through the channels. Under existing conditions of discharge but little advantage is taken of them since only a small proportion of the pure water ever reaches the shores of Manhattan, as is shown by the equations of tables 4, 5 and 6. These equations indicate, however, that the nearer the sewage is carried to the harbor entrances, the greater will be the amount that can be cared for without undue pollution of the waters.

The existing population in New York and vicinity, whose sewage is emptied into the various areas is shown in the following table, which has been compiled from the best available sources; the sewage discharge is computed at 100 gallons per capita per day.

TABLE 7.

Locality.	Estimated Population.	Estimated Sewage for Twenty-four Hours in Million Cubic Feet.	Estimated Sewage for Six Hours in Million Cubic Feet.
A—Lower Bay	50,195	.7	.17
B—Upper Bay	367,816	4.9	1.23*
C—Hudson River, Battery to Ninety-sixth street..	755,992	10.1	2.53
D—Hudson River, Ninety-sixth street to Spuyten Duyvil	165,260	2.2	.55
E—East River, Battery to Hell Gate	2,212,295	29.6	7.40
F—East River, Hell Gate to Throgs Neck	246,601	3.3	.82
G—Harlem River	651,098	8.7	2.18
Total	4,449,257		

*To this will be added the sewage from the Passaic Valley System, when completed, 4.28 million cubic feet, which, when discharged, will be freed from 20 per cent. of its putrescible organic contents.

If we assume that the total oxygen of the waters is not to be reduced more than 30 per cent., there will be 20.4 pounds of oxygen available for each million gallons of pure water contained in each area during any tidal period. Reaeration in 12 hours would increase the oxygen contents by 0.6 pounds per million gallons of the total volume of water. This would make the following additional amount of oxygen available for each area for each six-hour period.

TABLE 8.

A =	11,131.2 million cubic feet	=	83,261.4 million gallons	=	49,956 pounds oxygen.
B =	12,273.7 million cubic feet	=	91,807.3 million gallons	=	55,084 pounds oxygen.
C =	5,390.8 million cubic feet	=	40,323.2 million gallons	=	24,194 pounds oxygen.
D =	4,842.5 million cubic feet	=	36,221.9 million gallons	=	21,733 pounds oxygen.
E =	3,315.9 million cubic feet	=	24,802.9 million gallons	=	14,882 pounds oxygen.
F =	7,536.1 million cubic feet	=	56,370.0 million gallons	=	33,822 pounds oxygen.
G =	253.0 million cubic feet	=	1,892.4 million gallons	=	1,135 pounds oxygen.

Were it not for the circulation of the waters back and forth between the different areas it would be a simple matter to determine the amount of sewage the waters of each area could care for without undue pollution, or the average pollution of these waters under existing conditions with the sewage thoroughly diffused through them.

Under conditions as they exist, however, it is necessary to compute the dilution through a number of successive tides.

Using the formulae in Table 4 and the figures for sewage in Table 7, the amount of sewage received in each area from the various sources was computed. To this was added the additional amount of sewage from the various waters, computed by means of the same formulae, through successive tides.

With the amount of sewage thus obtained the percentage of dilution for each tide was obtained. The change in the dilution ratio for each area for successive tides of the same character was found to be a decreasing one. These ratios were then plotted and the points joined by a regular curve. From these curves the ultimate dilution ratio was then taken. These ratios are given in Table 9.

In considering these dilution ratios, it must be remembered that a safe ratio for dilution for one waterway cannot be assumed as safe for another. It is evident that if the flow of the waterway is in one direction only, the pollution added at a given point affects only the waters down stream from that point, whereas in a tidal stream, the polluted waters may return past the original point of pollution many times before being finally removed. Again for safety, this ratio must be a function of the rate of reaeration of the waterway, or of the time before its waters are further purified by an additional supply of unpolluted water. Other considerations such as the uses to which the polluted waters are put and the character of the territory through which they flow have also weight in determining the safe ratio.

As shown by studies of Brooklyn sewage, for reduction to a stable form each million gallons of sewage will require the consumption of between 1,500 and 6,000 pounds of oxygen under summer conditions, of which from 500 to 2,000 pounds is taken up in twelve hours. If we assume an average oxygen consumption of 2,000 pounds per million gallons of sewage and an increase of oxygen supply of .475 per cent. of saturation value for reaeration in six hours, the oxygen contents may be calculated; these values are given in Table 9. They are approximate and for summer conditions only.

TABLE 9.

Area.	Dilution Ratio.	Per Cent. of Oxygen Present. Without Reaeration.	With Reaeration.
	Flood		
A	....	100	100
B	1 in 120	75.0	75.5
C	1 in 65	54.0	54.4
D	1 in 58	48.4	48.9
E	1 in 63	52.5	53.0
F	1 in 100	70.1	70.6
G	1 in 50	39.4*	40.6
	Ebb		
A[1]	1 in 100	70.1	70.6
B[1]	1 in 65	54.0	54.4
C[1]	1 in 57	47.5	47.9
D[1]	1 in 55	45.6*	46.0
E[1]	1 in 100	70.1	70.6
F[1]	1 in 150	80.0	80.5
G[1]	1 in 60	50.1	50.6

* Largely result of pollution of Hudson above limits of Greater New York.

Calculations were then made on the assumption that all the sewage discharged into the Hudson within the limits of Greater New York and into the Harlem as well as that discharged into the Upper Bay from the Passaic Valley sewer is reduced two-thirds by purification. These computations were made in the same manner as the foregoing and the results are given in the table below, which are also approximate and for summer conditions.

TABLE 10.

Area.	Dilution Ratio.	Per Cent. of Oxygen Present. Without Reaeration.	Per Cent. of Oxygen Present. With Reaeration.
	Flood		
A	....	100	100
B	1 in 200	85.0	85.5
C	1 in 80	62.6	63.0
D	1 in 80	62.6	63.0
E	1 in 75	60.0	60.5
F	1 in 120	75.0	75.5
G	1 in 70	57.2*	57.7
	Ebb		
A[1]	1 in 190	84.3	84.8
B[1]	1 in 77	61.1	61.6
C[1]	1 in 80	62.6	63.0
D[1]	1 in 62	51.7*	52.2
E[1]	1 in 120	75.0	75.5
F[1]	1 in 180	83.4	83.9
G[1]	1 in 90	66.7	67.2

* Result of pollution of Hudson River above limits of Greater New York.

Computations were next made to show what would result if the discharge of sewage were made at the two entrances of the harbor, at the Narrows and near Throgs Neck.

Assuming that the sewage discharged into areas B, C, D, ½ E and ½ G is discharged at the Narrows, and that from areas ½ E, F and ½ G at Throgs Neck, computations were made by means of the same formulae and in the same manner as before. The results for summer conditions are shown in the following table:

TABLE II.

Area.	Dilution Ratio.	Per Cent. of Oxygen Present. Without Reaeration.	With Reaeration.
	Flood		
A	....	100	100
B	1 in 210	85.8	86.3
C	1 in 200	85.0	85.5
D	1 in 140	78.6	79.1
E	1 in 240	87.5	88.0
F	1 in 220	86.4	86.9
G	1 in 90	66.7*	67.2
	Ebb		
A^1	1 in 210	85.8	86.3
B^1	1 in 240	87.5	88.0
C^1	1 in 130	77.1	77.5
D^1	1 in 72	58.4*	58.9
E^1	1 in 220	86.4	86.9
F^1	1 in 240	87.5	88.0
G^1	1 in 150	80.0	80.4

* Result of pollution of Hudson River above limits of Greater New York.

Table 11 shows the results of the concentration of the discharge of the sewage of the entire drainage area of the harbor at the Narrows and at Throgs Neck, with the existing population. Referring to the computations of available oxygen given on page 34, about two-thirds of the amount would be available at the Narrows and one-third at Throgs Neck.

CHAPTER II.

The Absorption of Atmospheric Oxygen by Water.

Quiescent Water.

Discussion of the Problem.

Atmospheric oxygen is soluble to a limited extent in water, the maximum amount which can thus be dissolved under any given set of conditions being known as the "saturation value." Under the fairly uniform conditions of pressure with which we have to deal the saturation value is chiefly a function of temperature. Like other gases oxygen is practically insoluble in boiling water and the solubility increases progressively with decreasing temperature. The composition of the water has also some influence, salt water dissolving less oxygen than fresh water under the same conditions. We may confine our attention for the present to the behavior of oxygen in water, although the laws of diffusion and solubility which we shall consider are of general application to other gases such as nitrogen and carbon dioxide.

If a given column of water, containing less oxygen in solution than it can take up under the existing conditions, is exposed to the atmosphere, it begins to absorb oxygen. This process proceeds at a decreasing rate, governed by certain fixed laws, until a condition of saturation is reached. The rate of this absorption has been the subject of several investigations, the latest and best known of which were made by Adeney, (1) in connection with his investigations of the pollution of waters by sewage. Adeney exposed long tubes of partially deaerated water, *i. e.*, water containing in solution less oxygen than would be required to saturate it, to the atmosphere. After various intervals of time and from various depths specimens of the water were removed for analysis. In this way, valuable information was obtained as to the amount of oxygen, and other gases, absorbed by a column of water under the conditions of the experiment. Adeney presented his full experimental results without any attempt at generalization or any expression of the underlying physical law. His results, valuable as they are, are applicable to the practical case only when that case happens to coincide in all the variable factors, with the experimental condition. What these variable factors are was not shown by this work and serious misuse of Adeney's figures has been made by others, as will be pointed out later, through overlooking these obvious facts, and applying the figures in a way which finds no justification in the original paper. The writer some years ago undertook an investigation of this same question at the Sewage Experiment Station of the Massachusetts Institute of Technology, the results of which are presented here for the first time. (2) It was apparent at the outset that the fundamental physical law of absorption of atmospheric oxygen by water was so complex that a satisfactory generalization could only be arrived at

(1) Fifth report Royal Commission on Sewage Disposal. Appen. VI., 1908, p. 54. Trans. Royal Dublin Soc., 1905, p. 161. Phil. Mag., Mar., 1905.

(2) The experimental work involved in these investigations was carried out by Mr. Francis E. Daniels, to whose skill in technique and in the designing and making of the special apparatus required, the successful outcome is in a large measure due.

through a mathematical study of the law itself, coupled with an experimental investigation to determine the constants involved. This experimental work must be so planned as to eliminate successively the various variable factors developed in the mathematical study, and thus fix the constants involved for all conditions. A check upon both the mathematical and the experimental work would be had if satisfactory constants could be obtained. Because of the wide interest and discussion which Adeney's results have created among investigators of pollution problems and because both the theoretical and the experimental portions of the writer's studies have led to quite different conclusions, it will be necessary to describe our early methods and results and also certain experiments undertaken by the writer later to explain the apparent discrepancies.

Theoretical and Experimental.

The physical theory of absorption will first be briefly stated. In order that there shall be absorption it is always presupposed that the water contains less oxygen than is required to saturate it. Let it be assumed, as an initial condition, that such a body of water, having a uniform oxygen content throughout its depth, be exposed on its surface to the atmosphere. At once the surface begins to absorb oxygen at a definite rate. This rate is dependent upon the relation between the initial oxygen concentration and the saturation concentration. In other words, water at 80 per cent. of saturation, *i. e.,* containing 80 per cent. as much oxygen as it can contain, will start to absorb twice as rapidly as will water at 90 per cent. of saturation. This is the well-known law of rate of solution and is the first physical principal involved in this discussion. The absorption of oxygen would therefore come to a speedy end through saturation of the surface layer, were it not for a second and more important principle known as the law of hydro-diffusion. This principle shows that any dissolved substance existing in different concentrations at different parts of the solution tends to diffuse toward the point of low concentration. In its full quantitative expression the law of hydro-diffusion, known from its discoverer (3) as Fick's law, states that the rate of diffusion of any dissolved substance through the liquid and between two proximate points is proportional to the difference in concentration of the substance at those two points. The proportionality is designated by a constant known as the diffusion coefficient. A consideration of this law will show that after the absorption and the diffusion have been going on for any definite time the curve of concentration within the liquid will start at practically the saturation value at the very surface and run down to practically zero at some point within. This zero point will move deeper and deeper into the liquid with increasing time. The mathematical form of this curve can be determined in terms of the time, the depth, and the diffusion coefficient. The area under the curve taken between suitable limits representing the total depth of water gives the total amount of dissolved oxygen contained in the tube after any stated time interval. This area is obtained in the usual way, by integration between limits. The final result is expressed also in terms of time, depth, and the diffusion coefficient. The final working formula is:*

(3) Nernst, Theoretische Chemie., 2d German Ed., p. 156.
* The full mathematical derivation of this formula is given in the appendix.

$$D = 100 - \left[\left(1 - \frac{B}{100}\right) \cdot 81.06 \cdot \left(0.779^K + \frac{0.105^K}{9} + \frac{0.0019^K}{25} - -\right) \right]$$

B Initial value of dissolved oxygen.
D Final value of dissolved oxygen.
K A constant for each experiment $= \frac{\pi^2 at}{L^2}$
t Time in hours.
L Depth in centimeters.
a Diffusion co-efficient.

All oxygen values are expressed in the unit, "per cent. of saturation." This equation permits the evaluation of the coefficient, "a," from the determinations of the total amount of dissolved oxygen in a sample before and after exposure to the air, the time of exposure and length of tube being noted. This procedure therefore greatly facilitates the experimental determinations of the coefficient. In terms of the units that have been employed, "a" is the amount of oxygen expressed in per cent. of saturation, which would pass through a plane one square centimetre in area in one hour if the concentration gradient at that point were 1 per cent. of saturation per linear centimetre. After the value of "a" is known this equation also permits a calculation of the actual rate of reaeration under any given conditions of time, depth, and initial oxygen content. In determining the values of the coefficient it was found necessary to develop a special method of determining dissolved oxygen in water, and one was finally devised that is about ten times as sensitive as the present standard Winkler Method.* Special apparatus and refined technique were necessary to secure successful results. One of the greatest sources of error in tests of this kind lies in changes of temperature. Even minute changes will cause a circulation within the tube which will vitiate the results. Therefore, the work was done throughout in a carefully regulated water bath in which the temperature was held practically constant during the test.

Determinations of the coefficient were made with tubes of varying lengths and under exposures of varying periods of time, to test the two variables of the formula. The results were reasonably concordant, and when plotted against their corresponding temperatures, showed a distinct relation to the temperature. From a smooth curve representing the best average values at all points the following summary of values of the coefficient over the temperature range investigated were obtained.

Values of Diffusion Coefficient of Oxygen in Distilled Water at Various Temperatures.

Temperature C.	"a"
5	0.65
10	0.75
15	1.00
20	1.42
25	2.43

* This method is described in the appendix

Results.

Having utilized the formula in the experimental determination of the coefficient, we may now reverse the process and apply our calculations to the practical problem of absorption. Since the law governing the course of this absorption has been formulated, and is seen to contain factors for the variable conditions to be met with, such application may be made with assurance of reasonable accuracy. Consider, first, conditions in quiescent fresh water Other conditions will be treated later. It is obvious that the rate of absorption into a given volume of water must be a function of the depth of water. One million gallons of water exposed in a one-foot layer would absorb oxygen faster than it would if exposed in a five-foot layer. The equation shows in what way the depth is related to the problem. A second factor is the time allowed for absorption. This requires no discussion. A third factor is the initial condition. The more nearly saturated the body of water, the slower will be the rate of absorption. This principle of rate of solution has already been discussed.

The equation has been solved for a number of sets of conditions in order to illustrate its application. The actual solution is a matter of no small difficulty. It is necessary to employ forty terms of the converging series in the case of the smaller " K " values to secure accuracy. For purposes of greater practical use the quantities are given in pounds of oxygen per million gallons of water as well as in the original form, per cent. of saturation. The latter form of expression is the more useful to illustrate the magnitude of the reaeration effect. The former will be of use in our calculations of the capacity of the water to oxidize sewage. The three variables of depth, time and initial concentration are considered separately.

TABLE 12.

Amount of Oxygen Absorbed from the Atmosphere by a Quiescent Body of Fresh Water at 20° C. During Stated Periods of Time, at Stated Depths and with Stated Initial Concentration; Expressed in Per Cent. of Saturation.

Initial Concentration. Per Cent. Saturation.	Time in Hours. 1	6	10	12	20	24
	Depth Five Feet.					
0	0.83	2.17	2.80	3.05	3.93	4.45
10	0.74	1.95	2.52	2.74	3.53	4.00
30	0.58	1.52	1.96	2.14	2.74	3.12
50	0.42	1.08	1.40	1.52	1.96	2.22
70	0.25	0.65	0.84	0.92	1.18	1.34
90	0.08	0.22	0.28	0.31	0.39	0.45
100	0.00	0.00	0.00	0.00	0.00	0.00
	Depth Ten Feet.					
0	0.30	1.05	1.45	1.53	1.97	2.17
10	0.27	0.94	1.30	1.38	1.77	1.95
30	0.21	0.74	1.02	1.07	1.38	1.52
50	0.15	0.52	0.72	0.76	0.98	1.08
70	0.09	0.32	0.44	0.46	0.59	0.65
90	0.03	0.11	0.18	0.15	0.20	0.22
100	0.00	0.00	0.00	0.00	0.00	0.00
	Depth Fifteen Feet.					
0	0.15	0.60	0.87	0.96	1.30	1.45
10	0.14	0.54	0.78	0.86	1.17	1.30
30	0.10	0.42	0.61	0.67	0.91	1.02
50	0.08	0.30	0.44	0.48	0.65	0.72
70	0.04	0.18	0.26	0.29	0.39	0.44
90	0.02	0.06	0.09	0.10	0.13	0.15
100	0.00	0.00	0.00	0.00	0.00	0.00
	Depth Twenty Feet.					
0	0.10	0.40	0.57	0.67	0.93	1.05
10	0.09	0.36	0.51	0.60	0.84	0.94
30	0.07	0.28	0.40	0.47	0.65	0.74
50	0.05	0.20	0.28	0.34	0.46	0.52
70	0.03	0.12	0.17	0.20	0.28	0.32
90	0.01	0.04	0.06	0.07	0.09	0.11
100	0.00	0.00	0.00	0.00	0.00	0.00

TABLE 13.

Amount of Oxygen Absorbed from the Atmosphere by a Quiescent Body of Fresh Water at 20° C. During Stated Periods of Time, at Stated Depths and with Stated Initial Concentration; Expressed in Pounds Per Million Gallons.

Initial Concentration. Per Cent. Saturation.	Time in Hours. 1	6	10	12	20	24
	Depth Five Feet.					
0	0.636	1.66	2.14	2.34	3.00	3.41
10	0.566	1.49	1.93	2.10	2.70	3.06
30	0.444	1.16	1.50	1.64	2.09	2.39
50	0.322	0.827	1.07	1.16	1.50	1.68
70	0.193	0.497	0.643	0.704	0.904	1.03
90	0.064	0.166	0.214	0.234	0.300	0.341
100	0.00	0.00	0.00	0.00	0.00	0.00
	Depth Ten Feet.					
0	0.229	0.804	1.11	1.17	1.51	1.66
10	0.207	0.720	0.995	1.06	1.36	1.49
30	0.161	0.566	0.781	0.820	1.06	1.16
50	0.115	0.398	0.551	0.581	0.750	0.827
70	0.069	0.245	0.331	0.352	0.452	0.497
90	0.023	0.080	0.111	0.12	0.151	0.166
100	0.00	0.00	0.00	0.00	0.00	0.00
	Depth Fifteen Feet.					
0	0.115	0.459	0.666	0.735	0.996	1.11
10	0.107	0.413	0.597	0.658	0.896	0.995
30	0.077	0.322	0.467	0.513	0.696	0.781
50	0.061	0.230	0.337	0.367	0.497	0.551
70	0.031	0.138	0.199	0.222	0.299	0.337
90	0.012	0.046	0.067	0.074	0.100	0.111
100	0.00	0.00	0.00	0.00	0.00	0.00
	Depth Twenty Feet.					
0	0.077	0.306	0.436	0.513	0.712	0.804
10	0.069	0.276	0.390	0.459	0.643	0.721
30	0.054	0.214	0.306	0.360	0.497	0.566
50	0.038	0.153	0.214	0.260	0.352	0.398
70	0.023	0.092	0.130	0.153	0.214	0.245
90	0.008	0.031	0.044	0.051	0.071	0.080
100	0.00	0.00	0.00	0.00	0.00	0.00

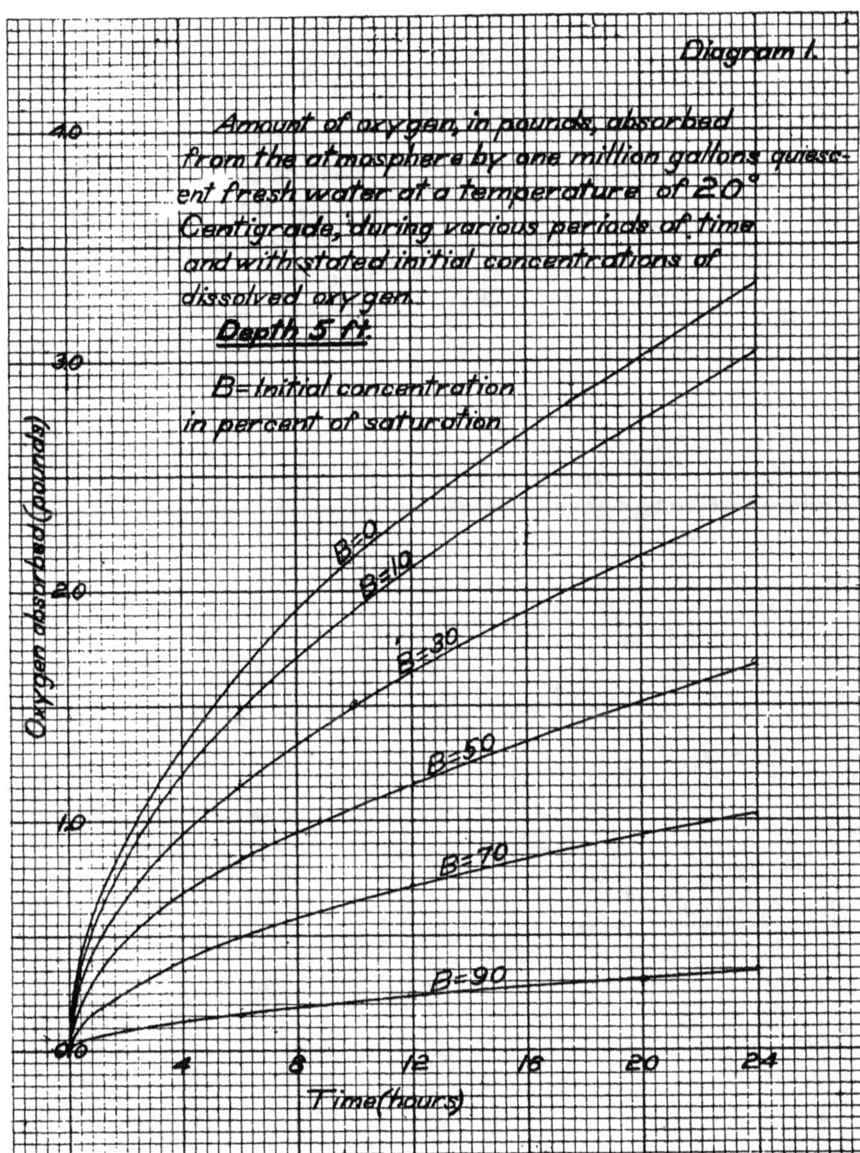
Diagram I.
Amount of oxygen, in pounds, absorbed from the atmosphere by one million gallons quiescent fresh water at a temperature of 20° Centigrade, during various periods of time and with stated initial concentrations of dissolved oxygen.
Depth 5 ft.
B = Initial concentration in percent of saturation
B=0
B=10
B=30
B=50
B=70
B=90
Oxygen absorbed (pounds)
40
30
20
10
0
4
8
12
16
20
24
Time (hours)

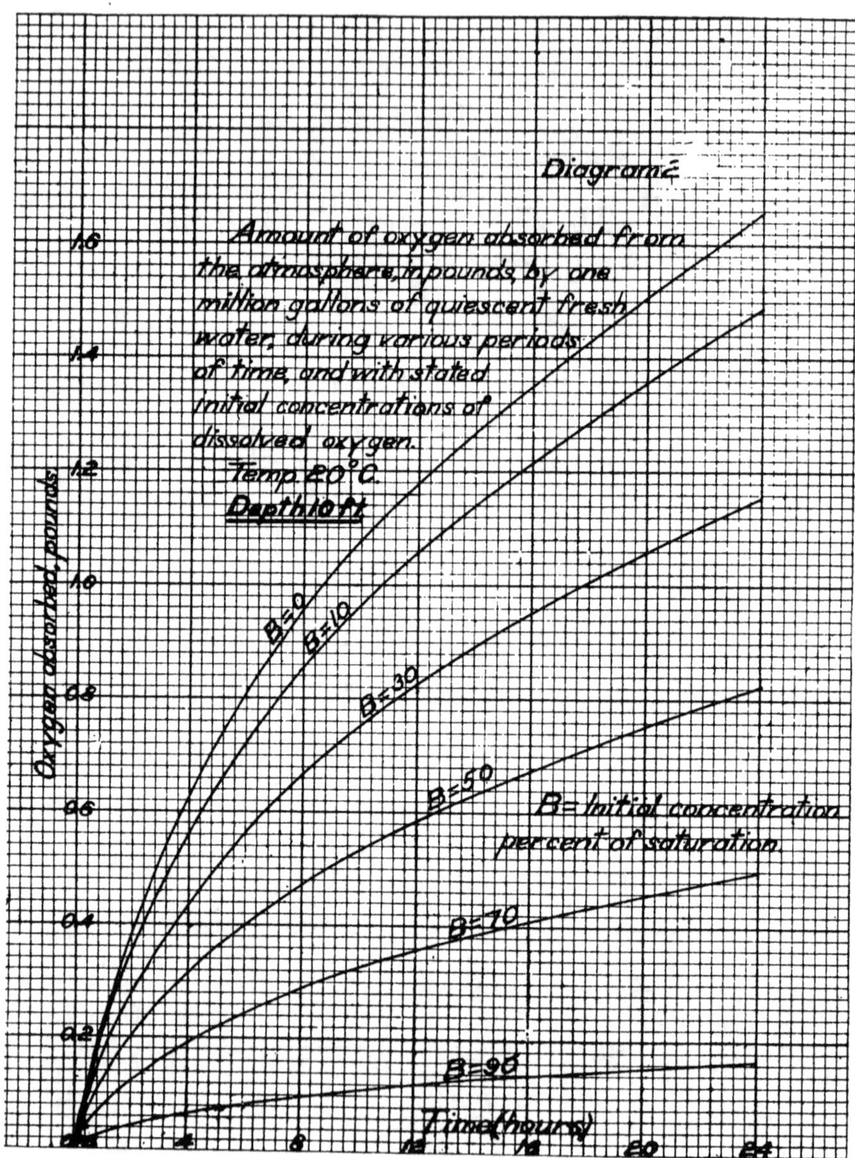
Diagram 2
Amount of oxygen absorbed from the atmosphere, in pounds, by one million gallons of quiescent fresh water, during various periods of time, and with stated initial concentrations of dissolved oxygen.
Temp. 20° C.
Depth 10 ft.
Oxygen absorbed, pounds
1.6
1.4
1.2
1.0
0.8
0.6
0.4
0.2
B=0
B=10
B=30
B=50
B=70
B=90
B= Initial concentration percent of saturation.
Time (hours)
4
8
12
16
20
24

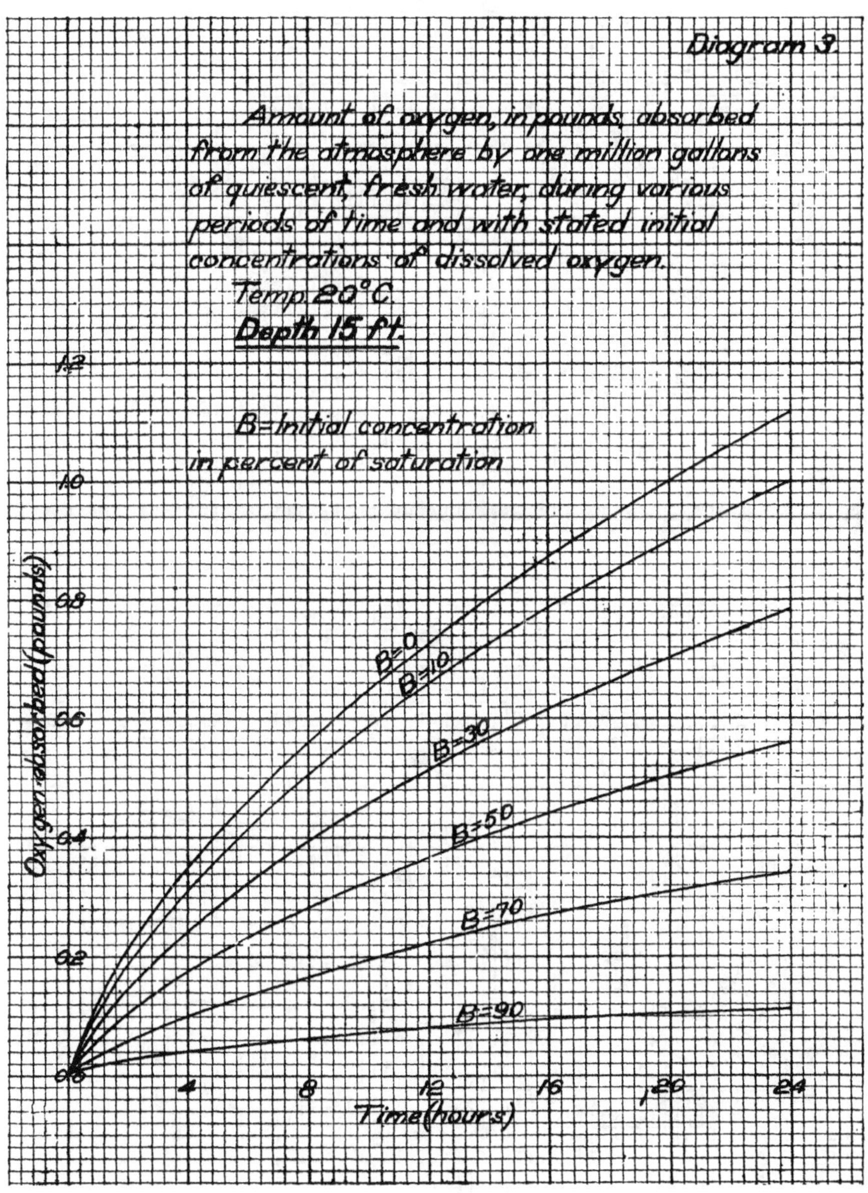
Diagram 3.
Amount of oxygen, in pounds, absorbed from the atmosphere by one million gallons of quiescent, fresh water, during various periods of time and with stated initial concentrations of dissolved oxygen.
Temp. 20°C.
Depth 15 ft.
B=Initial concentration in percent of saturation
1.2
1.0
0.8
0.6
0.4
0.2
0.0
B=0
B=10
B=30
B=50
B=70
B=90
Oxygen absorbed (pounds)
4
8
12
16
20
24
Time (hours)

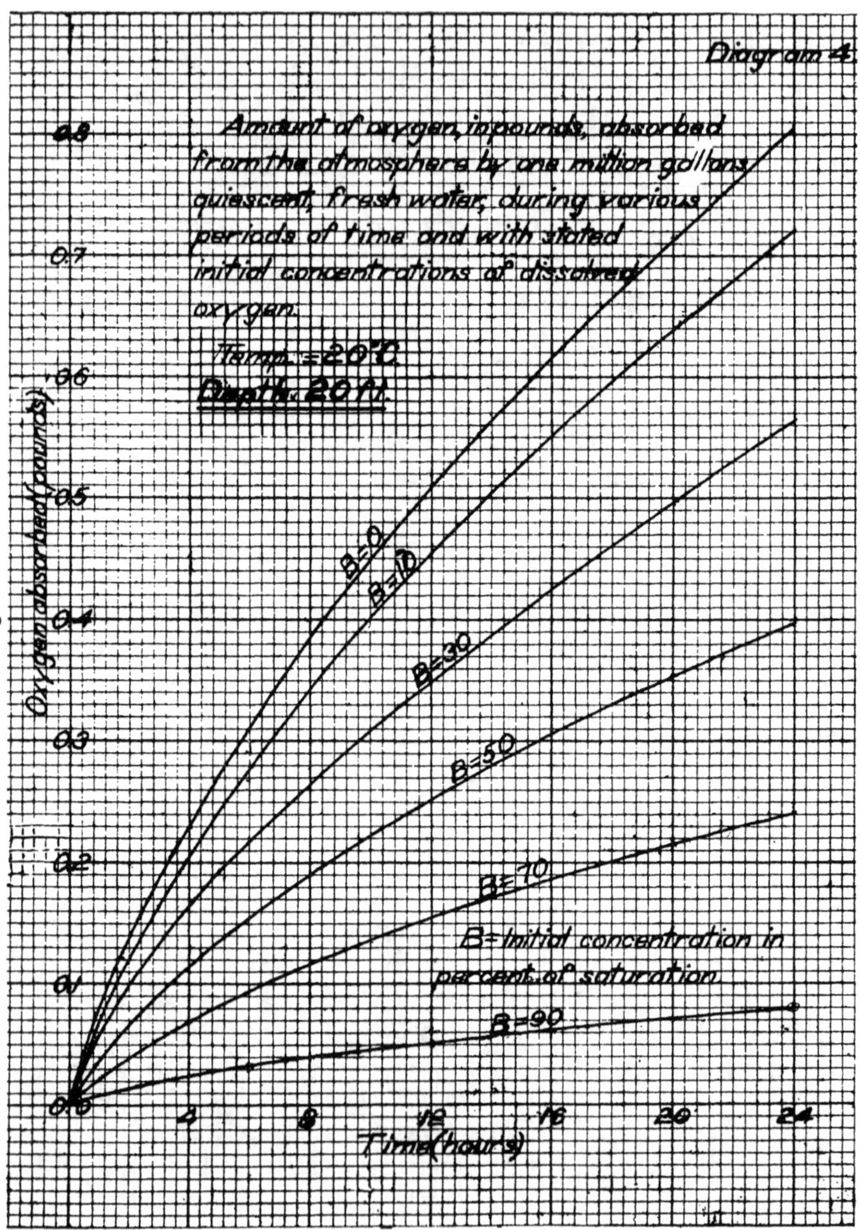
Diagram 4.
Amount of oxygen, in pounds, absorbed from the atmosphere by one million gallons quiescent, fresh water, during various periods of time and with stated initial concentrations of dissolved oxygen.
Temp. = 20°C.
Depth. 20 ft.
B=0
B=10
B=30
B=50
B=70
B=90
B = Initial concentration in percent. of saturation.
Oxygen absorbed (pounds)
0.0
0.1
0.2
0.3
0.4
0.5
0.6
0.7
0.8
4
8
12
16
20
24
Time (hours)

The results of the calculations are given in Tables 12 (per cent. of saturation) and 13 (pounds per million gallons). The same information is given graphically in Diagrams 1 to 4.

It is seen that, in quiescent fresh water at least, the rate of absorption is so low that reaeration in this case cannot play an important part in self-purification. A ten-foot column of water, for example, starting at 50 per cent. of saturation, would absorb only enough oxygen in 24 hours to bring its average oxygen content up to 51 per cent. The dependence of the rate of absorption upon the initial condition is also clearly shown. For example, the amount of oxygen which will be absorbed from the atmosphere in one hour by a ten-foot column of water containing only 10 per cent. of the saturation value of oxygen is nine times as great as is the case with an initial value of 90 per cent. It should also be noted that the rate of reaeration is rapid at first and diminishes quickly with time. This rapid initial absorption involves an initial condition of uniform mixing in the column of water under consideration. In practice such a condition seldom obtains, and it is in general the absorption occurring after the first or later hours that are of practical value. In a quiescent body of water the average hourly rate after 24 hours or even longer periods and not the rate during the first hours after uniform mixing, is the proper value for use. This point, which distinguishes the condition of quiescent water from that of water having vertical movements, will be referred to again in the discussion of the effect of winds and boats.

Application.

A serious misuse has been made of the results reported by Adeney in that his rates of absorption into fully deaerated water of comparatively shallow depths have been used to determine the rate of reaeration of a natural body of water which in the nature of things would have much greater depth and would never be permitted to approach a condition of complete deaeration. For example, a recent writer has stated (4) " In tidal salt water the results may be, on the whole, better, for while half fresh water and half salt water will contain less oxygen when saturated, its powers of reaeration are almost double fresh water. At 64° F. it will draw from the air 0.62 of a pound per hour per million gallons of its volume, and at increasing rate as the salt increases.

" The basin of New York harbor inside the Narrows, and below 140th Street on the Hudson, and Hell Gate on the East River, leaving out Kill von Kull, contains, at mean tide, 203,467 million gallons. At the known rate of absorption of 0.62 pounds per million gallons, its hourly reaeration amounts to 126,150 pounds, enough to destroy the organic matter in the sewage of sixty million people, at 100 gallons per head per day, provided the sewage is properly delivered to the water, without reducing the normal oxygen."

Passing by for the moment the reference to the effect of dissolved salts in water upon the rate of reaeration, a question which will be fully discussed later, it must be pointed out here that the depth and condition of aeration of the water, essential factors in the rate of reaeration, have been ignored in the above calculations. Any statement of the magnitude of absorption or reaeration must, to have any weight at all, be limited by

(4) Edlow W. Harrison, Proc. 35th Ann. Meeting, N. J. Sanitary Assn., 1909, p. 77.

considerations of the three fundamental variables of the problem—time, depth and initial condition.

It is this same point which is of such predominating influence in running streams. A stream five feet deep, which is completely mixed but once in an hour, will absorb oxygen three times as fast as would a body of water which is mixed but once in twelve hours. If our tables showed the facts for 15-minute intervals after mixing, a condition more nearly that of even sluggish streams, the effect would be still more striking.

Salt Water Conditions.

Thus far this discussion has referred to fresh water. Actual data for the determination of the diffusion coefficient in sea water are lacking. The known facts concerning the physical properties of solutions would indicate a slower rate of absorption. On the one hand the solubility is less, so that smaller concentration gradients and consequently less diffusion would necessarily follow even with the same value of the diffusion coefficient, "a." Our diffusion law refers to "per cent. of saturation," so that with the same value of "a" the absorption, expressed in this unit, is the same. If the saturation value be diminished by any cause, the actual amount of oxygen absorbed is correspondingly decreased. In the second place diffusion coefficients in general are decidedly reduced by increased viscosity of the fluid, so that, judging by analogy, the value of "a" in salt water would be decreased. All told, the rate of diffusion into salt water is certainly not greater and is probably much less than into fresh water. These statements are apparently confirmed by certain experiments of Adeney's, in which tubes of fresh and salt water were exposed under similar experimental conditions.

The "Streaming Effect."

On the other hand, under certain conditions, salt water apparently dissolves atmospheric oxygen more rapidly than fresh. Adeney and others have noted that, while in fresh water there is a tendency toward accumulation of the oxygen near the surface (as would be indicated by the mathematical formula), in the case of salt water the oxygen tended to distribute more evenly through the tube. This phenomenon has been called the "streaming effect" and was first noted by Hufner. (5) Adeney found it always present when salt water was used but most markedly so when a jet of air was introduced just below the surface of the water. In the case of fresh water there was no such effect. There was no circulation of the water produced mechanically by the jet. Adeney found further that the so-called "streaming effect" was due to some unknown property of the air and that that property was lost after passing once through water. So that if the same air was passed successively through the top layer of two tubes of water a streaming would take place in the first, but only slightly or not at all in the second. It was concluded that this effect was due to dust particles in the air acting possibly as electrical condensation points, or to some other electrical property of the air, such as ionization, which property was capable of being washed out, and that in connection with the ionized salts of the

(5) Ann. Phys. Chem. LX., 1897, 134.

water this electrical property in some way produced a downward streaming of the oxygen molecules. Adeney attempted to show that there was no actual circulation of the liquid, but his test was not a conclusive one in that it was not sufficiently sensitive.

This phenomenon assumes importance in view of the results that have now been described. This " streaming effect " of the oxygen amounts virtually to a continuous mixing of the water so that the oxygen values resulting would correspond with those initial rates of absorption already referred to in the case of running streams. It is upon this basis of very rapid absorption, as determined quantitatively by Adeney, that Mr. Edlow Harrison's estimate of 0.62 pounds per hour per million gallons was based.

The logical deduction from Adeney's investigation was that, owing to the peculiar streaming effect, salt water would reaerate itself at a rate many times greater than that observed in fresh water.

The writer became interested in the great practical importance of this aspect of the matter and during the past year undertook an investigation of the streaming effect. It was decided to employ a most sensitive detector of circulating currents, since the evidence on this point was not conclusive. Adeney had used a crystal of bichromate dropped into his tube. Under these conditions a thin layer of a very heavy saturated solution forms on the bottom, and the contents of the tube would have to be stirred quite vigorously to remove it. Our test for circulation was the addition of a solution of methylene blue in the same water as that under investigation. So delicate was this test that the addition of 1 per cent. of methylene blue to sea water gave the mixture a density sufficient to cause it at once to descend to the bottom of a tube of the same water. This colored mixture was therefore diluted until it would just float on the surface of the tube. The slightest tendency toward circulation was made manifest at once by streaks of blue water descending. With tubes of fresh and salt water thus prepared, and others similarly prepared with the indicator water on the bottom, Adeney's experiments were repeated and exactly confirmed. In every case where he obtained streaming there was a visible streaming of the blue color. In the case of fresh water and also of salt water, if treated with air that had already passed through one tube of water, there was no streaming. It was demonstrated that the streaming of oxygen was only a secondary effect, due to the streaming of the liquid as a whole. Furthermore, the real source of the streaming now became apparent. It was due to the evaporation of the top layer of solution, leaving a slightly denser solution on top which then descended. Within one hour after turning on the air this descent frequently began. No streaming occurs in fresh water, for obvious reasons. Adeney's other results are also clear in the light of these experiments. The property which was washed from the air by passing through the first tube was its dryness. The air became saturated and evaporation no longer took place. A sample of such washed air was used in our experiments, but was first passed through a drying tube. It had regained its streaming properties, more vigorously than ever before. In this experiment the water evaporated from the first tube was collected in the drying bulb and weighed. The increased concentration of the top layer of liquid was then calculated at the instant when streaming began. A solution was then made up of this strength and colored. When placed on the top of the standard salt water it immediately descended to the bottom. In brief, it was shown conclusively that the so-called streaming effect was due entirely to evaporation of water from the surface and the consequent increase in the specific gravity of the top layer of the solution. This layer then descended to the bottom. In practice no such results would be observed, since the upper layers of an estuary are always somewhat fresher than the lower.

Therefore, there is no apparent reason to believe that the reaeration of salt water follows any other laws than those which we have determined mathematically and experimentally for fresh water. In the absence of fuller information on the effect of increased viscosity, upon the diffusion coefficient, it can only be stated that the rate of reaeration of salt water is less than that of fresh, in proportion to the respective solubilities of oxygen in the two waters, and still less, but to an unknown extent, by reason of the greater viscosity and consequent small value of the diffusion coefficient.

TABLE 14.

Average Rate in Pounds Per Hour at Which a Quiescent Body of One Million Gallons of Fresh Water in Stated Depths Will Absorb Oxygen from the Atmosphere at 20 Degrees C., at Stated Intervals of Time After a Condition of Uniform Mixing and With an Initial Concentration of Oxygen of 70 Per Cent. of Saturation.

Depth Feet.	Time in Hours.					
	1	6	10	12	20	24
5	0.193	0.083	0.064	0.059	0.045	0.043
10	.069	.041	.034	.029	.023	.021
15	.031	.023	.020	.019	.015	.014
20	.023	.015	.013	.013	.011	.010

In summary Table 14 is presented to show the essential facts for use in our further studies. This is compiled from Table 13, the 70 per cent. initial condition alone being considered. Under these conditions the rate of oxygen absorption in pounds per million gallons of water per hour in various depths of water and during various intervals of time are shown. These figures represent our best present knowledge of the absorption of oxygen into quiescent fresh water and are excessive for quiescent sea water.

The figures in Table 13 are made the basis of the plot in Diagram 5. This table and the diagram show the total amount of absorption during stated intervals of time. For the purposes of the calculation which follows it is of advantage to have the same data expressed in average hourly rate over stated intervals, rather than total amount. This form of expression is used in Table 14 and in the plot, Diagram 6. A third form of expression is also needed, namely, rate of absorption after any stated interval, as distinguished from average rate during that interval. This form is used in Diagram 8.

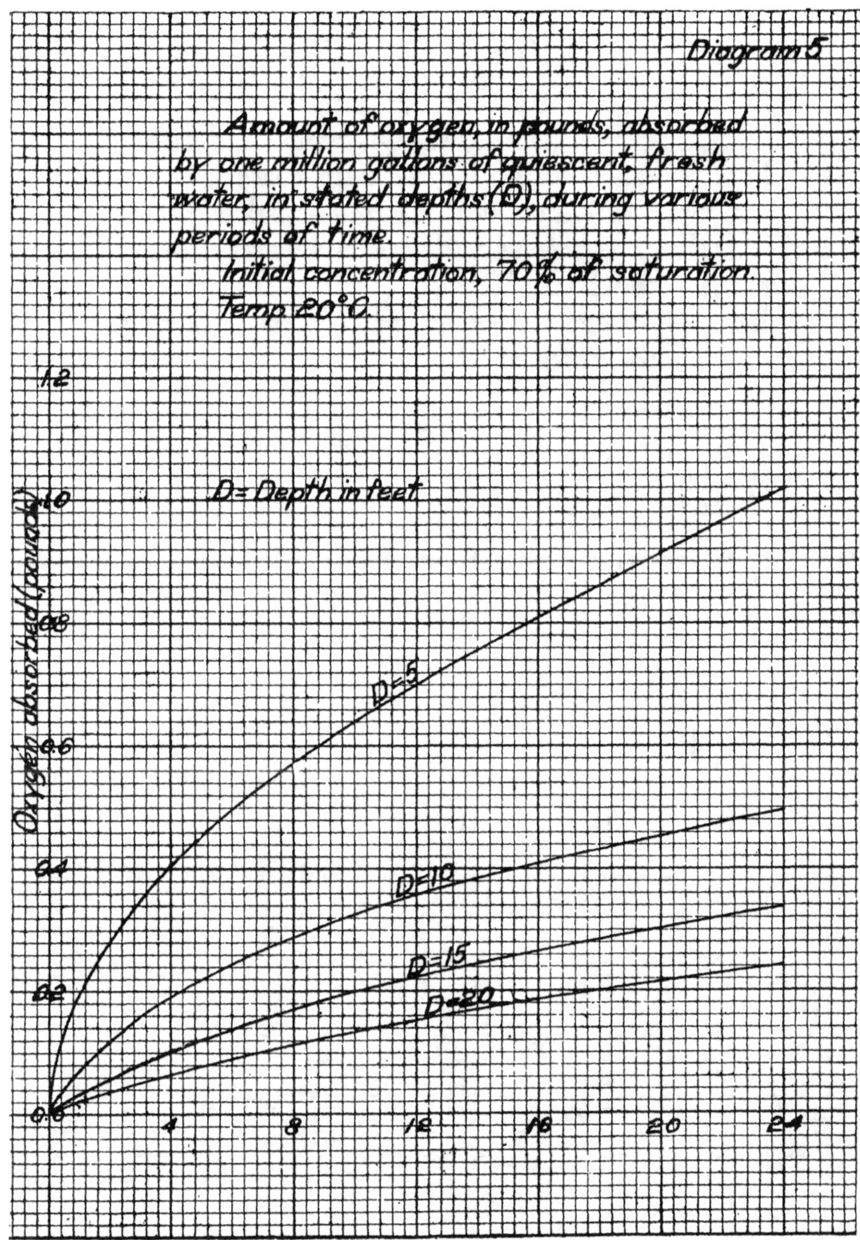
Diagram 5
Amount of oxygen, in pounds, absorbed by one million gallons of quiescent, fresh water, in stated depths (D), during various periods of time.
Initial concentration, 70% of saturation.
Temp. 20°C.
D = Depth in feet
Oxygen absorbed (pounds)
1.2
1.0
0.8
0.6
0.4
0.2
0.0
4
8
12
16
20
24
D=5
D=10
D=15
D=20

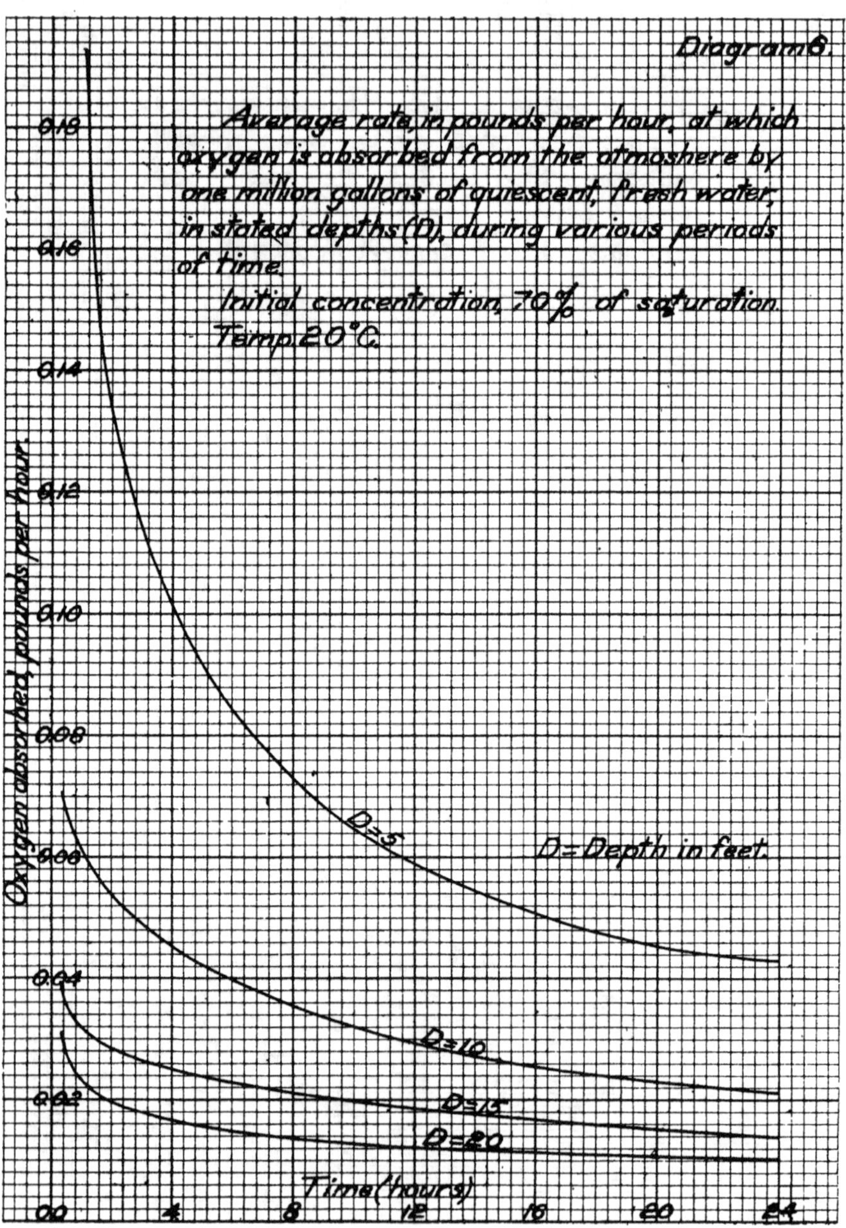
Diagram 6.
Average rate, in pounds per hour, at which oxygen is absorbed from the atmoshere by one million gallons of quiescent, fresh water, in stated depths (D), during various periods of time.
Initial concentration, 70% of saturation.
Temp. 20°C.
D=5
D=Depth in feet.
D=10
D=15
D=20
Oxygen absorbed, pounds per hour.
Time (hours)
0.18
0.16
0.14
0.12
0.10
0.08
0.06
0.04
0.02
0.0
4
8
12
16
20
24

The Effect of Currents and Other Disturbing Factors Upon the Rate of Absorption.

The discussion of the rate of absorption has thus far been based upon the assumption that the body of water in question is quiescent. The effect of departures from this assumption must now be considered. This brings up the question of currents, in the broad sense of the word, including eddies,

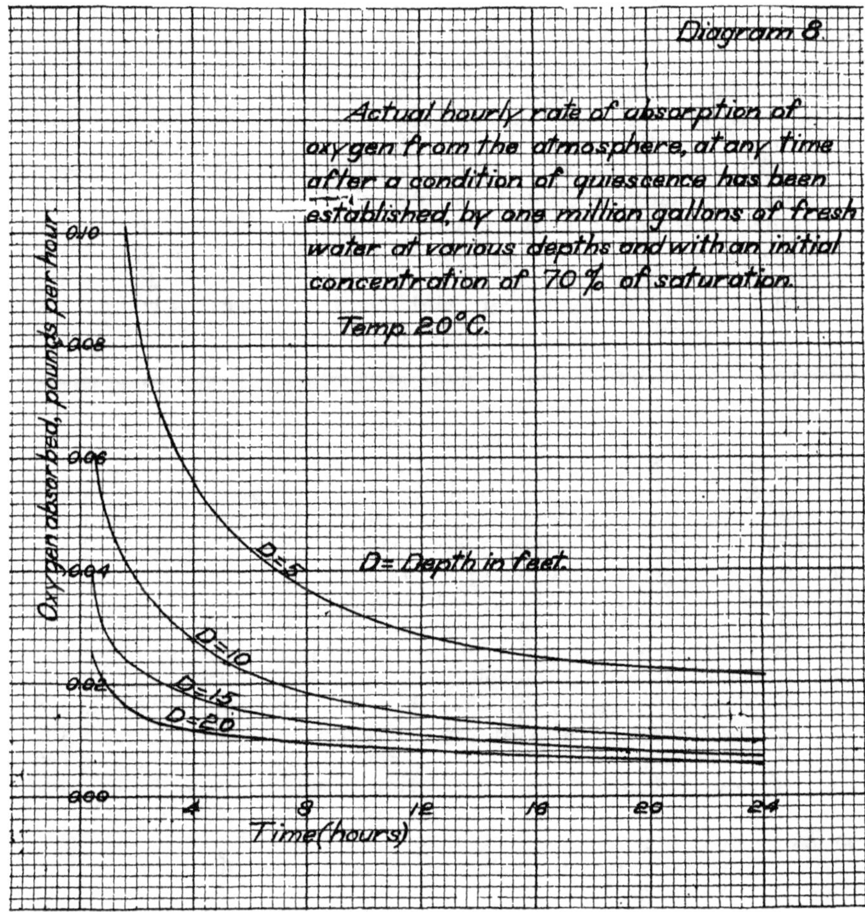

tide and wave action and brief local disturbances such as are caused by passing vessels. More specifically it is the vertical components of these currents only that enter the problem, since these alone induce a vertical circulation. The effect of wind will be first considered.

Effect of Wind.

The wind is generally looked upon as an important factor in the aeration of water. The very obvious agitation of the surface, produced by moderate breezes, and the more violent effect of storms, would seem at first glance to lend strength to this view. More careful analysis, however, in the light of the theory of aeration which has been developed makes it possible to test this hypothesis and determine the manner in which wind action must affect aeration, if at all, and approximately at least, the extent of such effect.

Since the fundamental law of aeration is one of diffusion, and furthermore, since the surface of any body of water is practically saturated at all times, it must be evident that no mere surface action can by itself affect the rate of diffusion. In order to assist the latter there must be an actual mechanical mixing of the water. If such mixing occurs to any given depth by reason of wind action the facts which have been developed thus far permit the following quantitative analysis to be applied.

It has been seen that a body of water starting with a uniform initial concentration of oxygen, B, less than saturation will absorb oxygen, and that by diffusion a concentration gradient is established, from saturation at the surface to the value, B, at some depth within. This process is continuous, but the rate of absorption is a constantly decreasing one. Starting with a condition of uniform mixing the absorption per hour is a maximum at the start and decreases steadily, as is shown in Table No. 3, and more strikingly in Diagram 8.

The immediate effect of wind upon a body of water is to produce wave action. A definite relation exists between the wind velocity, the "fetch" of the wind, i. e., the distance, windward, to the shore, and the size of the wave. The wave in turn sets the water beneath in motion, each particle moving in an eliptical path, whose minor axis, depth, is a function of the wave height. An excellent analysis of the relation between wind velocities, "fetch" and wave height is given by Gaillard (1).

Through the relation between wind action and height of wave, and the secondary relation between height of wave and depth of the movement of the water, it would appear that the velocity of wind would bear some definite relation to the depth of stirring. This relation is not one that can be deduced upon any of the present theories of wave action. In all such theories the principal of "continuity" is a primary assumption. That is, any given plane in the body of water at rest may, owing to wave action, become distorted but must remain continuous and unbroken. This mathematical conception is of course impossible of actual realization and the departure from the ideal condition is in fact the measure of the mixing of the water with which we now have to deal.

The relation between wind velocities and depth of mixing has been recently demonstrated in an ingenious and thorough manner by M. F. Sanborn.* The opportunity for such a study was rather unique. The Charles River Basin had been made by the construction of a dam by which the water within was maintained always at nearly high water mark. A lock in constant service, admitted enough sea water to prevent the complete freshening

(1) Professional Paper, Engineer Corps, U. S. A., No. 31. Wave Action. D. D. Gaillard, 1904.

* Distribution of Sea Water in the Charles River Basin, after Excluding Tidal Water, M. F. Sanborn, Eng. News, 63, 272.

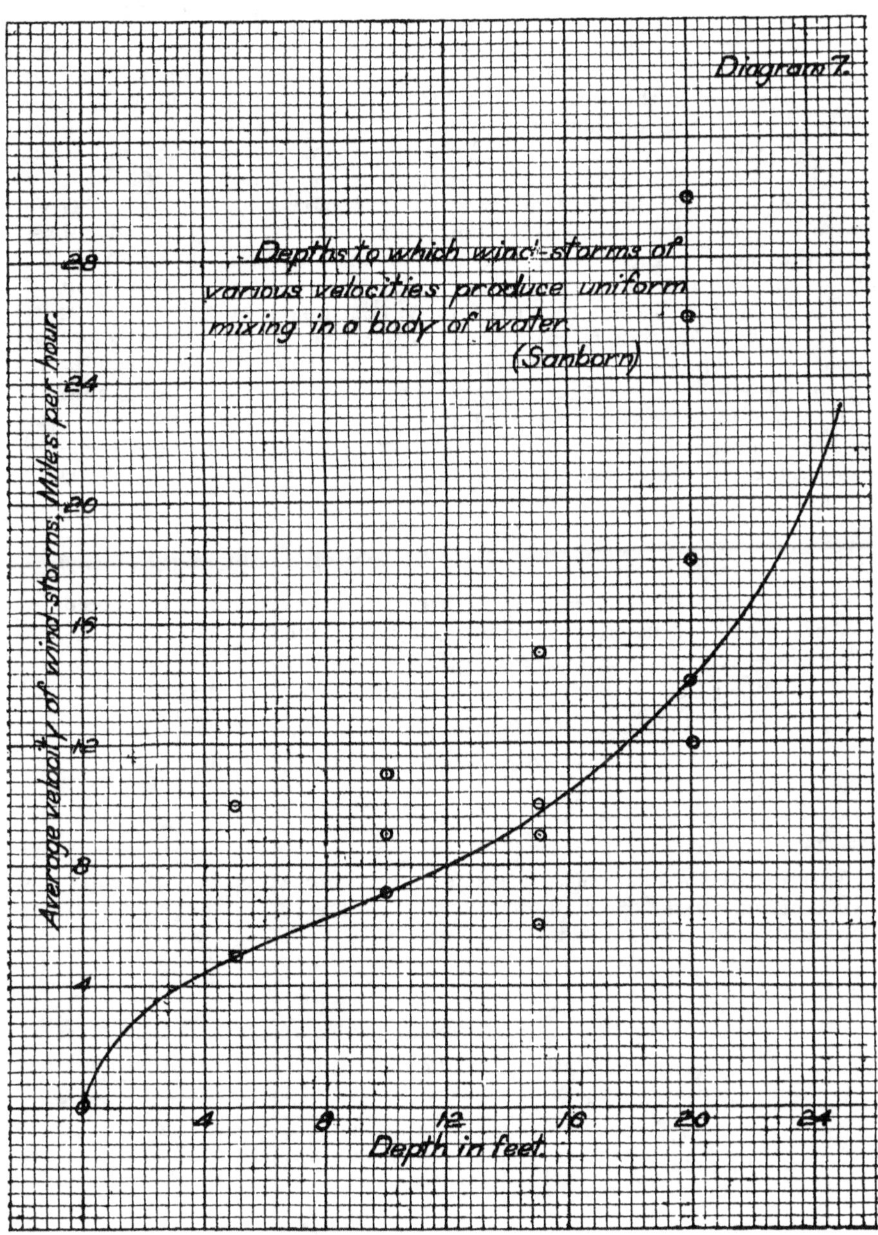
Diagram 7.
Depths to which wind-storms of various velocities produce uniform mixing in a body of water.
(Sanborn)
Average velocity of wind-storms, Miles per hour.
28
24
20
16
12
8
4
4
8
12
16
20
24
Depth in feet.

of the basin and a permanent condition of stratification with regularly increasing salinity with increasing depth has resulted. Disturbances due to wind were therefore easily and quickly recognized by a study of the salinity after wind storms. The condition of uniform mixing thus brought about speedily gave way to the stratified condition normal to the basin and conditions were ready for another test. Sanborn tested the results, all told, of twenty-one storms, ranging in wind velocities from five to thirty miles per hour. The direction of wind was in every case up or down stream with a fetch of one or two miles. The accompanying plot (Diagram 7), is from Sanborn's paper. Stevenson (1) shows that the wave height and consequently the depth of the movement is proportional to the square root of the fetch, so that we may assume that depths approximately twice as great as those found in the Boston experiments will be disturbed by wind storms of corresponding velocities, in New York Harbor. The following values therefore represent the best of our present knowledge and are probably not far from the truth. Since the total effect of wind will be shown to amount only to a minor correction to our figures, approximate values in this case are all that is required. They are for average conditions over the Bay and are excessive for the rivers except during wind storms blowing directly up or down stream.

TABLE 15.

Effect of Wind Producing Vertical Mixing in Water of New York Harbor.

From results of Sanborn upon Charles River (Boston), corrected by observations of Stevenson upon relation of fetch and wave height:

Wind Velocity, Miles Per Hour.	Depth of Uniform Mixing, Feet.
5	10
10	31
15	42
20	48

A study of the statistics of the United States Weather Bureau, has shown that during the four summer months, June to September, inclusive, the frequency of wind storms of varying intensities are as follows:

TABLE 16.

Frequency of Wind Storms of Stated Velocities.

(Compiled from Weather Bureau Chart.)

Wind Velocity, Miles Per Hour.	Average Frequency (Hours), June to September.
5	2.7
10	8.7
15	32.6
20	240.6

(1) Quoted by Gaillard, p. 67.

Combining these figures with those of Table 15, the frequency with which the water is disturbed to any given depth is determined. These depths and frequencies have been plotted, a smooth curve drawn through the points, and the following values reduced from the curve.

TABLE 17.

Frequency With Which the Waters of New York Harbor Are Uniformly Mixed to Stated Depth by Wind Action.

Depth of Mixing (Feet).	Frequency (Hours), June to September.
12	2.8
20	3.0
30	8.0
40	24.0

Discussion of the effect of this mixing by wind action will be postponed until the added effect of some other causes have been investigated. The slight breezes which always ruffle the surface have no material effect upon the result. They keep the surface and a few inches below in a state of constant admixture. The result is virtually to decrease the total depth by this amount. Reference to the figures in Table 13 will show that in depths of 20 feet or over a change of one foot in depth has but slight effect upon the rate of absorption.

Effect of Passing Vessels.

The currents produced by the movements of vessels are necessarily considered in a discussion of this kind. Vessels are commonly believed to exert considerable effect upon the aeration of the water. To determine this matter quantitatively the following procedure was adopted. If at any moment of observation, the total number of vessels in motion in the harbor is known, together with their respective speeds, drafts and breadth of beam (at water line), then the area disturbed per unit of time will be the sum of the products of the respective speeds and beams expressed in common units. For example, a vessel having a beam of 40 feet moving at a speed of ten miles per hour, will disturb a water area of 35,000 square feet per minute. The total area of water being disturbed in this way at any unit of time has been determined by averaging the results of a careful observation and classification of the vessels to be seen at any one time in the Hudson and East Rivers, between the Lackawanna Station, Hoboken, the Navy Yard, and Governor's Island. These observations were made at various hours during the day for a period of two weeks. The most used waters were purposely selected for these determinations in order that a maximum value might be obtained. For the same reason the hours of heaviest traffic only were taken and no attempt was made to get night observations. The results of the inspection and the average speeds and dimensions are given in Table 18. In this case as in the case of wave action the sum total of the effect is found to be of minor value, so that approximate accuracy only is required.

TABLE 18.

Statistics of Vessels.

Hudson River and East River between Lackawanna Station, Navy Yard and Governor's Island.

Average of daily observations at various hours for two weeks.

Type of Vessel.	Visible at One Time.	Speed Miles.	Beam Feet.	Draft Feet.	Area Disturbed Per Minute. Square Feet.
Ferries	7.5	14	40	12	369,000
Tugs	16.9	10	22	12	327,000
Tugs and Tow	6.6	7	100	12	407,000
Ocean Steamers	0.23	14	70	24	20,000
Schooners	0.39	7	30	14	7,000
Total					1,130,000

The total area disturbed calculated as described was found to be 1,130,000 square feet per minute. The total area of waters under observation is approximately 108,000,000 square feet. The proportion disturbed per minute is therefore 1/105 and the average time elapsing between successive disturbance of the same point is the reciprocal of this, or 105 minutes. The average draft is twelve feet so that it may be said that once in 1.75 hours any particular portion of the water of the Hudson or East River is stirred to a depth of 12 feet. Assuming such stirring to represent complete mixing, the data is now in form for reference to our absorption table. The effect of vessels amounts to but a few per cent. of the total effect due to all disturbances.

Effect of Tidal Currents.

The third important agency in the mixing of waters like those of New York Harbor is one which is least noticeable in its action and which is consequently overlooked in general discussions of this subject. This is the vertical circulation due to tidal action. Tidal currents act in at least two distinct ways. There is first the effect of the velocity of the moving stream in passing through a changing cross-sectional area and second the effect of under-run produced at the meeting of fresh and salt water.

When any body of water moves through a cross section which is changing in area or direction local differences in pressure arise which cause vertical and horizontal circulation. To a minor extent, movement in uniform sections, is, owing to bottom resistance, a process of rolling rather than one of strict translation. This effect is aggravated by rough bottoms and by high velocities. In extreme cases "rips" result even where there are considerable depths. Less vigorous action leads to "boils," common upon rivers with irregular sandy bottoms, or in the vicinity of bends.

Mixing due to these causes is always quite complete throughout the depth, and owing to the large volumes which pass during a tidal cycle, this agency, where it is active at all, is of importance in the aeration of tidal waters.

In New York Harbor the waters which flow into the East River from the Upper Bay, either through the Buttermilk Channel or around the west side of Governor's Island, are visibly subject to this action. At Hell Gate also there is complete vertical mixing of all the water passing. It happens that the volume of water in the East River between Hell Gate and the Battery is approximately equal to that which enters from each end during a half tidal period of six lunar hours, so that the average time between mixings of the waters of this river is about six hours. Some slight additional advantage is also derived from the relatively narrow cross-section and consequent pressure gradients across the current at maximum flow, from the bends and from the influence of Blackwell's Island. These all produce minor partial mixings through the vertical plane so that for these waters an average mixing period of five hours is probably conservative, and will be assumed.

The waters of the Hudson are less subject to action of the kind here described. Its width precludes any material cross-stream pressure gradients due to velocity of flow and side resistance and its uniform depth is not favorable to "boils." A portion of its flow is subject to overturning at Governor's Island, but the amount is inconsiderable. The second class of tidal effect mentioned, however, is predominant in the Hudson, namely the effect of under-run. A careful study throughout the tidal cycle, as given by the U. S. Coast and Geodetic Survey (1), shows that at least once during each flood tide there is a fairly complete commingling of the waters throughout the depth of the stream. This effect is confined to those waters in which there is distinct stratification and is probably immaterial below Spuyten Duyvil, as indicated in the salinity tables published by the Metropolitan Sewerage Commission (2).

Above Spuyten Duyvil, therefore, an average time between mixings of twelve hours may be safely assumed.

That portion of the tidal prism of the bay and tributaries which passes through the Narrows may similarly be assumed to receive a thorough mixing at that point, but as this incoming water will be composed largely of pure sea water, with an oxygen content approaching saturation the advantage in this case is slight.

In the main body of the Upper Bay and Lower Hudson the mixing from tidal effect is slight at best and cannot be estimated even roughly. The effect of tides rising and falling upon sloping shores, of waves breaking upon those shores, and of minor irregularities in current leading to eddies and boils is at least small in comparison with the effect of Hell Gate for example, and the small additional aeration given to waters passing the latter point serves excellently to indicate the infinitesimal results due to these minor causes.

---

(1) U. S. Coast & Geodetic Survey, Rep. for 1887, Append. No. 15.
(2) Rep. Met. Sew. Comm. of New York, 1910, p. 529, Table IX.

SUMMARY AND CONCLUSION.

These various results may now be summarized and added, as indicated in Table 19. It should be noted in particular that the effect of boats is the maximum effect found in the river and is largely excessive for the upper bay. Similarly the wind action is probably excessive for the Hudson and certainly largely so for the East River. The values are also all excessive in that fresh water coefficients of absorption only were available. It has been purposely intended to give results which shall be maximum values in every case.

TABLE 19.

Average Rate of Absorption of Atmospheric Oxygen in Various Parts of New York Harbor and Tributary Waters When 70 Per Cent. Saturated.

Body of Water.	Average Time Between Mixing (Hours).				Rate of Absorption. Pounds Per Million Gallons, Per Hour.
	Wind.	Boats.	Tide.	All Causes.	
Upper Bay, Middle and Lower Hudson:					
Depth of 12 feet	2.8	1.75	....	1.1	0.045
Depth of 20 feet	3.0	....	....	3.0	0.045
Depth of 30 feet	8.0	....	....	8.0	0.040
Depth of 40 feet	24.0	....	....	24.0	0.035
Upper Hudson:					
Mean depth 30 feet	8.0	....	12	4.8	0.012
East River:					
Depth of 12 feet	2.8	1.75	5	0.89	0.048
Depth of 20 feet	3.0	....	5	1.9	0.049
Depth of 30 feet	8.0	....	5	2.3	0.051

The last column of Table 19 is obtained in the following manner: The upper twelve feet in the bay is completely mixed in the summer time on the average of once in 1.1 hours. Obviously the maximum effect of such mixing would result from a uniform distribution of the mixing periods. In assuming such a distribution therefore, which is the only possible assumption in a general analysis of this kind, the results will show a degree of aeration somewhat in excess of the truth. Similarly we may allow an average period of mixing of 8 hours for the 30-foot, and 24 hours for the 40-foot depths. Referring now to Diagram 6, it is seen that the average rate of absorption in 12-foot depths by water 70 per cent. saturated, during a period of 1.1 hours is approximately .045, and in 20-foot depths during a period of three hours 0.018 pounds per hour per million gallons of water. The values for greater depths have not been plotted, but at 30 feet during an 8-hour period the value is found to be 0.01, and at 40 feet during 24 hours approximately 0.005 pounds per million gallons.

In 20-foot depths one million gallons will therefore absorb altogether 0.018 pounds per hour plus the amount absorbed by twelve-twentieths of one million gallons in the upper twelve feet, or 0.027, making a total of 0.045 pounds. Similarly in 30 feet there will be an absorption per million gallons of 0.01 pound, plus two-thirds of 0.045 pound, a total of 0.040 pound, and in 40 feet, 0.005 pound plus three-fourths of 0.040 pound, a total of 0.035 pound.

In the Hudson River above Spuyten Duyvil a mean depth of 20 feet is assumed which with an average mixing interval of 2.4 hours gives a rate of absorption of 0.019 pound per million gallons. The treatment of the East River is the same as that outlined above.

In each case the absorption in deep layers is determined as defined by their degree of quiescence, and to this the absorption by the upper layers due to their more frequent periods of mixing is added.

It is of interest to note that the action of the wind and tide reverses the conditions found in quiescent water, in that the rate of absorption of oxygen per million gallons of water increases slightly with increasing depth down to about 30 feet. With the added action of boats this effect is not so noticeable, and in the final results the combined effect results in a very even rate of absorption so that special treatment of the 12-foot depths need no longer be considered and for all practical purposes the average rate of absorption in the bay and lower Hudson may be taken at 0.045, in the East River at 0.050, and in the upper Hudson at 0.019 pound per hour per million gallons of water in all depths less than 40 feet. The effect of aeration in depths greater than 40 feet may safely be disregarded.

There remains only the discussion of minor tributaries. Of these the Harlem is of the greatest interest. This rapid-flowing stream is undoubtedly more thoroughly mixed throughout its course and throughout most of the tidal cycle, than any other body of water dealt with here. The relatively small volume of water passing through the Harlem makes it of minor consequence. Of the other bodies of water tributary to the Bay there is none that is as favorably affected either by wind or tide or vessels as are the Hudson and East Rivers. There are doubtless many small bays that have shallower depths, but reference to diagram 6, plate 16, will show that even in depths of ten feet, with periods of mixing of twelve hours or more the rate of aeration is not greater than those that have been found in the bay.

CHAPTER III.

Investigations Upon the Aeration of Sewage.

General.

The purification of sewage by biological means may be carried out to any degree of perfection desired and at costs that vary with the efficiency of the process. The most economical of such processes, and the least efficient, as measured by the degree of oxidation resulting, aims at producing complete stability in the organic matter. The effluent from a trickling filter for example, if discharged into a stream, will cause little or no reduction in the dissolved oxygen and natural purifying power of such stream.

Between this condition of practically complete stability and the condition of crude sewage, which is highly decomposable, lies a great range of possible conditions of partial oxidation which may be denoted numerically as lying between the limits of zero and 90 per cent. relative stability upon a scale in which complete stability would be represented by 100 per cent. In studies of sewage disposal by dilution this relative stability factor is one of prime importance since it measures directly the resulting effect upon the waters in question. Hitherto, little if any attention has been given to the problem of producing effluents having stabilities within the range indicated.

The experiments here reported were undertaken to determine if by some suitably arranged plan of artificial aeration, such partial purification could be accomplished at reasonable cost. Since biological filters are but mechanical devices for bringing together in close contact the three elements which enter into the oxidizing reactions, namely sewage, oxygen and bacteria, it was hoped that by increasing the ratio of sewage to oxygen volumes within a given tank space, and thus reducing the space required for purification, partial oxidation would result which would be of value under the peculiar local condition. These experiments were divided into three series. Series I. included investigation in shallow tanks upon both crude and septic sewage. Series II., investigations in a deep tank with septic sewage alone, and Series III., investigations, with a modified septic tank known as a biolytic tank. The first two series were made at Brooklyn and the last at Boston.

Series I.—Aeration of Crude and Septic Sewage in Shallow Tanks.

Plan of Investigation

The purpose of these experiments was to determine, first, whether the stability of raw or septicised sewage could be increased by forced aeration, and, secondly, under what conditions, with what volumes of air and at what cost the maximum economic efficiency of such a process could be attained. For this purpose arrangements were made at the sewage disposal works located in East New York for pumping directly from the outfall sewer a continuous flow of sewage sufficient for these investigations. This sewage was first pumped to an elevated supply tank from which it flowed by independent lines to a septic tank and to an aerating tank. The sewage from the septic tank overflowed to a second aerating tank; we were thus enabled to aerate both the crude sewage and the septic sewage. During a portion of this period of investigation aeration of the septic tank effluent was accomplished by pumping compressed air to the bottom of the tank through six parallel lines of pipe, each furnished with a row of ⅛-inch holes along its top line. For the purpose of better distribution of this air a fine mesh copper gauze was soldered around the air pipe so that the space between the pipe itself and this gauze became virtually an air chamber. During the second period of the investigation in addition to the arrangement just described, the tank was provided with frames upon which common laths were nailed in such a way that vertically and horizontally these laths were about one inch apart and at an angle of 45 degrees. The rows of laths were also staggered both vertically and horizontally. This arrangement gave throughout the body of the tank a very large surface for the development of bacterial growths upon which we relied for improved efficiency and it also served to improve the distribution and delay the passage of the air as it flowed upward. The aerating tank used with the crude sewage was constructed in exactly this same way at the beginning. The total capacity of the septic tank was 3,200 gallons; of the septic aerating tank 1,495 gallons; and of the raw sewage aerating tank 740 gallons. The average rate of flow through the raw sewage tank was maintained throughout at 13,000 gallons per day, making the period of treatment 1.4 hours. The septic tank and aerating tank were first operated at the rate of 13,000 gallons per day, making the period of septic action 5.9 hours and of aeration 2.8 hours. Later the capacity of the septic tank was decreased one-half as was also the rate of flow, thus maintaining the rate of septic treatment at the same figure but increasing the time of aeration to 5.6 hours. Considerable difficulty has been experienced in maintaining a steady flow of air through these two tanks and in particular in apportioning that flow in the desired ratio. It is believed, however, that the average conditions of air flow and the average results obtained are fairly representative.

Chemical Methods.

Chemical analyses have been made of the raw sewage before and after aeration and of the septic sewage after aeration. In changes in the character of the sewage with reference to its stability or its oxidizability, the ordinary methods of chemical analysis do not indicate the significant factors. One factor of importance is the dissolved oxygen contained in the liquid in question. Of chief importance, however, is that factor which we call the stability of the sewage which is the reciprocal of its tendency to withdraw oxygen from a stream. This stability factor we have estimated in two different ways. The first is known as the relative stability method or more commonly the putrescibility. In this method the liquid is mixed with the different proportions of water containing a known amount of dissolved oxygen. A sensitive indicating dye known as methylene blue is added to the mixture and the whole is preserved in a stoppered bottle and kept under constant observation. This blue dye has the property of losing its color when the dissolved oxygen of the liquid has entirely disappeared. The time required to so decolorize a sample is a somewhat complicated logarithmic function of the stability. This function has been determined as the result of an extended series of investigations upon all classes of sewages and effluents so that we now have a well-defined relation between the time required for decolorization and the so-called relative stability. This relative stability is the ratio between the amount of oxygen available in the diluted sample and the total amount of oxygen which would be utilized by that sample in its complete oxidation. Thus a sample of such a mixture which had a relative stability of 50 per cent. would contain just half the amount of oxygen which would be required to render it perfectly stable. This method is easy of application and is the one most commonly employed in sewage work. A more delicate method for obtaining the same information, and one which was devised for this work and used here for the first time is the following:

Suitable mixtures of the sewage in question with oxygen-saturated water are made and the total amount of oxygen in the mixture determined immediately. The sample is then stored in a tight bottle for a suitable period of time and a redetermination of the amount of dissolved oxygen present is made. The rate at which the oxygen disappears under these conditions gives us an index of the oxidizability of the organic matter and a more direct measure of the probable effect upon the stream than is given in the methylene blue method. The theoretical basis for this method will therefore be discussed in some detail.

Considering the reaction taking place between the organic matter of the sewage and the oxygen dissolved in the water the following relation should hold

$$\frac{dO}{dt} = KOC$$

In which O is the amount of oxygen present in unit volume, C the amount of organic matter oxidizable, t the time allowed for the reaction to proceed, and K a constant determined by the character of the organic matter and in turn defining the oxidizability of that organic matter. Integrating

$$\log \frac{O'}{O} = KCt$$

O′ being the initial and O the final amount of oxygen present.

The constant K defines mathematically the rapidity with which the oxygen is used up in a mixture of water and sewage. It depends upon the character of the sewage matter and the concentration of that material in the sewage and is independent of the extent of dilution or character of diluting water. A value of K = .0030 would indicate a sewage which in 25 per cent. admixture with water would reduce the oxygen content of the mixture 50 per cent. in four hours. Similarly for K = .0020 the reduction in a 25 per cent. admixture in four hours would be 37.5 per cent. and with K = .0015, 28.5 per cent.. These figures are tabulated in column A below to serve as a standard for interpreting the results of our experimental work.

In column B a set of figures are given which show the percentage of sewage of given K value which could be discharged into a stream under the condition that the oxygen of that stream shall not be reduced more than 20 per cent. in six hours.

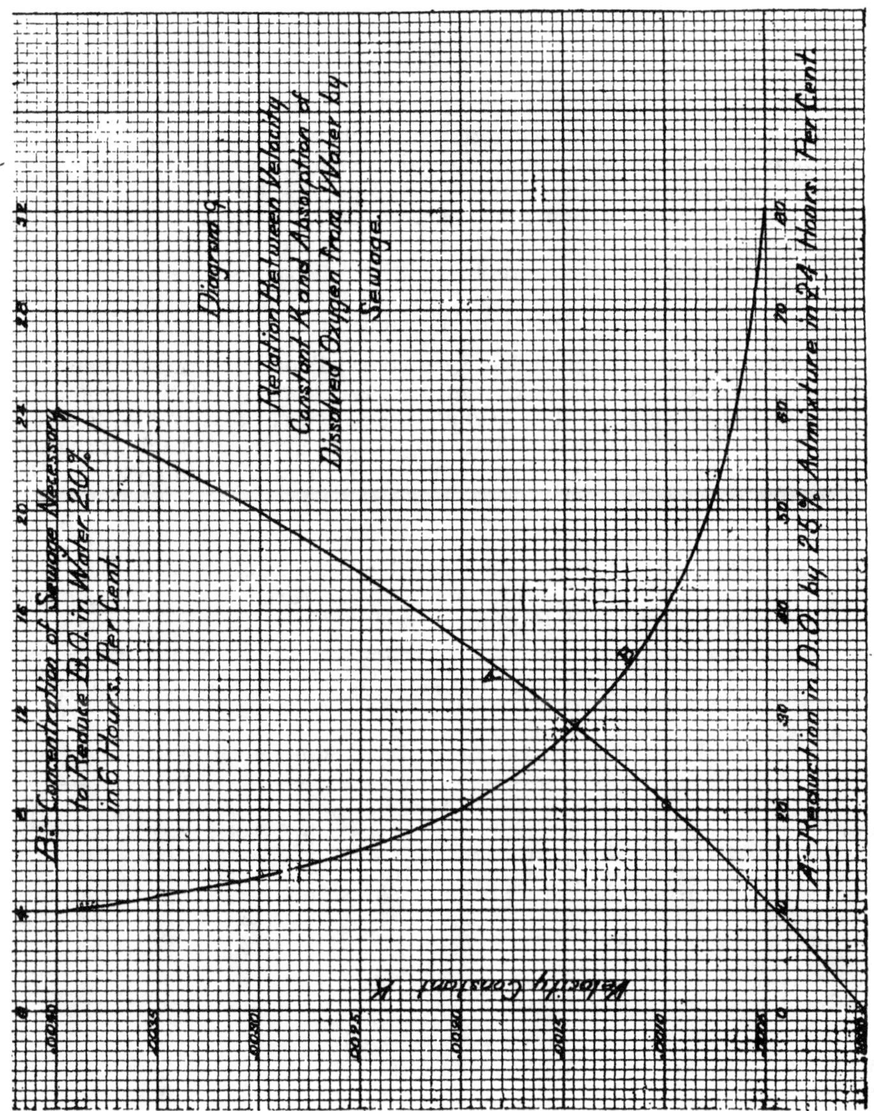
Diagram 9.
Relation Between Velocity Constant K and Absorption of Dissolved Oxygen from Water by Sewage.
B: Concentration of Sewage Necessary to Reduce D.O. in Water 20% in 6 Hours. Per Cent.
0 4 8 12 16 20 24 28 32
A: Reduction in D.O. by 25% Admixture in 24 Hours. Per Cent.
0 10 20 30 40 50 60 70 80
Velocity Constant K
.0040 .0035 .0030 .0025 .0020 .0015 .0010 .0005 .0000
A
B

K	A	B
.0030	50.0%	5%
.0020	37.5%	8%
.0015	28.5%	11%
.0010	20.0%	16%

A—Reduction in dissolved oxygen which would result at the end of four hours in a 25 per cent. admixture of sewage in water.

B—Maximum concentration of sewage permissible if the oxygen shall not be reduced more than 20 per cent. in approximately a half tidal period of six hours.

The relationship is shown more fully in Diagram 9.

Results Obtained.

Chemical Analyses—Samples were collected daily throughout most of the period covered by the work. During the latter part of the period they were collected every other day. Composite samples, preserved with chloroform, were analyzed weekly. The results are given in Table 20 in the form of monthly averages. For comparison an average analysis of Boston sewage is given.

TABLE 20.

Monthly Averages of Sewage Analyses Made on Samples Collected Daily at East New York, Before and After Experimental Treatment, and Average Analysis of Boston Sewage.

Month.	Suspended Solids.			Oxygen Consumed.			Nitrogen as Organic.			
	Total.	Vol.	Fixed.	Total.	Dis.	Susp.	Free Amm.	Total.	Dis.	Susp.
Crude Sewage.										
April	73	48	25	90	71	19	38	29	22	7
May	52	38	14	73	61	12	57	14	10	4
June	53	35	18	71	63	8	53	14	10	4
July	71	46	25	76	60	16	46	16	12	4
August	92	61	31	64	58	6	40	16	12	4
***September**	113	86	27	76	65	11	46	28	22	6
Average:										
1st Series	68	44	24	75	63	12	46	18	14	4
Grand Av.	75	52	23	76	63	13	46	20	15	5
Crude Sewage Aerated.										
April	78	47	31	68	51	17	39	23	19	4
May	54	34	20	53	42	11	33	16	13	3
June	101	57	44	56	46	10	33	15	12	3
July	56	34	22	55	46	9	36	15	12	3
August	94	65	29	57	47	10	34	15	12	3
Average	76	47	29	58	47	11	35	17	13	4

*Second series of experiments begun.

Month.	Suspended Solids.			Oxygen Consumed.			Nitrogen as Organic.			
	Total.	Vol.	Fixed.	Total.	Dis.	Susp.	Free Amm.	Total.	Dis.	Susp.
				Septic Sewage Aerated.						
April	54	38	16	57	38	19	24	21	17	4
May	34	23	11	52	40	12	26	16	11	5
June	58	34	24	56	40	16	27	17	15	2
July	54	26	28	56	41	15	27	16	12	4
August	42	31	11	42	38	4	26	14	11	3
*September ..	72	51	21	49	46	3	24	25	20	5
Average:										
1st Series..	49	26	23	53	39	14	26	17	13	4
Grand Av.	51	32	19	52	41	11	25	18	14	4
				Boston Sewage.						
Sept.-Dec. ...	185	130	55	66	27	33	21	3.1	1.7	1.4

* Second series of experiments begun.

The high nitrogen values indicate a sewage much stronger than the average and possibly containing nitrogenous manufacturing wastes, such as brewery waste. The low suspended solids on the other hand indicate a considerable deposit in the outfall sewer. Considering the strength of this sewage its stability is high. The sewage of Boston is fully as putrescible as this sewage, measured in terms of oxygen absorption from water, but in chemical composition it is much weaker. This bears out the indication of some relatively stable manufacturing waste. It would appear that we are dealing with a sewage which, although strong according to our analytical results, is not more decomposable than an average city sewage. Improvement by aeration would, therefore, be relatively more difficult.

The analyses of the crude sewage after aeration and of the same sewage after having passed the septic tank and the aeration tank are also given in Table 20. No changes are noted other than those which can be ascribed to the action of the tanks themselves.

Relative Stability—The relative stability results as determined by the methylene blue test are given in Table 21.

TABLE 21.

Relative Stability, Dissolved Oxygen and Putrescibility Results and Other Data.

Series I.

Sewage.	Period.	Air., Cu. Ft. Per Gal.	Time of Contact, Hours.	Relative Stability Dilution %. 15	20	25	30	35	Putrescibility Coefficient K Dilution %. 5	25	Dis. Oxygen.
Crude	1	..	..	80	66	53	45	..	.0029	.0035	1.9
Crude, Aerated	1	.20	1.4	95	96	77	69	61	.0020	.0020	2.3
Crude	2	..	..	75	57	43	..	..	.0054	.0060	2.8
Crude, Aerated	2	.09	1.4	..	..	74	63	52	.0023	.0044	1.1
Crude	3	..	..	86	70	60	..	..	.0059*	.0040*	1.2
Septic, Aerated	3	.36	2.8	95	95	79	61	48	.0027*	.0026*	.34
Crude	4	..	..	82	68	60	..	..	.0028	.0026	2.7
Septic, Aerated	4	.67	5.6	..	..	68	56	45	.0017	.0023	.37
Crude	5	..	..	74	58	48	..	..	.0038	.0036	3.1
Septic, Aerated	5	.77	5.6	..	..	78	70	68	.0014	.0021	1.2
Crude	6	..	..	79	59	44	..	..	.0076	.0104	2.5
Septic, Aerated	6	.23	2.8	..	..	83	80	69	.0018	.0054	.22

* These dilutions are 10 and 50 instead of 5 and 25.

Period 1—March 25 to May 17.
Period 2—May 18 to August 19.
Period 3—March 25 to April 21.
Period 4—April 22 to May 12.
Period 5—May 13 to June 26.
Period 6—June 27 to August 19.
Baffle screens used during Periods 1, 2, 5 and 6.

The raw sewage shows a constantly decreasing stability as is always the case during this season of the year. Direct aeration at the rate of .20 cubic feet of air per gallon of sewage increases the stability by about 45 per cent. in a 25 per cent. mixture, and 53 per cent. in a 30 per cent. mixture. During the second period the rate of application of air was decreased to .09 and the increased stability for this period in a 25 per cent. mixture was 72 per cent. It is possible that still less quantities of air would give results approximately as good, but upon the basis of this work it is evident that no greater quantities than 90,000 cubic feet per million gallons will be required.

The septic sewage results must be considered in four separate periods. During period "3" the rate of application was .36 cubic feet per gallon, and the increased stability over the raw sewage for the corresponding period was 32 per cent. in a 25 per cent. mixture; during the fourth period the time of contact with the air increased from 2.8 to 5.6 hours, the other conditions remaining the same except that now the rate of application of air was .67 cubic feet per gallon. The stability in 25 per cent. mixture was increased only 13 per cent. During the fifth period screens were installed similar to those already in use with the crude sewage, the rate of application and time of contact remaining the same, which resulted in an increased stability of 62 per cent., calculated on the crude sewage for this period.

During the sixth period the air was diminished to 0.23 cubic feet per gallon, and the time of contact to 2.8 hours, with a resulting improvement in stability at 25 per cent. dilution of 89 per cent., the highest value recorded during these studies. A part of this improvement is doubtless due to the decreased stability of the sewage itself already noted, and the same statement may be made in regard to the second period of the raw sewage experiment, in which decreasing the amount of applied air did not materially affect the result. The results of these last periods are approaching summer conditions and it is doubtless true that with the coming of warm weather and the consequent lessened stability of the crude sewage, high percentages of improvement are more readily obtained. As it is summer conditions that really limit any dilution process of sewage disposal, these warm weather results have the greatest significance in this present study.

Putrescibility Coefficient—The results obtained by the putrescibility coefficient are, when suitably interpreted, the most satisfactory basis for determining the results of the work of this character. In Curve B, Diagram 9, the maximum permissible concentration of sewage in a body of water is given for all values of the coefficient, under the condition that the dissolved oxygen shall not be reduced by more than 20 per cent. in six hours. For purposes of comparison any other value might have been selected. Measured by this practical test the percentage improvements in the sewage under treatment as shown by the data of Table 21 were as follows:

TABLE 22.

Percentage Improvement in Condition of Sewage Brought About by Aeration, as Measured by Concentration of Sewage Required to Reduce the Oxygen Content of Water, 20 Per Cent. in Six Hours.

Summary.

Period.	Improvement, Per Cent.
1	45
2	136
3	118
4	65
5	177
6	320

Full discussion of these results will be reserved for a later place.

Series II.—Aeration of Septic Sewage in a Deep Tank.

Our investigations up to this time had shown that a satisfactory partial oxidation of crude sewage could be accomplished under the conditions prevailing in the experiments. The volume of air required relative to the sewage flow was considerable, however, and the cost of such treatment seemed unnecessarily high. Examinations of the air leaving the aeration tank showed conclusively that the oxygen content was far from being exhausted. In fact, the air was practically of normal composition upon leaving the tank as far as we could learn from chemical analysis. In other words, the actual amount of oxygen absorbed from this considerable volume of air was infinitesimal. It seemed therefore that the same body of air might to good advantage be used to treat a larger volume of sewage at a consequent decreased cost of pumping. This result could only be obtained by increasing the depth of the tank. In two tanks of unequal depth through each of which sewage is flowing at a stated velocity and into each of which a stated volume of air is passing, the sewage in that tank having the greater depth will obviously receive exactly the same treatment as that in the smaller tank, but the relation of air volume to sewage will be inversely as the depths.

Plan of Investigation.

To test the efficiency of this procedure, a tank twenty-one feet in depth to the water line was built out of two-foot lengths of 24-inch vitrified sewer pipe set up in a vertical stack. Through the central axis of this stack a three-quarter-inch iron pipe passed from top to bottom and upon this pipe circular discs of No. 12 expanded metal lathing were placed at one-foot vertical intervals. Sewage was admitted to this stack through a two-inch pipe at the bottom, this pipe coming from the overflow in the septic tank used in our previous experiments. The sewage overflowed from a pipe at the top of the stack. Compressed air was pumped through the three-quarter-inch iron pipe mentioned and was distributed at the bottom of the stack through one-eighth-inch holes spaced two inches on centers upon four cross arms 90 degrees apart, extending from the center to a point near the periphery. Compressed air was supplied by the compressor used in the previous experiments. The capacity of the air compressor was determined under the working conditions by inserting a pressure air meter in the line and calibrating the pump by revolutions. Subsequently the rate was controlled by pumping as nearly as possible at a fixed number of revolutions and wasting the desired amount through a by-pass which was metered. The actual amount of air used was then taken as the difference between the original pump rate at the given speed and the amount of air measured in the waste line. The experimental portion of this work was divided into two periods:

During the first, a four-hour period of septic treatment and a one-hour period of aeration were allowed. The rate of flow of sewage through the tank during this period was 486 gallons per hour and of air about 110 cubic feet, so that air was being applied at the rate of approximately 0.23 cubic feet per gallon.

During the second period, the rate of flow throughout the system was reduced one-half, so that the time of septic treatment was made eight hours and of aeration two hours. The volume of air was decreased proportionately, so that the net effect of this change was to increase the time of treatment only.

Results Obtained.

These experiments were controlled by the same chemical tests as were made in the first series. They extended from September 10 to September 23, in the first period, and from September 23 to October 6 in the second period. As the sole purpose of this series of experiments was to determine whether results comparable with those obtained in Series I. could be obtained in the deeper tank at a correspondingly less volume of air relative to sewage, it was not continued longer than was necessary to demonstrate the facts. The average results of each period as measured by the two methods already described are summarized below.

TABLE 23.

Relative Stability, Dissolved Oxygen and Putrescibility Results and Other Data.

Series II.

Sewage.	Period.	Air, Cubic Feet Per Gallon.	Time of Contact, Hours.	Relative Stability. Dilution Per Cent.					Putrescibility Coefficient K, Dilution Per Cent.		Dissolved Oxygen.
				20.	25.	30.	35.	40.	5.	15.	
Crude	1	....	..	78	60	49	..	..	.0054	.0058	2.0
Aerated septic	1	0.23	1	..	..	94	85	77	.0011	.0015	6.2
Crude	2	....	..	80	68	52	..	..	.0069	.0080	.80
Aerated septic	2	0.23	2	..	..	77	62	44	.0028	.0044	4.4

In interpreting these results it is necessary to bear in mind the fact already developed early in these investigations—that the putrescibility of the sewage itself changes greatly from season to season, largely owing to temperature changes. Therefore the ratio of improved stability obtained in this series of experiments is the point of particular significance. No direct comparison of actual K values or of stabilities as determined by the methylene blue test can be made between these results and those of the first series which were made during the warmer summer months.

The improved stability as measured by the methylene blue test at 30 per cent. is 93 per cent. in period one (1) and 48 per cent. in period two (2), and as measured by the putrescibility coefficient 380 per cent. and 145 per cent., respectively.

On the whole, it is seen that the relative improvement is decidedly greater than was observed in Series I. It is not certain that results of maximum efficiency are obtained in this case, owing to the comparatively small amount of air necessary; the compressor in use could not be controlled at any lower rates, but the evidence indicates that satisfactory results could be obtained with relative air volumes somewhat less than those actually used.

Analyses of the air escaping from the top of the tank were made on several occasions and showed that about 2 per cent. by volume of the total amount of air passed, or 10 per cent. by volume of the oxygen content of that air had been exhausted in its passage through the tank. It is therefore apparently only a matter of engineering economy in the construction of deep tanks which will determine the most economical depth to be employed. Obviously the economy of this treatment increases in direct proportion to the depths of the tank.

Series III.—Experiments Upon the Aeration of a Biolytic Effluent, at Boston, Mass.

The two series of investigations which have been reported thus far made use of a septic tank effluent which was at all times devoid of oxygen and was throughout a considerable period of this work exceedingly putrescible. It is a well-known fact in sewage chemistry that with increasing age of sewage there is a corresponding decrease in oxygen dissolved values and that this change does not end when the zero value is reached. Under the anaerobic conditions which then result, the sewage becomes exceedingly avid for oxygen so that an old septic effluent will oftentimes absorb almost immediately more oxygen than the original sewage would have absorbed in many hours. There is reason to believe that this increased avidity for oxygen is due in a large measure to easily oxidized gaseous or mineral compounds, so that oxygen used up in accomplishing such oxidation is largely wasted. On the other hand, it is quite possible that this increased avidity is a direct measure of the ease of oxidation of the entire mass of the organic matter, in which case these conditions are distinctly favorable. The results of the first series of investigations reported seemed to indicate that other things being equal a septic effluent would rapidly use up a larger amount of oxygen than with a corresponding crude sewage with no additional beneficial results in the matter of stability than those which could be ascribed to the partial loss of suspended solids which is incidental to the septic process. It was thought best, therefore, to obtain more data upon the question of the desirability or otherwise of first septicizing the sewage before aeration.

Plan of Investigation.

At the Sewage Experiment Station of the Massachusetts Institute of Technology, a tank of somewhat novel design has been in operation under the direction of one of the writers for about eighteen months. This tank has been called a " biolytic " tank. It is essentially a deep rectangular tank with a hopper-shaped bottom. The sewage enters through a pipe down the center and is discharged at a point near the bottom of the tank. It flows upward in a column whose cross section is constantly increasing and whose velocity is consequently decreasing, overflowing at eight points about the periphery. The purpose of this tank and of this peculiar mode of operation is to prevent the accumulation of the products of decomposition in the bottom layers and to keep the sewage as fresh as possible consistent with satisfactory sedimentation. The tank effluent is well clarified and in much more satisfactory condition for treatment upon sand filters or other oxidizing mechanisms than is the effluent of the septic tank.

The aeration system was installed in the upper two feet of this tank, essentially similar to the arrangements used in the first series of these experiments. Our results thus far having indicated the possibility of increased economy with increased depth, the question of depth and relative volumes of air are not deemed of importance in these experiments. If satisfactory results could be obtained during a stated period of treatment such as one or two hours the economy in air compression which would result from the use of deeper installations could easily be determined. The installation, therefore, consisted of a series of seven horizontal air distributors essentially like those already described, above which was a system of inclined slats like those used at Brooklyn, two feet in depth. This tank had a cross-sectional area at the top of approximately 50 square feet. The rate of flow through the tank was eight thousand gallons in twenty-four hours, which gives an upward velocity in the upper section of 0.88 feet per hour. The time of exposure to the air was therefore approximately two and a quarter hours.

Results.

Results by the putrescibility coefficient only were obtained in this series. During the experiments putrescibility coefficients were obtained at a great many dilutions in order to determine thoroughly the significance of this test. The averages of all coefficients obtained during the period, October 1 to December 31, 1910, were

Crude sewage..............................	.0022
Septic aerated..............................	.0020

which by Diagram 1 gives an improvement of 10 per cent., as measured by the dilution of these sewages which will reduce 20 per cent. of the oxygen of the water in six hours.

This poor showing is evidently due to difficulty in getting aerobic conditions established in the tank which had been anaerobic for over a year.

During the months of November and December, when improvement was most difficult in Brooklyn, the average results of the Boston tests made at 5 per cent. dilutions were

Crude sewage..................................	.0023
Septic aerated.........	.0012

The improvement here, measured as before by Diagram 9, is 92 per cent. These results show strongly the necessity for a separate aeration tank following the septic treatment. The two processes cannot be combined in one tank.

CONCLUSIONS.

Amount of Air Required and Improvement Effected.

The amount of oxygen necessary to give significant results has been determined regardless of cost or other considerations. In the case of the crude sewage it was found that a rate of application of 110 thousand cubic feet per million gallons gave an excess of dissolved oxygen in the sewage which indicated that no further advantage would be obtained by increasing the air supply. In the case of the septic sewage an equal rate of application gave no such evidence of excess and an effort was made to add the air at a sufficiently high rate to show some excess. This effort was only partially successful and in no case was the excessive oxygen in this effluent as great as in the raw sewage effluent. For this reason also the time of contact was doubled without any appreciable results in the excess of oxygen. It was soon discovered that it was useless to attempt to get any noticeable excess in this septic sewage and that even at the lower rates the stability of the septic sewage was increased and at the higher rates of application was fully equal to that of the aerated crude sewage. Analysis of the air leaving the liquid also showed that the absorption of oxygen from this air was very little indeed so that it seemed desirable to decrease rather than to further increase the amount. The result obtained during period 6 amply justified this conclusion. These results are so far superior to those obtained with crude sewage, that there is every indication that highly satisfactory results could have been obtained at still lower rates of treatment.

Imperfect distributing apparatus made it impossible to further reduce this rate and study this matter further in the limited time that was available. The results of Series II. are of especial interest in indicating still further economy in air. The much greater efficiency obtained during the first period of treatment indicates a distinct advantage in favor of shorter period of septic treatment. Again it was found impossible with the large capacity of the air compressing machinery and meters to reduce the air flow to what was strongly indicated as the point of maximum economy.

The Boston experiments were not planned to determine possible economy in air since only a shallow depth was available, but the result of all this work taken together enabled conclusions to be drawn that were not indicated in any single series. Period 6 of Series I. gave the best results in a shallow tank with an air consumption of 0.23 cubic feet per gallon and a contact period of 2.8 hours. Series II. shows that economy in air and tank space, and efficiency increase with the depth, other conditions being equal. Together with Series III. it indicates a great advantage in short septic periods. All the data taken together plainly show that, during the hot weather months, the critical period in harbor conditions, the stability of a sewage as measured by its withdrawal of oxygen from the diluting waters, can be increased from two to three fold by the application of short period septic action, and by aerating in a deep tank; and that an air consumption of approximately 0.1 cubic feet per gallon will doubtless be sufficient under these conditions. This means that under any stated conditions of permissible pollution in the harbor waters the maximum amount of sewage which can be disposed of in the harbor is increased two to three fold by this treatment.

Sludge.

The question of sludge disposal is one which is common in all sewage treatment and has not been investigated here. The Biolytic tank in use at Boston is designed with special reference to this problem. Its function is to reduce the sludge problem to a minimum by providing for maximum liquifaction in the tank. Results of the operation of the tank will soon be published in another place. It can be stated that the sludge problem will at least be not greater than in other processes and can by proper design of tanks be very much reduced if desirable. The amount of finely divided suspended matter which the tank will discharge is controlled by the design. The amount which should be discharged under any given local conditions can only be determined by local studies. It will be found advantageous to discharge a maximum quantity as determined by stream flow and dilution in any case. The remainder will have to be dealt with by methods now in vogue, most likely by removal in scows.

Cost of Aeration.

The relative costs of low pressure air compression by means of compression and rotary blowers has not been gone into in detail. There would seem to be some advantage in the use of deep tanks and higher pressures, up to possibly thirty feet. On the other hand for lower pressures, up to five or six feet, the blower type of air pump is highly efficient.

A blower of this type having a capacity of fifty thousand cubic feet of air per hour under a five-foot head of water requires about 25 K. W. of current, net.

At the rates of aeration which we have finally adopted, this blower would care for a sewage flow of half a million gallons per hour. At a cost of 4 cents per K. W. hour these costs for current alone would be two dollars ($2) per million gallons. This refers to small electrically operated plants at sewer outfalls. For larger installations, the cost of power would not exceed one-half this amount. We estimate the total cost of installation of plant in the neighborhood of two thousand dollars ($2,000) per million gallons daily capacity, or about one twenty-fifth the cost of sprinkling filters after deducting land costs. Labor charges should be exceedingly low.

It should further be noted that under conditions in which such a process might be necessary and sufficient, the necessity for its use would arise only during the summer season, of perhaps four months each year. If winter conditions demand treatment at all then the summer conditions would not be met by aeration, since the variations we have noted between summer and winter sewages are greater than the improvements obtained.

Under certain local conditions also less perfect results than have been obtained here might be ample. The merits and possibilities of this process have only been barely indicated in this investigation and a fruitful field has been opened up for future investigation.

CHAPTER IV.

Studies for Sewage Disposal From Certain Districts.

*Flushing Drainage District**—This district is bounded on the south by the ridge near Hillside road, which forms the divide of the watershed to north and south; on the west by Flushing Bay and the high land west of Flushing Creek; on the north by the Sound and on the east by Little Neck Bay and the low lands extending from the head of that bay to the ridge first mentioned. The total area is 14,923 acres, and the estimated future population on a basis of 50 persons per acre for the towns and 25 persons per acre for suburban districts, is 423,425. For the purpose of determining possible points of discharge a trunk sewer system had to be designed, on the separate system for the unsewered parts and with storm water overflows where the combined system is now installed. This system as designed serves all of the district and is adequate to the needs of the estimated future population. A water consumption of 125 gallons per capita per day was assumed and an allowance of .003 cubic feet per second per acre was made for ground water flow, based on the practice of the Borough Engineer of Brooklyn. Further assumptions made were as follows: that of the total flow per 24 hours, half would pass in eight hours; that the maximum velocity with sewer 0.8 full should not exceed 7.5 feet per second; and that the minimum velocity with sewer 0.2 full should not be less than 1.50 feet per second.

It was found that the drainage from the entire area could be brought to a point in the East River east of Powells Cove and then discharged, and that five-sevenths of the area could be drained by a high level gravity system to the point of discharge, with a low level gravity system for the remainder, discharging into the high level system by pumping. Possible sites for purification works were found should such prove necessary. Details of the recommendations made are given in the special report rendered March 20, 1910.

*Corona Drainage District**—This district comprises the territory between the Flushing District on the east, the dividing ridge on the south, the Borough of Brooklyn and Newtown Creek on the west and the East River on the north. Its area is 14,535 acres and the estimated future population on the basis described for the Flushing District is 628,200. This includes an area of 756 acres with an estimated future population of 37,800 for which the natural drainage is through the sewers of Brooklyn. Another portion containing 1,290 acres with an estimated future population of 64,500 along the water front from Astoria south and west to Newtown Creek and lying below the 20-foot contour, is now drained into Newtown Creek and the East River. Eventually its sewers will have to be intercepted and discharged by pumping into the main system.

For the remainder of the district a gravity system of trunk sewers has been designed by which all of the sewage is carried to and discharged into deep water of the East River from a point approximately to the southeast of Berrian's Island.

*See map showing Drainage Districts of Jamaica, Corona, Flushing and Westchester following p. 148. The writers are indebted to Mr. E. F. Robinson for valuable assistance in the Drainage District Studies.

Should purification works become necessary, these can be located on Riker's Island, to which the system can be prolonged.

The sewers were designed on the same assumptions as those for the Flushing District. Provision for storm water overflows has been made at points where the proposed interceptors receive the discharge of existing combined systems, and at two points along Flushing Bay and one point near the head of Newtown Creek. While the sewers were designed for sanitary and ground water flow only, they are of capacity sufficient for the estimated future population and until the present population shall have increased greatly they can be utilized for storm water flow.

There is now a sewage purification plant at Elmhurst, which is capable of caring for the sewage of the district tributary to it for the present and if improved can be utilized for the increasing population for some years and thus render unnecessary the immediate construction of a portion of the projected system.

Full details of the system as projected are given in the special report dated May 24, 1910.

*Jamaica Drainage District**—This district comprises the areas draining naturally into Jamaica Bay as well as Coney Island, Rockaway Beach and a small area near the head of Little Neck Bay, within the limits of Greater New York, but cut off by a ridge from the Flushing District system. In general it is bounded on the north by the ridge which forms the southern limit of the Corona and Flushing Districts, on the east by Nassau County, on the south by Jamaica Bay and on the west by Gravesend Bay.

The estimates for future population were made as in the other districts. Inasmuch as it is expected that the portion of the district contiguous to Jamaica Bay, for which a population of 50 per acre has been assumed, will be developed chiefly for manufacturing and commercial purposes, a water consumption of 100 instead of 125 gallons per day has been allowed, which gives an equivalent population of 40 per acre with a water consumption of 125 gallons per day. In the cases of Coney Island and Rockaway Beach, the permanent population is small in comparison with the number of daily visitors throughout the summer months. For Coney Island a maximum population of 500,000, with an average daily water consumption of 15 gallons per capita, has been assumed, and it is further assumed that the total run-off will take place in 12 hours. These assumptions when reduced to terms corresponding to those used for other districts would give a permanent population of 70 per acre with a daily per capita water consumption of 125 gallons. Similar assumptions for the Rockaway section give an equivalent permanent population of 50 per acre, with a daily water consumption of 125 gallons. Other assumptions as to population, water consumption, ground water run-off and ratio of maximum to average discharge are the same as for the Flushing District.

The total area in the Jamaica District is 48,916 acres. The total estimated future population is 1,661,495.

Jamaica Bay is a land-locked tidal basin of slight depth, in which the entire tidal prism is filled and emptied during each tidal period. Partial purification of the sewage discharged into it will be required, but even with

*See map showing Drainage Districts of Jamaica, Corona, Flushing and Westchester, following p. 148.

such purification, to secure an adequate degree of diffusion there must be several points of discharge. For the portion of the Jamaica Bay drainage area of the Borough of Queens, the system as projected gathers all of the sewage by gravity at two main concentration points, one at the present Twenty-sixth Ward Pumping Station, and one on Cornell Creek, from which it will be discharged through iron force mains into Fishkill and Broad Channels, respectively. When under the proposed project for improvement of Jamaica Bay, a thirty-foot channel has been formed along the north side of the Bay as far as these discharge mains, they must terminate in that channel, and it will then be essential to provide the most efficient means of diffusion practicable on discharge in order to avoid the formation of local nuisances. Storm water overflows are provided whenever existing sewers of the combined system are intercepted.

The eastern section of the Borough of Brooklyn comprised in the Jamaica District already had approved plans for sewerage, and the project had to be formed with due regard to these plans. The project contemplates the collection of the sewage by gravity at three points where it is lifted to a higher level and conveyed by gravity to proposed purification works in Riches Point Meadow, and then lifted and discharged into Rockaway Inlet, the ebb currents from which pass seaward, without touching the bathing beaches of Coney Island or Rockaway Beach.

The western sections in the Borough of Brooklyn are already provided with approved projects partly carried out. In the complete project only a few additions were required.

Two distinct systems of disposal are practicable for the Coney Island sewage. One is to force the sewage north to the concentration point established for the sections to the north and thence to lead and discharge it into the Narrows, through the interceptor already constructed. The second is to discharge it to the south by pumping into the sea, not less than 2,000 feet from shore, and at a point from which currents do not lead to the beach. The latter plan is recommended, since the inadvisability of increasing the pollution of the harbor in any case where it can be avoided is manifest.

The Little Neck Bay section is of a limited area. It is proposed to concentrate the sewage from it at the head of Little Neck Bay and after purification to discharge it into the bay.

The Rockaway section is low and flat. It is proposed to collect the sewage from it at three points, and after coarse screening and sedimentation with liquefaction for a short period in hydrolytic tanks, to discharge it into the sea at least 1,000 feet from the shore line, from which there is no probability of its being brought back to any appreciable degree.

Disposal in Jamaica Bay—As stated earlier, Jamaica Bay is a landlocked tidal basin, of which the tidal prism is filled and emptied during each tidal period through Rockaway Inlet. After passing the fanshaped bar between Rockaway Point and Coney Island, outside the outer extremity of the inlet, the inlet has a deep channel of ample width which extends as far east as Barren Island. There this main channel is divided into several minor channels. One follows the north shore of Rockaway Point, others pass northeast between the islands of the bay, and the most westerly follows generally the west shore of the bay. These channels are formed and maintained by the tidal currents. But there is no current circulation between the heads of the channels along the north side of the bay other than such as may be produced temporarily by wind action. Excepting as moved by the winds, the waters on the north and east shores are quiescent. Under such conditions it is evidently necessary that the sewers be extended into the channels as in the project.

The total flow through Rockaway Inlet as determined by the observations of the Engineer Department, U. S. Army, is for flood 4,550,000,000 cubic feet. This is the measure of the tidal prism. From the map of the bay the portion of the tidal prism tributary to each channel was determined and from this the mean velocities of flow in the channels calculated. Assuming the sewage discharge through each of the outlets on the basis as calculated for the project and beginning with pure water in the bay, the amount of partially polluted water due to the discharge at the close of an ebb tide and remaining in the channel at the beginning of the flood period was determined and the ratio of sewage to pure water obtained. It is evident that this ratio is at first too large, since at first no previous pollution is assumed. By continuing the process the ratio grows smaller by decreasing decrements until the decrement practically vanishes and the ratio then represents the true proportions of the average admixture of sewage and sea water which result from the discharge of the assumed volume of sewage. While the dilution figure fairly represents an average condition, the pollution in the immediate vicinity of the sewer outlet will be much greater even with the best process for diffusion possible, and to avoid local nuisance, it will be necessary to have the dilution ratio large. We believe that this figure should not be lower than 1 part sewage to 117 parts sea water at 63 degrees Fahrenheit.

The sewage discharged into Rockaway Inlet from Riches Point Meadow, if considered alone, would have an ultimate dilution, determined as indicated, of one part in 2,670, but when considered together with the discharge into other portions of the bay the average ultimate dilution is 1 in 209. The discharge into Big Fishkill Channel will have an average ultimate dilution of 1 in 75. That discharged into Broad Channel will have an average ultimate dilution of 1 in 95. These figures are based upon an assumption of thorough diffusion. At periods of slack water the percentage of pollution will be much greater.

The dilution ratio of 1 in 117 was adopted as necessary in view of the volume of oxygen absorbed by sewage under summer conditions (1,950 pounds per million gallons in 12 hours), the available supply in the tidal basin, and the consideration that under the worst conditions this supply must never be reduced below 50 per cent. of the saturation value, which would make an average reduction to 75 per cent. of saturation value a standard with a small margin of safety.

Complete purification before discharge is evidently never necessary under the conditions prevailing in Jamaica Bay with sewage concentrated and discharged under the project outlined in this report. During the winter season even partial purification will probably be unnecessary. Therefore, we recommend for this district purification by aeration as described in this report as being most economical and advantageous. Even this treatment will probably be unnecessary until the proposed drainage system shall have been developed to at least one-half of its ultimate capacity.

Details of the project are given in the special report dated November 18, 1910.

*Borough of Richmond Drainage District**—This district includes all of Staten Island with an area of 36,623 acres, shaped roughly in triangular form with its vertex to the south and its greatest length from the vertex to near the centre of the base at the outer end of the Kill von Kull, on a line running northeast and southwest. It is bounded on the north by the Kill von Kull and the Upper Bay; on the east by the Narrows and the Lower Bay; on the south by the Lower Bay and on the west by the Arthur Kill. The total length of coast line is 36 miles, of which 18 miles border on the two Kills and 5 miles on the Upper Bay. Both Kills are now polluted by sewage from the cities of New Jersey to an extent which probably makes further discharge of sewage into them inadmissible. Tidal and current data are meagre, but the following discussion of the circulation in the Arthur Kill, based on the best information obtainable, confirms this opinion. An examination of the tidal curve of the current charts in Appendix No. 9 of the report for 1886 of the U. S. Coast and Geodetic Survey shows that the tide has risen to 1.51 above mean low water at the beginning of the flood currents and that the plane of the water rises to high water (+4.1) and falls to an elevation of +2.35 before the current begins to run ebb.

It is estimated that the amount of water in the Arthur Kill below the low water plane is about 1,973.5 million cubic feet; that the tidal area is about 123.34 million square feet; and that the ebb and flood flow through the cross-section at Elizabethport is 319.0 million cubic feet.

TABLE 24, SHOWING DATA FOR ARTHUR KILL.

Area.		Elevation at Beginning of	Maximum or Minimum Elevation	Elevation at End of Period	Tidal Area Million Sq. Ft.	Tidal Prism Volume Million Sq. Ft.	Total Volume at End of Period Million Cu. Ft.
P-Arthur Kill	Flood	+1.5	4.1	2.35	123.34	289.9	2,263.4
P′ " "	Ebb	+2.35	0.0	1.50	123.34	185.0	2,158.5

Let M = clean water from the Lower Bay

Let K = water received from the Kill von Kull or Newark Bay

Let n = tide under consideration, flood or ebb

n−1 = the previous tide, ebb or flood

Then P_n = 2,263.4 million cu. ft. = 1,839.5 million cu. ft. (P'_{n-1}) + 423.9 million cu. ft. (M) = 8.28% (P'_{n-1}) + 18.72% (M)

= .8522 P'_{n-1} + 423.9 million cu. ft. (M)

P'_n = 2,158.5 million cu. ft. = 839.5 million cu. ft. (P_{n-1}) + 319.0 million cu. ft. (K)

= 85.22% (P_{n-1}) + 14.78% (K) = .8128 P_{n-1} + 318.0 million cu. ft. (K)

*See map of Richmond Drainage District following p. 182.

Under present conditions it is estimated that the amount of sewage emptied into Arthur Kill amounts to 18.5 million gallons in 24 hours or 0.623 million cubic feet in 6 hours. Using this value in the above formulae we get the following approximate figures for summer conditions:

Area	Dilution Ratio	Per Cent. of Oxygen Present. Without Reaeration	With Reaeration
P	1 in 127	76.5	76.9
P′	1 in 105	71.5	72.0

If the sewage from the Borough of Richmond be added to the sewage now discharged into the Kill from New Jersey, the figures will be as follows:

Area	Dilution Ratio	Per Cent. of Oxygen Present. Without Reaeration	With Reaeration
P	1 in 98	69.4	69.9
P′	1 in 76	60.6	61.1

The waters of the Upper Bay are so intimately connected by circulation with the waters of the Hudson and East Rivers that no increased pollution there is permissible. The Lower Bay, however, has its tidal prism filled and emptied in each tidal period from and into the waters of the ocean and has a capacity for sewage reduction greater than is necessary for all of the areas of its drainage basin. The safe points for the discharge of unpurified sewage from Staten Island are then into the deep channel of the Narrows and into the Lower Bay at those points lying near the channels of the bay through which the circulation of its waters takes place, including the lower half of the coast line between Great Kills and the southern end of the island.

The configuration of the land in Staten Island is not such as to render the concentration of the sewage and its discharge at the points named a simple matter. The natural drainage is to the east into the Lower Bay and to the north and west into the Kill von Kull and the Arthur Kill. The divide between the two watersheds is a bold ridge. At the north it rises abruptly from the water to a height of 200 feet opposite the entrance to the Kill von Kull. From this point it runs slightly west and south with steep side slopes and gradually increasing elevation until about 4 miles from its northern extremity it attains a height of over 400 feet. It then inclines to the southwest and two miles further on drops to a height of 50 feet and gradually rises again to an average height of 100 feet, terminating near the south part of the island. The gap mentioned above affords a means of leading the drainage from a large part of the north watershed into the Lower Bay without the necessity for expensive tunnelling. Along the

Arthur Kill there are extensive areas lying at an elevation of less than 10 feet above mean sea level, which must be drained into the Arthur Kill, unless expensive pumping plants are installed. The general configuration of the north watershed is such that an economical design will require minor lifts and long trunk lines, so as to permit of sewer discharge without purification, but the drainage system as projected has been designed with a view to a minimum expense for installation and operation.

The future population has been estimated at 25 per acre; the volume of sewage at 125 gallons per capita; ground water flow is assumed to be 0.003 second-feet per acre; other assumptions are similar to those of the other districts.

Seven outfalls are projected. The first serves the north and northeast shores and discharges into the deep water of the Narrows near the Quarantine Station. The second serves the area to the west of the ridge lying above the 50-foot contours and also the area east of the ridge above the 40-foot contours between the Narrows on the north and Great Kills on the south. The third serves the low land about Great Kills and discharges off shore in 12 feet of water by means of a pressure main.

The fourth serves the eastern slope of the ridge between Great Kills and Princes Bay and discharges 800 feet off Seguine's Point at the head of Princes Bay in a 21-foot channel running parallel to the shore. The fifth serves the south end of the island and discharges 1,600 feet off shore below Princes Bay into the same channel. A portion of the sewage discharged here will have to be pumped over the ridge whence it will discharge by gravity and another portion will have to be lifted from a sump to the gravity discharge main.

No purification will be required for the sewage discharged from these five outfalls.

The two areas of low land along the Arthur Kill will have to be provided with distinct systems, each concentrating in a sump, from which the sewage must be lifted and after partial purification, discharged into the Arthur Kill. Complete purification will be unnecessary, since once the waters have reached the Lower Bay there will be ample capacity there to receive and care for the sewage carried by them.

Full details of the system as projected are contained in the special report dated February 15, 1911.

Bronx District Sewage—Since the drainage from this district can be carried to the East River at points near Throgs Neck, where the capacity of the waters is ample to care for it without purification, it has not been deemed necessary in the limited time at our disposal to do more than indicate the possible points of concentration and discharge.

The drainage lines recommended for all of the districts are shown on the accompanying map.

CHAPTER V.

In making the studies reported in the preceding chapters, the lack of means to obtain more accurate maps of the districts reported on, more complete data as to the volume of sewage now being discharged into the various parts of the harbor, greater detailed knowledge of current velocities and a more complete set of determinations of the average existing pollution were keenly felt by the authors. They feel confident, however, that true conclusions can be derived from the work accomplished.

Table 6 in Chapter 1 shows clearly how pollution in one part of the harbor affects the remaining areas. At the end of the flood current period the Hudson below Ninety-sixth street is filled by waters of which 3 per cent. were in the Lower Bay at the end of the last ebb and 97 per cent. in the Upper Bay at the same tidal period; the Hudson between Ninety-sixth street and Spuyten Duyvil received 17 per cent. of its contents from waters of the Upper Bay of the preceding ebb and 83 per cent. from below Ninety-sixth street; the East River, from the Battery to Hell Gate, is filled with the waters of the Upper Bay of the last ebb tidal period; the wafers of the East River beyond Hell Gate are 7 per cent. from the Upper Bay of the preceding ebb, 41 per cent. from the lower East River of the preceding ebb, 50 per cent. from its own waters of the preceding ebb and 2 per cent. from the Harlem of the preceding ebb; and the Harlem is made up 25 per cent. from its own waters of the preceding ebb, and 75 per cent. from the waters of the Hudson of the same period. During this period the flow has been from Sandy Hook toward Throgs Neck, via thc East River direct and via the Hudson, Harlem and East Rivers; the clean sea water entering but for a short distance, the remainder of the flow being composed of water more or less polluted from its earlier stay in the harbor.

During the ebb period the flow is in the opposite direction. Pure water enters from the Sound and penetrates but a short distance into the East River. Thus at the end of the period it is seen that only 20 per cent. of the volume east of Hell Gate is pure, the remainder being of water which has been in the area for from 6 to 12 hours longer; the Harlem contains 65 per cent. of water from the earlier East River flood and 35 per cent. from its own preceding flood volume; the Hudson above Ninety-sixth street is composed 81 per cent. of water which had been in it in the second preceding ebb, 3 per cent. of Harlem water of the preceding flood and 16 per cent. of water from the Hudson above Spuyten Duyvil; below Ninety-sixth street the waters are 25 per cent. preceding ebb, 14 per cent. from the Hudson above of the preceding ebb and 60 per cent. of those of the preceding flood plus 1 per cent. of Harlem water of the preceding flood; the Upper Bay is a mixture from the Hudson and East Rivers and from the Kill von Kull.

The resultant movement of the circulation is towards Sandy Hook, but this movement is not continuous nor at a fixed rate (the formulae being based on mean tidal conditions). During all of the time of fluctuation through the various channels each cubic foot of water is giving up oxygen in sewage reduction, with no accessions save the small amount received by reaeration.

A study of Table 9 shows the danger of continuing longer the present system of conveying sewage to the nearest waterway and there discharging it without treatment. Tables 9, 10 and 11 show that, while the capacity of the harbor waters to receive and reduce sewage without undue pollution is ample for the present population, such is the case only when the sewage is discharged near the harbor entrances; and further that even with full diffusion, it is unsafe to discharge sewage into the river waters without treatment. Either conveyance to the harbor entrances or treatment before discharge is feasible, but either course would entail a heavy expenditure. The selection of the more economical can not be made without further and detailed investigation.

The effect of the pollution of the Hudson River above the limits of the City on the waters of the upper Hudson and the Harlem is shown clearly in the formulae of Table 6, and in the oxygen percentages of Tables 9 and 10. Table 10 shows that were it not for the pollution of the Hudson above the city limits, the average oxygen contents of all of the harbor waters would be made over 60 per cent. of saturation by partial purification of the sewage now discharged into the Hudson and Harlem Rivers alone. Table 11 shows this even more forcibly.

The investigations into the method of partially purifying the sewage by aeration, described in detail in Chapter III., show the possibility of obtaining at small cost and with a plant requiring little space a degree of purification ample for sewage emptying into waters under conditions similar to those of Jamaica Bay and of the Arthur Kill. The authors feel sufficient confidence in the results obtained to warrant them in recommending that the existing Twenty-sixth Ward Pumping Station in Brooklyn be fitted with a plant for sewage treatment by this method, with the belief that with greater experience the method can be further developed, so as to warrant a more extended application.

The studies of the harbor capacity warrant them further in recommending that no purification be now made of sewage from the Flushing, Corona and Bronx Districts discharged into the deep water of the channels of the East River at points east of Riker's Island.

In order to avoid a local nuisance, from such discharge, it is necessary that a complete diffusion of the sewage be made immediately on discharge. They know of no method now in use which will secure such diffusion and recommend that experimental work be carried on to develop the best form of outlet for this purpose.

Finally, they would state that it is their belief that radical measures are now necessary for the prevention of injury to the harbor by sewage pollution. Since to be effectual such measures must be applicable to all communities from which sewage is discharged, they believe that joint action in the matter is necessary bv the States of New York and New Jersey; that a standard of purity should be adopted for the harbor waters; that the measures necessary to attain and maintain that standard should be determined; and that such further action as may be necessary to carry such measures into effect should be taken.

Respectfully submitted,

W. M. Black,
Earle B. Phelps.

New York, February 16, 1911.

APPENDIX.

Determination of the Rate of Absorption of Atmospheric Oxygen by Water.

In the text of this report brief reference was made to the relationship existing between time, depth and initial degree of aeration and the amount of atmospheric oxygen absorbed by a given body of water. The mathematical derivation of these relationships and the technique involved in the experimental determination of the diffusion coefficient will be given here in full.

Mathematical.

Assume a column of water, not fully saturated with dissolved oxygen, and exposed to the atmosphere at one end. This is essentially the condition found in a lake.

An infinitely thin layer at the surface of the water becomes saturated with oxygen in an infinitely short time, i. e., at once. This layer can absorb no more oxygen until a portion of that which it contains has passed, by diffusion, to the deeper layers. The rate of absorption therefore is governed wholly by the rate at which oxygen diffuses through the liquid.

The diffusion law:

Fick's law of hydro-diffusion (Nernst, Theoretische Chemie, 2nd German Ed., p. 150) expresses the rate of diffusion of dissolved substances in terms of the concentration gradient as follows:

$$\frac{ds}{dt} = -aq \times \frac{dc}{dx}$$

ds is the amount of substance passing any point, x, through a cross-sectional area, q, in time, dt, when the concentration gradient is $\frac{dc}{dx}$; c is the concentration at any point, varying with x, and a, is a constant for the given substance at given temperature called the coefficient of diffusion.

The first problem is to derive from the fundamental equation an expression which will permit the experimental determination of "a."

At the point x + dx the concentration gradient becomes

$$\frac{dc}{dx} + \frac{d}{dx}\left(\frac{dc}{dx}\right) dx = \frac{dc}{dx} + \frac{d^2c}{dx^2} . dx$$

and the amount of substance passing that point is determined by

$$\frac{ds}{dt} = aq\left(\frac{dc}{dx} + \frac{d^2c}{dx^2} . dx\right)$$

The difference between the amount passing point x and that passing point x + dx is the increase in the amount of substance present in the volume qdx during the time dt. This is

$$aq \frac{d^2c}{dx^2} . dx$$

The increase in concentration in this section is the increase in amount divided by the volume, or

$$\frac{dc}{dt} = \frac{d^2c}{dx^2}$$

which states that the rate of change in concentration of dissolved substance occurring at any point, x, is proportional to the differential of the concentration gradient or the second differential of the concentration itself with respect to the distance. If the gradient be uniform, differential zero, there is no change in concentration occurring at any point.

It will be convenient to express concentration in the usual form, milligrams per liter, or parts per million, distances in centimeters and time in hours which will result in giving the constant "a" a fixed value. As thus defined, "a," the diffusion coefficient, is the rate per hour at which the concentration of dissolved substance is changing at any instant, under the condition that the concentration gradient is changing at a rate of one milligram per liter, per centimeter per centimeter.

The relations are almost exactly those exisiting in the case of the transfer of heat through a conductor.

The solution of the differential equation given above requires the establishment of certain limiting conditions, although the equation itself applies to all conditions.

Case I.

The water contains no oxygen at the start. A surface film becomes saturated instantly, concentration, s. The column has a definite length (L).

to solve

$$\frac{dc}{dt} = a\frac{d^2c}{dx^2} \qquad (1)$$

Under the given conditions when

$$t = 0 \qquad c = 0 \qquad (2)$$

$$x = 0 \qquad c = s \qquad (3)$$

$$x = L \qquad \frac{dc}{dx} = 0 \qquad (4)$$

The reason for applying condition (4) requires discussion. Since no oxygen is passing the closed end, the gradient obviously becomes zero at that point, after the oxygen has diffused to the end of the column. But mathematically a gradient of zero at x = L implies a positive gradient at all other values of x less than L, which in turn implies some oxygen at all points from the start, or, in other words, an infinite rate of diffusion for the first diffusing molecule. This conception could only be realized if the diffusing gas itself were infinitely divisible. At concentrations with which we deal analytically matter is practically divisible in this way and the inconsistency vanishes. After deriving the experimental constants involved it will be possible to calculate the actual magnitude of the inconsistency noted.

A general solution of equation (1) is

$$c = -e^{-ab^2t} \sin bx + \text{const.}$$

or any multiple of such a term or the sum of any series of such terms.

Substituting condition (3) we have

$$\text{const.} = S$$

Giving

$$c = -e^{-ab^2t} \sin bx + S$$

Differentiating and substituting condition (4) we obtain

$$\frac{dc}{dx} = -e^{-ab^2t} \,.\, b \,.\, \cos.\, bL = o$$

which is true if

$$b = \frac{(2\eta + 1)\pi,}{2L}, \text{ n being any positive integer.}$$

Finally to satisfy condition (2) we have

$$S = \sin bx$$

Since the general solution given above may contain a series of terms of the same form as the one developed, Fourier's series is available for determining this function.

We may write

$$S = \frac{4s}{\pi} \sum_{\eta=\infty}^{\eta=o} \frac{1}{2\eta+1} \sin .\, (2\eta + 1)\, y \text{ by Fourier's series.}$$

$$\text{Put } y = \frac{\pi x}{2L}, \text{ and the expression, } \frac{2\eta+1}{2L} = b,$$

$$S = \frac{4s}{\pi} \sum_{\eta=\infty}^{\eta=o} \frac{1}{2\eta+1} \sin .\, bx$$

Since this expression is the sum of a series of multiples of sin bx, it may be substituted for sin bx in the general solution. Making all substitutions:

$$c = s - \frac{4s}{\pi} \sum_{\eta=\infty}^{\eta=o} \frac{1}{2\eta+1} \,.\, e^{-ab^2t} \,.\, \sin bx$$

$$\text{when } b = \frac{2\eta + 1}{2L}, \ \eta \text{ being any integer.}$$

This equation expresses the relation existing between concentration of dissolved oxygen at any point. (c), distance of that point from the exposed surface, (x), and time of exposure, (t). With a fixed time it is the equation of the concentration curve, giving concentrations at all points from surface to bottom. Experimentally we can best determine the average concentration in the column. The determination of a concentration at any given depth would be analytically difficult. We may, therefore, determine from this equation the total amount of oxygen contained in a given differential volume and by the summation of all these amounts arrive at an expression for the total amount of oxygen in the column.

Let the area of the cross section of the column be q. The volume of a differential strip will then be q dx. The amount of oxygen in this volume is the concentration times the volume or

$$dO = cqdx = Sqdx - \frac{4\,Sq}{\pi} \sum_{\eta=\infty}^{\eta=0} \frac{1}{2\,\eta+1}\, e^{-ab^2t} \sin bx \, . \, dx$$

We may now obtain the total amount of oxygen in the column by integrating this equation between limits, o and L;

$$O = Sq \int_L^0 dx - \frac{4\,Sq}{\pi} \sum_{\eta=\infty}^{\eta=0} \frac{1}{2\,\eta+1} \, . \, e^{-ab^2t} \int_L^0 \sin bx \, . \, dx$$

$$= SqL - \frac{4\,Sq}{\pi} \sum_{\eta=\infty}^{\eta=0} \frac{1}{2\eta+1} \, . \, e^{-ab^2t} \, . \, \frac{1}{b}$$

Substituting the value of $\frac{1}{b}$ and simplifying

$$O = SqL\left(1 - \frac{8}{\pi^2} \sum_{\eta=\infty}^{\eta=0} \frac{1}{(2\,\eta+1)^2} \, . \, e^{-ab^2t}\right)$$

But SqL represents a condition of saturation in the volume qL, so we may express the oxygen in terms of "per cent. saturation" by dividing by the saturation value, SqL, and multiplying by 100.

$$O\,(\%\ Sat) = 100 - \frac{800}{\pi^2} \sum_{\eta=\infty}^{\eta=0} \frac{1}{(2\,\eta+1)^2}\, e^{-ab^2t}$$

Whence we derive as a working formula

$$D.\ O. = 100 - \left(81.06\, e^{-K} + 9.007\, e^{-9K} + 3.242\, e^{-25K} + 1.654\, e^{-49K} - - - -\right)$$

$$\text{In which } K = \frac{a\,t\,\pi^2}{4\,L^2} = \frac{2.467\,a\,t}{L^2}$$

e = 2.718, base of natural logs.
a = diffusion coefficient (to be determined).
t = time in hours.
L = length of column in centimeters.

Case II.

Similar to I. except that the concentration at the start is B, throughout. To solve

$$\frac{dc}{dt} = -\frac{d^2c}{dx^2} \qquad (1)$$

Under the conditions

$$\text{When } t = 0 \qquad c = B \qquad (2)$$
$$x = 0 \qquad c = S \qquad (3)$$
$$x = L \qquad \frac{dc}{dx} = 0 \qquad (4)$$

The procedure is exactly the same as in I. until condition (2) is treated. Here we get

$$S - B = \sin bx$$

When the final equation becomes

$$C = S - \frac{4(S-B)}{\pi} \sum_{\eta=\infty}^{\eta=0} \frac{1}{2\eta+1} \cdot e^{-ab^2t} \sin bx$$

This equation is integrated in the same way, giving

$$O = SqL - \frac{4(S-B)q}{\pi} \sum_{\eta=\infty}^{\eta=0} \frac{1}{2\eta+1} \cdot e^{-ab^2t} \cdot \frac{1}{b}$$

Whence the final working formula becomes

$$O\ (\%\ \text{sat.}) = 100 - \left(1 - \frac{B)}{100} \cdot (81.06\, e^{-K} + 9.007\, e^{-9K} + 3.242\, e^{-25K} + 1.654\, e^{-49K} - - -\right)$$

$$= 100\left[\left((1 - \frac{B}{100}\right) \cdot 81.06 \cdot \left(0.779^{K} + \frac{0.105^{K}}{9} + \frac{0.019^{K}}{25} - - -\right)\right]$$

B = initial value of dissolved oxygen.
D = final value of dissolved oxygen.
K = a constant for each experiment $= \frac{\pi^2 a t}{L^2}$
t = time in hours.
L = depth in centimeters.
a = diffusion co-efficient.

The determination of K from this equation, with O, S and B given is not possible by any workable method. The sum of the series was therefore determined with varying values of K and the results plotted. It was observed that by plotting the logarithms of the sums against corresponding

Apparatus
Used in Determining
Diffusion Coefficient.

Diagram I
(Appendix)

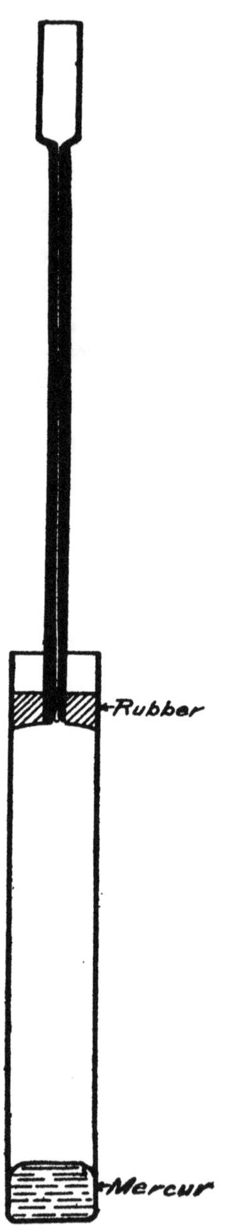

values of K the result was nearly a straight line for the higher values. This method of plotting was therefore employed. This line deviates from a straight line more and more in the lower values when the solution requires a greater number of terms of series. Forty terms of the series were employed in the computation at K = .0001. In the range over which the plot will be of greatest practical value, the determinations are quite accurate and interpolations can be satisfactorily made.

Experimental.

The experimental determination of *a* is now made possible. If a column of water, whose initial content of oxygen is known, be exposed to the air for a definite time and the final content of oxygen be then determined, data are available for calculating the coefficient *a*. It is essential that during the test there shall be no circulation of the water within the tube. The rate of absorption is so slow that results of maximum accuracy are obtainable only in tubes of short length, exposed for a few hours. Lengths of 7 to 8 centimeters were found most satisfactory. To test the depth factor, L, in the formula a few determinations were made in tubes of four centimeters. The determination of dissolved oxygen in such small volumes required more delicate methods than those in common use. The method which was finally adopted is the result of a long investigation of possible methods. It depends upon the reoxidation of decolorized indigo.

A detailed description of the method employed is as follows: A quantity of "iron-excelsior," made of fine iron turnings was placed in a flask of water which was then vigorously boiled. After boiling for some time the flask was connected with a hydrogen generator through an absorption bottle containing pyrogallate solution, and the flame was removed. The flask was allowed to cool in this condition over night. The next morning water could be drawn which contained three to ten per cent. of the saturation value of dissolved oxygen. Water with less oxygen than this is exceedingly difficult to prepare.

The apparatus employed for the determination of absorption is shown in the sketch. It consisted of a test tube, into which a rubber stopper was fitted with extreme care, so as to slide plunger-fashion within the tube. This stopper was wet with a very dilute caustic solution to assist the sliding. The capillary glass tube passed through the stopper to its inner surface which was concaved slightly. The tube was expanded at its upper end into a straight-sided funnel. Two etched lines, one near each end of the tube, marked off a definite volume.

The tube was filled with mercury to slightly above the lower line. The stopper was then forced into the mercury, expelling all air and forcing mercury through the capillary to the upper funnel. A siphon from the bottom of the flask described above was then inserted into the funnel, its end projecting below the mercury, and the water was allowed to run for a minute or two, overflowing from the funnel. Then while the water was still running, and overflowing, the stopper was slowly withdrawn, allowing a small stream of water to enter the tube. In this way the water was transferred without contact with the air.

When the stopper had reached the upper mark, its movement was stopped and, while the water was still flowing above, a drop of mercury was added to the funnel to seal the capillary. The tube was then removed, the funnel emptied of water and dried and the whole apparatus set in a large water tank, previously brought to the temperature desired for the experiment.

The tube was left there one hour to acquire a uniform temperature. Then while still immersed nearly to its upper edge, the tube was exposed to the air by the removal of the stopper and capillary. The time was noted and during the exposure the oxygen in a set of "blank" tubes was determined. These blanks were prepared exactly as described here, but were not exposed. They furnished the initial value, B, in the formula.

After an exposure of from one-half to four hours the tubes were again plugged with the same stoppers and capillaries, the stopper being forced in until the capillary was filled and a seal of mercury was applied as before. The tube was now ready for an oxygen determination.

A solution of indigotine or soluble indigo was placed in the funnel, above the mercury seal. A solution of sodium hydro-sulphide was added in excess to completely reduce and decolorize the indigo. A glass tube connected with a carbon-dioxide generator was inserted into the funnel and a stream of carbon-dioxide blown through the reduced indigo. This gas, by accumulating over the liquid prevented the too rapid oxidation of the indigo by the air, at the same time there was enough oxygen in the carbon-dioxide to oxidize the indigo slowly and uniformly. Finally a faint blue color would return in the tube and when this color matched a standard tube which had been prepared of known value, the stopper was raised and the indigo added to the water. A new mercury seal was put in, the tube well mixed and put aside. The oxidation of the indigo was almost instantaneous but proceeded at a decreasing rate for some time. While still sealed from the air this tube was then compared with a set of standards in similar tubes, the latter having been prepared by diluting a standard indigo solution which was made up to match a single test made upon a saturated water of known oxygen content. Repeated tests of this method upon waters of known value showed that it could be relied upon to give results with these small amounts of water, that were free from reagent corrections and of much greater accuracy than could be had from the older method.

Results.

One hundred and fourteen tests were made at temperatures ranging from 6 degrees to 30 degrees, with tube lengths of from 3.8 to 8.4 centimeters and with exposures of from one-fourth to four hours. The results have been plotted in Diagram II., values of a being shown in relation to temperature. To avoid confusion, sets of closely agreeing results have been averaged and the average values shown as one value, the number of determinations included in the average being indicated by the number of radial lines about the circle. The values are somewhat scattering, and a closer analysis indicates that some unknown factor is involved. Exceedingly concordant results are readily obtained upon any one day, while upon the following day another group of concordant results will be obtained differing from the first. Barometric corrections were later applied without relieving the situation. It is quite likely that humidity conditions would explain the irregularities. Considering the variations in depth, time, and initial values, that were employed the results on the whole are satisfactorily uniform and the curve which has been drawn, being deduced from such a large number of results, probably gives a value of the diffusion coefficient at any temperature which is not far from the actual truth.

Within the range of values which have been employed in the computations in the text errors resulting from the maximum divergence of individual tests from the average value of the curve are less than 5 per cent. at the five-foot depths and less than 2 per cent. at the twenty-foot depths.

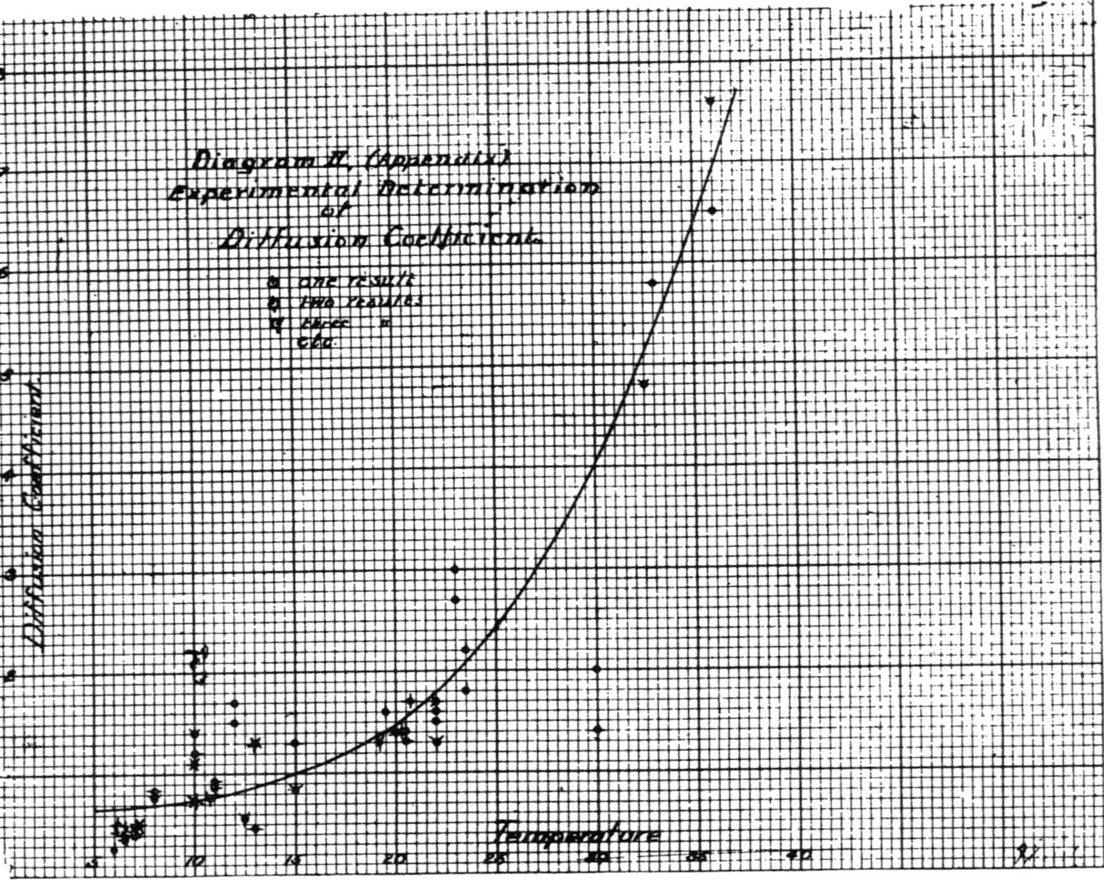
Diagram II. (Appendix)
Experimental Determination
of
Diffusion Coefficient.
one result
two results
three "
etc.
Diffusion Coefficient.
Temperature
8
7
6
5
4
3
2
5
10
15
20
25
30
35
40

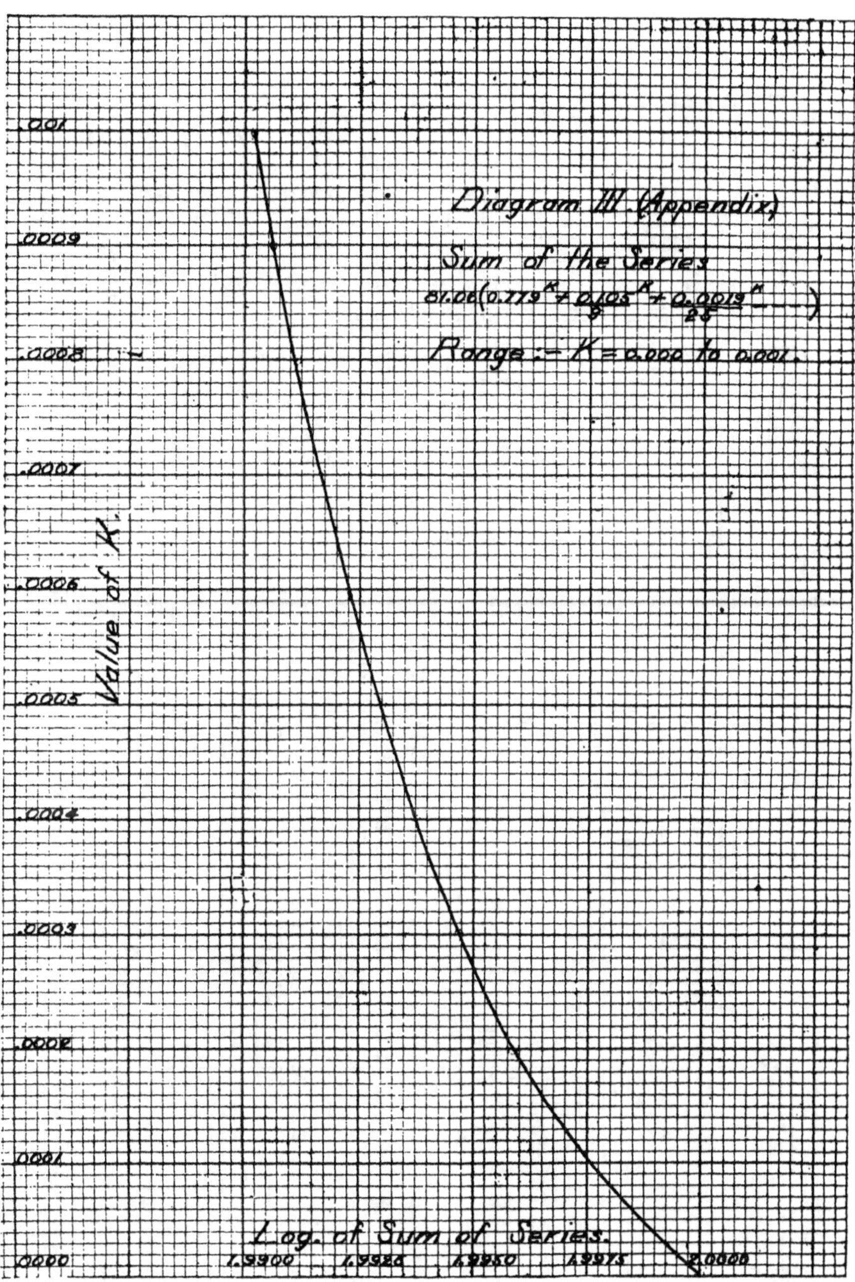
Diagram III (Appendix)
Sum of the Series
$81.06\left(0.779^{K}+\frac{0.105^{K}}{9}+\frac{0.0019^{K}}{25}\cdots\right)$
Range:— K = 0.000 to 0.001.
Value of K.
.001
.0009
.0008
.0007
.0006
.0005
.0004
.0003
.0002
.0001
.0000
Log. of Sum of Series.
1.9900
1.9925
1.9950
1.9975
2.0000

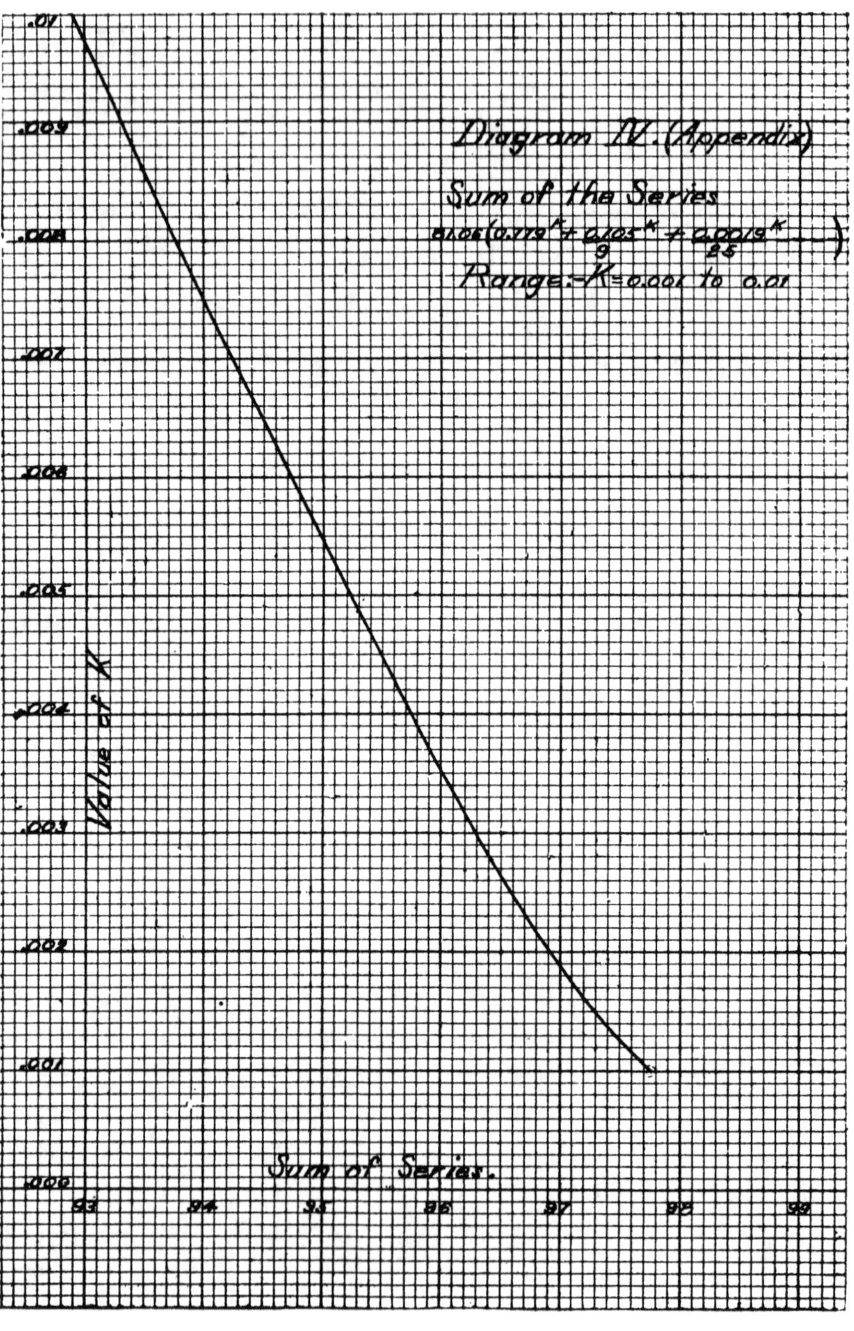
Diagram IV. (Appendix)
Sum of the Series
81.06(0.779^K + 0.105^K/9 + 0.0019^K/25 ....)
Range:–K=0.001 to 0.01
Value of K
Sum of Series.
.01
.009
.008
.007
.006
.005
.004
.003
.002
.001
.000
93
94
95
96
97
98
99

SPECIAL REPORT

ON THE

Corona Drainage District

SUBMITTED TO THE

BOARD OF ESTIMATE AND APPORTIONMENT

JUNE 17, 1910

CHIEF ENGINEER'S OFFICE,
BOARD OF ESTIMATE AND APPORTIONMENT,
CITY OF NEW YORK,
June 10, 1910.

Hon. WILLIAM J. GAYNOR, *Mayor,*
Chairman of the Board of Estimate and Apportionment:

SIR—Herewith is transmitted a report from Colonel William M. Black and Professor Earle B. Phelps, bearing date of May 24, 1910, relative to the treatment of the drainage of that portion of the Borough of Queens north of the ridge or backbone of the island, and extending from Flushing Creek to Newtown Creek.

The investigation of the matter of reference has been made pursuant to the authorization of the Board of November 12, 1909, under which Colonel Black was engaged to advise relative to the treatment of the drainage problem of the city in so far as it related to the pollution of the adjacent waters.

The result of the investigation of this problem for the territory between Flushing Creek and Little Neck Bay was made the subject of a report which was presented at the Board meeting of April 22, 1910, and which was thereupon referred to the President of the Borough of Queens for general guidance in the design of sewers for the locality. At this time attention was called to the fact that to establish its feasibility the plan submitted had been made to include a general subdivision of the territory considered into drainage districts and also the planning of the main trunk lines, but that the latter was based on making provision only for the sanitary flow with which the investigation was primarily concerned. It was suggested at this time that it would seem desirable to provide in the drainage plan for the removal of both the sanitary and storm water flow in a combined system of sewers, and that if such treatment were to be adopted it would probably be necessary to modify the plan in many particulars, although it was believed that the general scheme could be applied.

The report now presented relates to an area of about 14,535 acres, for which the sanitary requirements only have been considered other than in so far as an excess of capacity may have been provided to meet future growth and which may, for a limited time, be utilized for removing the surface water.

In general, the plan contemplates two main trunk sewers, these providing, respectively, for the independent drainage of most of the First and Second Wards, these sewers meeting at the junction of Riker avenue and Theodore street, from which point the main outlet would extend out to deep water off the foot of the latter street. This outlet is stated in the report to have been selected having in view the possibility of extending it by tunnel to Rikers Island in case it should be ultimately found necessary to install purification works.

It has not been found practicable to incorporate in the plan that portion of Long Island City immediately adjoining the water front and an area of considerable extent at the head of Newtown Creek, both of which are at such low elevation as to require pumping. The sewers in the former section have been largely constructed and it is evidently believed that their use can be continued for some time in the future. It is also understood that a portion of the low area may possibly find an outlet through sewers in the Borough of Brooklyn. A small area in the vicinity of Bowery Bay is also found to be of too low an elevation to secure a gravity outlet, but in the remaining subdivisions of the drainage area it is understood that no pumping will be required.

A number of sewers have already been built in the Elmhurst section, and the plan makes provision not only for continuing their use but also that of the purification plant already built until such time as it is found practicable to carry out what is suggested as the ultimate plan.

In the report it is pointed out that the studies relative to the capacity of the harbor to absorb sewage are still in progress and have not yet advanced far enough to warrant any recommendation in the matter. Attention, however, is called to the desirability of supplementing this work with independent investigation and experiment at various points which would bring out information not now available relative to the requirements which must be met before reaching a final determination as to the extent of the purification which will undoubtedly at some time be required.

I would recommend that a copy of this report be sent to the Presidents of the Boroughs of Brooklyn and Queens to be used for their guidance in the development of the drainage plan for the territory affected.

Respectfully,

NELSON P. LEWIS,
Chief Engineer.

May 24, 1910.

Mr. Nelson P. Lewis,

Chief Engineer, Board of Estimate and Apportionment:

Sir—In connection with our general studies of the sewerage problems of certain portions of Greater New York, we beg to submit herewith a second report, which deals with the main drainage problem of that portion of Queens Borough lying between Flushing Bay, Newtown Creek, the East River, and the division line between Queens and Brooklyn. For purposes of convenience and identification we have designated this district the "Corona Drainage District." Reference to the accompanying map marked "Corona Drainage District"* will facilitate the discussion which follows.

Divisions of the Drainage District.

For the purposes of this study we have divided the above designated district into eighteen drainage areas, numbered respectively 1 to 18, of which areas Nos. 3, 4, 5, 9, 10 and 11 are subdivided into two sub-areas designated by a and b respectively; and areas Nos. 6, 8 and 13 are similarly subdivided by a, b and c respectively. In the map the division lines between these areas are indicated by heavy dotted lines. Contour lines at 20-foot intervals are shown, but these are only approximate, by reason of the lack of detailed topographic surveys and of available time and funds for making such surveys, which has been commented upon in our first report. Our proposed sewer lines are indicated in red, and other features are sufficiently described in the legend. Estimates of future populations have been made upon a basis of either twenty-five or fifty persons per acre, depending upon the location of the area in question and the character of the country. The drainage areas dealt with are approximately as follows:

Area No. 1. This area is bounded on the south by a crest line which is practically the division line between two wards; it extends on the east to a crest line which has already been identified as the westerly boundary of the low level area in the Flushing Drainage District, and on the north to a crest which parallels the first crest mentioned for a distance of about seven thousand feet. Its westerly boundary is a broken line which has been determined by the requirements of existing sewer assessment districts. It contains 2,343 acres, from which we have deducted 793 acres of parks and cemetery land. The estimated future population is 38,750.

Area No. 2. This is a small area lying between the northerly boundary of No. 1 and the 20-foot contour line which separates it from the low level area of the Flushing Drainage District. It extends on the west to Dry Harbor road. It contains 482 acres, with an estimated future population of 24,100.

Area No. 3. This is a small area bounded practically by Metropolitan avenue, Dry Harbor road and North Hempstead Plank road on the south, east and north, respectively, and on the west by the natural crest line as indicated. It contains 500 acres, with an estimated future population of 25,000. It is subdivided into two sub-areas of 360 and 140 acres with 18,000 and 7,000 estimated future populations, respectively.

Area No. 4. This area lies to the north of No. 3 and extends to Woodside and Broadway on the north, and to Dry Harbor road on the east.

*Omitted. See general map of Drainage Districts of Jamaica, Corona, Flushing and Westchester, p. 148.

Its westerly boundary is a crest line just west of Fiske avenue. It is further divided by a crest line running northeast, as shown. It contains 613 acres, with an estimated future population of 30,650, of which 266 acres and 13,300 population are included in Sub-area a, and 347 acres and 17,350 population are included in Sub-area b.

Area No. 5. This area lies to the northwest of the low level area of the Flushing District already described, and above the 20-foot contour line. It extends on the north to Jackson avenue and on the west to a crest line running north and south as shown. It is subdivided as shown. It contains almost all the Corona section, having a total area of 959 acres, with an estimated future population of 47,950, of which 761 acres and 38,050 population are included in sub-area a, and 198 acres and 9,900 population are included in sub-area b.

Area No. 6. This area lies to the northwest of No. 5, extending to Flushing Bay on the northeast and following the 20-foot contour line on the northwest. It extends on the west to a crest as shown and on the south to Woodside. It is subdivided into three sub-areas: Sub-area a comprising the southeasterly half of the whole area; c comprising a strip about 1,500 feet in width along Flushing Bay; and b the remainder. It contains altogether 1,154 acres with an estimated future population of 57,700, of which 610, 359 and 185 acres, and 30,500, 17,950 and 9,250 population are included in sub-areas a, b and c, respectively.

Area No 7. This area is a narrow winding low-level strip lying to the northwest of No. 6, situated entirely below the 20-foot contour line. It comprises practically the low land surrounding the small inlet from Flushing Bay to the southeast of Sanford Point. It contains 381 acres, with an estimated future population of 19,050.

Area No. 8. This area is a similar narrow strip lying to the northwest of No. 7, extending to the waterfront on its easterly end and to a crest which is practically a projection of this same waterfront as far west as Wilson avenue. It includes also a larger area to the west of Nos. 6 and 7, bounded practically by Newtown road and Woodside. It is subdivided into three sub-areas. It contains 811 acres, with an estimated future population of 40,550, of which 569, 126 and 116 acres and 28,450, 6,300 and 5,800 population are included in sub-areas a, b and c, respectively.

Area No. 9. This area lies to the northeast of No. 8 and is bounded on the east by the 20-foot contour which practically parallels Winthrope avenue, and on the west by a crest line which follows Ditmars avenue closely. It extends on the north practically to the East River. It is subdivided into two sub-areas and contains 403 acres, with an estimated future population of 20,150, of which 207 and 196 acres, and 10,350 and 9,800 population are included in sub-areas a and b, respectively.

Area No. 10. This is a low-level area lying entirely below the 20-foot contour. It extends from Area No. 9 to the East River and includes on the east a narrow strip of shore front extending to Sanford Point; on the west a similar strip extending as far as Astoria. It is subdivided into two sub-areas. It contains 394 acres, with an estimated future population of 19,700, of which 197 acres and 9,850 population are included in each of the sub-areas.

Area No. 11. This area lies to the southwest of No. 9 and in part to the north of No. 8. It extends also to the west in a narrow point to Noble avenue in the Ravenswood district. It is bounded on the northwest by the 20-foot contour, which separates it from No. 10, and by a straight line which is practically identical with a continuation of that contour between Astoria and Ravenswood. The westerly point is bounded on the south by a crest line as shown. It is subdivided into two sub-areas. It contains 966 acres, with an estimated future population of 48,300, of which 374 and 592 acres and 18,700 and 29,600 population are included in sub-areas a and b, respectively.

Area No. 12. This area includes the waterfront from Astoria south and west to Newtown Creek. It is bounded on the east by a line which follows in general the 20-foot contour. It contains a portion of Astoria and all of Ravenswood and Hunters Point, with an area of 129,000 acres and an estimated future population of 64,500.

Area No. 13. This area lies between Areas Nos. 8, 11 and 12 as defined, and extends on the southeast to the crest line which runs in a southerly direction from the junction of Greenpoint avenue and Woodside to Newtown Creek. It is subdivided into three sub-areas. It contains 1,209 acres (of which 167 comprise parks and cemeteries), with an estimated future population of 52,100, of which 511, 382 and 316 acres, and 25,550, 19,100 and 7,450 population are included in the sub-areas a, b and c, respectively. The 167 acres of park and cemetery are within sub-area c.

Area No. 14. This area is a narrow strip lying to the southeast of Nos. 8 and 13. It extends on the east to Area No. 4 and on the south to a line which follows closely the 30-foot contour. It contains 335 acres, with an estimated future population of 16,750.

Area No. 15. This area lies to the southeast of No. 14, extends on the north and east to No. 4, on the west to the Long Island Railroad, and on the south to a line which practically marks the 35-foot contour. It contains 501 acres, with an estimated future population of 25,050.

Area No. 16. This area lies to the southeast of No. 15 and to the southwest of No. 3. It is bounded on the south by a crest line extending in an east and west direction as shown. It contains 909 acres of which 236 acres comprise parks and cemeteries, and its estimated future population is 33,650.

Area No. 17. This area comprises a narrow strip along the Newtown Creek and southwest of Areas Nos. 13 and 15. It is bounded on the south by a line which is practically identical with Grand avenue. It contains 255 acres, with an estimated future population of 12,750.

Area No. 18. This is a large area lying in the southerly corner of the drainage district. It extends from the Borough line on the southeast to the crests which have already been described as bounding Areas Nos. 1, 2 and 16.

The acreage and estimated future populations of these eighteen drainage areas are tabulated below. The total area of the district is 14,535 acres and the total estimated future population 628,200. This district as defined includes an area of 756 acres with an estimated future population of 37,800 (comprising areas 15 and 17), which is now, or will naturally become, tributary to the sewers of Brooklyn Borough.

Area	Acres	Poulation (Est. Future)
1	*1.550	38,750
2	482	24,100
3	500	25,000
4	613	30,650
5	959	47.950
6	1,154	57,700
7	381	19,050
8	811	40,550
9	403	20,150
10	394	19.700
11	966	48,300
12	1.290	64.500
13	*1.042	52,100
14	335	16,750
15	501	25.050
16	*673	33,650
17	255	12.750
18	1.030	51,500
	13 339	628.200
Park and cemetery	1.196	
Total	14.535	

* Includes park and cemetery land.

General Scheme of Sewerage for the District.

A general description of the scheme of sewerage which we have provided for the entire Corona Drainage District will now be given. The final point of discharge, as now provided, will be in deep water in the East River at a point approximately 1,500 feet to the southeast of Berrian's Island. The question of some form of treatment of this sewage will be considered in a later report. Having in mind the possibility that purification to some degree may be found desirable, this point of final discharge has been so located that if necessary the entire discharge can be carried by tunnel to Riker's Island, where suitable purification works can be installed. To bring the sewage to this point, we have provided two main intercepting systems which, for convenience, we will designate the East Interceptor and the West Interceptor. The main line of the East Interceptor may be considered to start at the junction of Myrtle and Tompkins avenues in Area No. 18, to flow in a westerly direction through that area to the Borough line, thence in a general northeasterly direction along the natural valley line which carries it eventually completely through the center of the district to a point on Flushing Bay, and thence following the shore to the point of discharge.

A main branch of this interceptor starts at nearly the same point between Areas Nos. 1 and 18 and flows through a second valley in a northeasterly direction to the low land near Flushing Creek, thence on the margin of this low land to the point of junction with the main line in Area No. 5.

The West Interceptor may be considered to start at the extreme southern point of Area No. 13c, and to run in a general northerly direction to the Pennsylvania Railroad yards, making a detour around these yards and thence northeasterly, following approximately the 40-foot contour to the north corner of Area No. 9b, and thence southeasterly to the point of discharge. Trunk sewers, designated in general by the number of the area served, will enter these interceptors as follows:

Trunk No. 3a enters the main branch where it crosses Trotting Course lane. This trunk is composed of two branches, draining the two sides of Sub-area No. 3a.

Trunk No. 3b enters this same branch near the point of crossing North Hempstead Plank road, and drains Areas 3b, 4a and 2.

Trunk No. 14 enters the East Interceptor at the corner of Maurice and Thompson and drains Area No. 14 and a portion of 4b.

Trunk No. 5a enters this same interceptor at Sycamore avenue and drains the northerly portion of Area No. 5a.

Trunk No. 5b enters this interceptor at Flushing and Newtown Turnpike, and drains Area No. 5b.

Trunk No. 6b enters this interceptor at the northern end of Area No. 6c and by its two branches drains Area No. 6b.

Trunk No. 7 enters the interceptor at the same point and drains Area No. 7. It will probably be necessary to pump from this trunk into the interceptor.

Trunk No. 8b enters the interceptor on the Shore road and drains directly Area No. 8b. It extends to the southwestern corner of Area No. 7, at which point branches draining Areas Nos. 8a and 6a, respectively, enter it.

At the corner of Laurel Hill and Skillman two small trunks enter the West Interceptor.

Design of Trunk Lines From Each Area.

As in our previous report, it has been deemed sufficient for our present purposes to investigate fully the approximate routes, grades, and maximum size of all trunk lines at the point of entrance into the interceptors. In this case, in addition, we have investigated the maximum size of the principal branches of trunk lines where they occur. It has not been deemed advisable to make a more detailed study of these trunks. Such a study would involve the detailed investigation of all existing sewers, information as to which is often meagre or totally lacking. Estimates of capacity of trunk lines are based upon water consumption and ground water flow, as previously described in our Flushing report. Provision for storm water overflows has been made at those points where these proposed lines intercept existing combined sewers, and at two points along Flushing Bay and Creek and one point at head of Newtown Creek. While the sewers have been designed for sanitary and ground water flow only, until the population has been greatly increased, these provisions will suffice for storm water. Assumptions as to the relation between maximum flow and total mean flow for 24 hours have been made as described in our Flushing report. Velocities and discharges have been computed for sewers flowing full, 0.8 full, 0.5 full and 0.2 full. Maximum flows are based upon the sizes necessary at 0.8 full. In the following table the principal items involved in the design of these trunks, including maximum discharge, available slope, maximum diameter, and velocities and discharges at 0.8 and 0.2 full are given:

Design of Trunk Sewers.

Trunk No.	Length, Feet.	Total Fall, Feet.	Elevation of Invert, Upper End.	Contributing Area, Acres.	Maximum Discharge, Sec., Ft.	Slope 1 Foot in	Maximum Diameter, Feet.	Sewer 0.8 Full.		Sewer 0.2 Full.	
								Velocity, Sec., Ft.	Discharge, Sec., Ft.	Velocity, Sec., Ft.	Discharge, Sec., Ft.
3a	5,000	40.00	81.84	360	6.28	125	1.83	5.75	12.30	3.00	1.08
3a, north	7,000	14.00	95.84	180	3.14	500	1.75	2.95	6.15	1.56	0.54
3a, south	4,500	15.00	96.84	180	3.14	300	1.67	3.45	6.15	1.80	0.54
2	3,000	25.00	46.84	482	8.41	120	2.00	6.33	16.49	3.30	1.45
3b	3,000	30.00	85.17	140	2.45	100	1.25	4.83	4.81	2.52	0.42
3b, 4a	6,000	33.33	55.17	406	7.09	180	2.00	5.28	13.90	2.76	1.22
3b, 4a, 2	2,700	4.50	21.84	888	15.50	600	2.67	3.45	15.50	1.80	1.36
14	9,000	18.00	50.44	335	5.85	500	1.75	3.88	5.85	1.50	0.51
14, 4b	4,000	10.00	32.44	508	8.88	400	2.00	3.45	8.88	1.80	0.78
5a	4,500	45.00	62.77	190	3.33	100	1.33	5.18	6.52	2.70	0.57
5b	4,500	15.00	30.34	198	3.36	300	1.67	3.45	6.59	1.80	0.58
6b	7,500	15.00	22.80	359	6.27	500	2.33	3.45	12.30	1.80	1.08
7	10,000	20.00	13.67	381	6.65	500	2.33	3.45	13.03	1.80	1.14
6a	3,600	18.00	34.25	610	10.65	200	2.33	5.53	20.90	2.88	1.81
8a	3,000	4.28	21.53	569	9.94	700	3.00	3.45	19.49	1.80	1.71
6a, 8a	4,500	3.75	16.25	1,189	20.59	1,200	3.17	2.99	20.09	1.56	1.74
6a, 8a, 8b	2,500	3.33	12.50	1,315	....	750	3.00	3.45	22.29	1.20	1.80

Design of the Intercepting Sewer.

The design of these sewers is determined by the available slope and by the points of entrance of the various trunk lines. To facilitate reference, the two interceptors and that third line which has been called the "main branch of the East Interceptor," have been sub-divided into sections designated by letters and beginning at the upper end in each case. These sections are described as follows:

The East Interceptor.

Section A, from the upper end of the eastern edge of Area 18, along Myrtle to Cypress, to Himrod, to Covert, to Willoughby, to Onderdonk, to Troutman, to Woodward.

Sections B and C, from the corner of Woodward and Troutman across Linden Hill Cemetery upon the 60-foot contour to Metropolitan, to Nurge, to Flushing, to Grand, to Hull, to Jay and Newtown road, thence following the 40-foot contour to Railway, thence to Maurice, along Maurice to junction with Trunk No. 14 on Thompson.

Section D, a short section on Thompson, from the junction with Maurice to the junction with the present Elmhurst sewer on Broadway, intercepting the latter.

Section E, from Maurice and Broadway, along Broadway to Court, to Suydam, to Junction, to National, to Vine, to Willow, to junction with Trunk No. 5a on Sycamore.

Section F, from Willow and Sycamore to Central and Willow at the junction with the Main Branch.

Section G, from the junction with the Main Branch along Central to Main, to Myrtle, to junction with Trunk No. 5b on Flushing and Newtown Turnpike.

Section H, from junction with Trunk No. 5b practically on the 20-foot contour to shorefront, thence along the shore to junction with Trunks 6b and 7.

Section I, from the above point, still following the shore line and Shore road, to junction with Trunk 8b at Ehret avenue and Shore road.

Section J, from Ehret avenue and Shore road along River avenue to junction with outfall sewer on Theodore.

Main Branch of the East Interceptor.

Section A, from upper end on Cooper, along Cooper to Trotting Course Lane at the junction with Trunk 3a.

Section B, from junction on Trotting Course Lane, following valley line to 40-foot contour, thence following swamp margin to junction with Trunk No. 2 at siphon entrance.

Section C, inverted siphon under Horseshoe Creek from Newtown to Corona.

Section D, from inverted siphon along Westside avenue to South, to Broad, to Myrtle, to Crown, to Central, to junction with East Interceptor at Central and Willoughby.

The West Interceptor.

Section A, from 50-foot contour line on Montgomery on southern edge of Area No. 13c, along Montgomery to Waters, to Washington, to Jones, to Laurel Hill Boulevard, to Borden, to Greenpoint and Borden.

Section B, from Greenpoint and Borden, along Greenpoint to Hunters Point, to Honeywell, to Thompson, to Rawson, to Foster, thence diagonally along proposed street to Skillman, skirting the Pennsylvania Railroad yards to Laurel Hill avenue at junction with two small trunks from Area No. 13a.

Section C, from last-named junction, still skirting the Pennsylvania Railroad yards, to Webster.

Section D, from Webster and Jackson along Webster to Prospect.

Section E, from Webster and Prospect, along Prospect to Pierce, to Crescent.

Section F, from Pierce and Crescent, along Crescent, to Grand.

Section G, from Crescent and Grand, along Crescent, to Hoyt.

Section H, from Hoyt and Crescent, along Hoyt to Howland, to Ditmars, to Barclay, to Winthrop.

Section I, from Winthrop and Barclay, along Winthrop to Blackwell, to River avenue, to junction with East Interceptor and outfall sewer on Theodore.

The total length, total fall of each section, elevation of invert at upper end of section, area contributing to each section, dimensions, slopes, velocities and discharges at 0.8 and 0.2 full, of the above-described sections of these three interceptors, are given in the following tables:

Section.	Length, Feet.	Total Fall, Feet.	Elevation of Invert, Upper End.	Contributing Area, Acres.	Maximum Discharge, Sec., Ft.	Slope 1 Foot in	Maximum Diameter, Feet.	Sewer 0.8 Full. Velocity, Sec., Ft.	Sewer 0.8 Full. Discharge, Sec., Ft.	Sewer 0.2 Full. Velocity, Sec., Ft.	Sewer 0.2 Full. Discharge, Sec., Ft.
Main Branch.											
A	2,200	5.0	41.84	1,172	7.68	440	1.75	3.20	7.68	1.70	0.68
B	7,800	19.5	36.84	1,910	21.63	400	2.75	4.48	21.63	2.34	1.90
C	1,000	0.9	17.34	2,798	37.13	1,100	3.16	2.60	37.13	Siphon.	
D	5,100	3.0	16.44	3,798	37.13	1,700	4.33	2.88	37.13	1.50	3.26
East Interceptor.											
A	12,000	25.00	79.44	1,030	18.00	500	2.67	3.91	18.00	2.04	1.58
B	11,000	22.00	54.44	1,703	29.75	500	3.16	4.27	29.75	2.18	2.56
C	4,000	10.00	32.44	1,876	32.78	400	3.16	4.73	32.78	2.52	2.88
D	1,400	1.17	22.44	2,374	41.66	1,200	4.25	3.45	41.66	1.80	3.66
E	7,200	6.00	21.27	2,764	48.31	1,200	4.50	3.56	48.31	1.86	4.29
F	700	0.50	15.27	3,145	54.96	1,400	5.00	3.45	54.96	1.80	4.82
G	2,700	1.35	13.44	5,943	92.09	2,700	6.33	3.45	92.09	1.80	8.08
H	9,000	4.29	12.09	6,327	98.68	2,100	6.50	3.45	98.68	1.80	8.65
I	6,300	2.63	7.80	7,183	113.63	2,400	7.00	3.45	113.63	1.80	9.96
J	3,500	1.40	5.17	8,892	139.36	2,500	7.75	3.56	139.36	1.80	12.23
West Interceptor.											
A	4,000	13.33	50.17	149	2.6	300	1.50	3.45	5.31	1.80	0.45
B	7,200	12.00	36.84	403	7.05	600	2.00	2.76	13.82	1.44	1.21
C	3 900	5.57	24.84	1,042	18.18	700.	2.84	3.45	18.18	1.80	1.60
D	2,500	2.50	19.27	1,042	18.18	1,000	3.00	2.99	18.18	1.50	1.60
E	1,400	1.17	16.77	2,519	43.95	1,200	4.33	3.45	43.95	1.80	4.16
F	3,600	3.00	15.60	2,706	47.21	1,200	4.50	3.56	47.21	1.86	4.14
G	1,800	1.50	12.60	2,706	47.21	1,200	4.50	3.56	47.21	1.86	4.14
H	5,700	3.80	11.10	3,298	57.53	1,500	5.00	3.45	57.53	1.80	5.50
I	5,300	3.53	7.30	3,691	64.39	1,500	5.33	3.56	64.39	1.80	5.65
Outfall.											
A	900	0.27	3.77	12,583	203.75	3,300	9.50	3.45	203.75	1.80	17.90

Provision for Storm Water.

At all points where the proposed intercepting sewers or trunks intercept existing combined systems of sewerage, present points of final discharge have been retained to serve as stormwater overflows. These points so far as our present information goes are as follows: On the West Interceptor overflows are provided at the corner of Hunters Point and Honeywell, and of Nott avenue and Honeywell; at Webster and Prospect; Washington and Prospect; Jamaica and Crescent; Newtown and Crescent; on Hoyt avenue; and Howland and Potter. Storm water overflows into Flushing Creek and Bay are provided on the East Interceptor for the sewage of Elmhurst Section. This matter will be discussed in some detail later in this report.

Provisions for Intercepting Existing Sewers.

On the West Interceptor it has been possible to provide for the greater part of the sewage now flowing into Newtown Creek and the East River from points at higher elevation than that of the interceptor. Such existing sewers as we have knowledge of, which can be provided for, are shown in purple ink on the accompanying map as connected with the proposed interceptor. Sewers on Graham and on Broadway in Long Island City pass under the proposed grade of the interceptor. They are, therefore, not provided for at present. It will be noted that a considerable portion of Long Island City, namely, that part of the East River front which is below the 20-foot contour, which we have called Area 12, is not provided for in this scheme. This section is so completely sewered that special future consideration will have to be given to it. Any plan which contemplates the concentration of the sewage now entering the waterfront from this area must involve a low-level interceptor following the line of Newtown Creek and the East River shore to a point in Astoria whence the sewage will have to be lifted about 25 feet to the West Interceptor. This same provision will apply to those few sewers already noted and doubtless to others of which we have no information which it is not possible to include in the present Interceptor as designed.

Disposition of the Present Elmhurst Sewage and Sewage Disposal Works.

The present plan contemplates the intercepting of the present flow from the Elmhurst Section by the East Interceptor at the corner of Broadway and Maurice avenue. It is believed that for many years to come the present plant at Elmhurst will provide satisfactorily for the disposal of all the sewage which may reach that point; and furthermore that with the advances which we may reasonably expect in the art of sewage disposal, this plant may be able to care for the entire flow from that section of the East Interceptor above Elmhurst. We therefore recommend that until conditions make necessary the further extension of this final plan, the Elmhurst plant be retained to receive all the sewage from such sections of this interceptor as may be connected up from time to time; and we further recommend that studies upon improved methods of disposal, looking particularly toward economy in space and time required for treatment, be continued either at this plant or at some suitable station along the lines that are already developed at the Twenty-sixth Ward Disposal Works, or along new lines which may suggest themselves to us from time to time in consequence of these installations. We urge the importance of continuing on a small scale the study of the special requirements and possibilities in this matter of sewage disposal for Greater New York. The accumulated data of such experiences will be of great value from time to time as such problems are met with.

Purification and Disposal Investigations.

Our more general studies of the ultimate capacity of New York Harbor and its tributary waters to dispose of sewage in an inoffensive manner are still in progress. We are not yet ready to report upon this matter. Before any final decision is arrived at it is desirable to carry our studies to such a point that our opinions shall be based upon a sufficient array of facts to justify them. If it be found that the waters of New York Harbor cannot continue to receive the sewage of the Metropolitan District in its crude form, but that some partial purification of a portion of that sewage at least will eventually be necessary, our plans contemplate such purification in those portions of the city where it can be carried out at a minimum expense. For this reason our studies of the two drainage districts upon which we have already reported have considered a possible necessity of some form of purification, and suitable sites for these works have been selected.

As a minimum requirement we think it necessary to provide for a proper admixture of sewage and water at the point of final discharge; such provision is of much greater importance in the case of these proposed large trunk sewers than it is with the present system of numerous small outlets. With this view in mind, we are investigating the possible methods of securing such admixture before the final discharge. If this can be accomplished it may be possible to so design our outfall works that the sewage will not rise to the surface of the stream, but will remain diffused in the lower strata. Such a result would do away entirely with one serious objection to the discharge of crude sewage into such waters as those we have to deal with, namely, the discoloration of the surface waters and other visible indications of sewage near the point of discharge.

Very respectfully,

W. M. BLACK,
EARLE B. PHELPS.

SPECIAL REPORT

ON THE

Flushing Drainage District

SUBMITTED TO THE

BOARD OF ESTIMATE AND APPORTIONMENT

APRIL 22, 1910

Chief Engineer's Office,
Board of Estimate and Apportionment, City of New York,
April 11, 1910.

Hon. William J. Gaynor, *Mayor,*
Chairman of the Board of Estimate and Apportionment:

Sir—At the meeting of the Board of Estimate and Apportionment held on November 12, 1909, attention was called to the need of expert advice relative to the location of points at the waterfront which might properly be used for outletting sewers, and acting on the recommendation made at that time the Board retained Colonel William M. Black, U. S. A., to investigate the matter, and with the understanding that his studies should be carried far enough to establish the extent of purification required in sections where the discharge of raw sewage would result in objectionable harbor pollution.

The desired investigation was begun early in January by Colonel Black, who had in the meantime associated with himself Professor Earle B. Phelps, and with the understanding that it would be completed during the coming summer.

After several conferences it was agreed that the field to be covered should include a general study of the districts for which no complete or permanent drainage plans have been devised and so far as required to establish the points of outlet which were practicable, both from the standpoint of sewer design and suitability for such use.

In recognition of the well-founded objections which have been raised to the use in this city of any of the methods now recognized for purification of sewage, it was also agreed that experiments should be made with a process heretofore untried but which had been suggested by Colonel Black in connection with his studies of the Passaic Valley drainage problem and which seemed to be along lines which could be advantageously followed. An experimental plant for determining the merits of this system has been installed in the East New York Purification Works, Borough of Brooklyn, and its operation has just been begun.

Several years ago the construction of a trunk system of sewers for the Ingleside section in the Borough of Queens was authorized by the Board of Estimate and Apportionment, and at a subsequent date it became necessary to abandon the plan for the outlet originally proposed, its unsuitability having been demonstrated. The sewers are now nearly completed, but no provision has yet been made for a permanent outlet; until this is obtained the system cannot be used. For this reason I suggested to Colonel Black that his attention be first given to the district in which these sewers have been built, and under date of March 30 he has submitted the accompanying report which is concurred in by Professor Phelps.

In this report it is demonstrated:

1st. That the drainage of the territory located between the backbone of the island and the East River, and extending from the westerly boundary of the Flushing Creek valley to the westerly boundary of the valley at the head of Little Neck Bay, comprising about 14,900 acres, should be considered as a whole.

2d. That the discharge from about 4,500 acres of low land within this area, or about 28 per cent. of the total flow, will have to be pumped, while a gravity outlet can be secured for the remainder of the district.

3d. That if further investigation should establish the feasibility of discharging all of the raw sewage directly into the East River, or if the experimental work now being conducted in the matter of an improved process of purification should give satisfactory results, practically all of the dry weather flow could be outletted about one-half mile west of Whitestone Point, and that in case of failure of the experiments and an establishment of the need of purification the discharge from the greater part of the area could be carried directly to Flushing Bay. In either case, it is believed that the lower areas of College Point, Whitestone, and Bayside can be carried to the Whitestone outlet without purification, it being held that the purification of the flow of the remaining area would permit of the discharge of the raw sewage from this territory, which forms only a small part of the whole.

4th. That if purification is required the site for the works would be located in the vicinity of Whitestone road and Bayside avenue, if the experimental process is satisfactorily developed, and otherwise in the low land north of Flushing.

5th. That the concentration point for the drainage of the low areas will be located in the vicinity of Myrtle avenue and Lawrence street.

6th. That pending the carrying out of the entire project and for a limited time the raw sewage from the Flushing section might be outletted, without purification, into the channel at the head of the bay.

7th. That all sewage should be screened before being outletted.

8th. That for the sections adjoining Flushing Creek, where combined sewers have already been built, provision should be made in the permanent plan for intercepting the dry weather flow and leading it to the outlet now recommended for the entire territory, the surplus flow during storms to be discharged as heretofore.

9th. That, where practicable, future plans for the territory in the vicinity of Flushing Creek should be based on using the separate system for so much of the area affected as is based on the outletting of the surface flow into the creek.

I would recommend that a copy of this report and of the acompanying plan be transmitted to the President of the Borough of Queens for consideration, and that his attention be directed particularly to the fact that the plan is intended to be used only as a general guide in the treatment of the problem and with the understanding that if provision is made for the removal of both storm water and the dry weather flow on the combined plan, as would seem desirable, it would doubtless be found practicable and advantageous to make radical changes in certain minor features.

Respectfully,

NELSON P. LEWIS,
Chief Engineer.

March 30, 1910.

Mr. Nelson P. Lewis, *Chief Engineer, Board of Estimate and Apportionment,* New York City:

Sir—In connection with our general studies of the sewerage problem of certain portions of Greater New York, we submit herewith the report upon the portion of our work which deals with that part of Queens Borough draining into Flushing Bay and adjacent waters. This section will be known in these studies as the Flushing Drainage Area.

Divisions of the Drainage Area.

For the purpose of this work the above described district has been divided into twelve sections numbered respectively one to twelve, and the section numbered "six" has been further subdivided into three divisions known respectively as 6a, 6b and 6c. In the estimation of populations we have allowed either twenty-five or fifty persons per acre depending upon the location of the area in question and the character of the country. Reference to the accompanying map * is invited to make clear the following description of these various drainage areas. The respective areas are marked off in heavy black lines except where such lines coincide with contour, street or stream lines, in which case they are indicated by dotted lines. Contour lines at 20-foot intervals are shown, but these are only approximate.

Maps of detailed topographical surveys were not to be obtained and funds and time for the preparation of such maps were not available. Under these conditions we were obliged to use the general map of the City of New York, prepared by the Topographical Bureau of the Board of Public Improvements, dated January 1, 1900, the topography of which is understood to have been compiled from maps issued by the United States Geological Survey.

Area No. 1—This area is situated along the shore between Whitestone Point and the point at the head of Little Neck Bay. It consists of 1,575 acres, having an estimated future population of 42,250.

Area No. 2 includes that portion of the College Point district which is above the 20-foot contour. It contains 493 acres with an estimated future population of 24,650.

Area No. 3 is a suburban district lying between No. 1 and Flushing Bay, having 1,350 acres, with an estimated future population of 35,600.

Area No. 4 includes that portion of Flushing to the north of Franklin and Sanford avenues, which lies above the 20-foot contour. It consists of 524 acres, with an estimated future population of 26,200.

Area No. 5 includes that portion of the Ingleside district of Flushing, lying to the south of Franklin and Sanford avenues and extending to the crest line west of the Flushing Cemetery, which is above the 30-foot contour. It consists of 636 acres, with an estimated future population of 31,800.

Area No. 6 is the large suburban district south of Flushing extending on the south to the crest of the entire drainage area and on the west to the limits of the Flushing Creek Valley. It includes a portion of Bayside and

*Omitted. See general map of Drainage Districts of Jamaica, Corona, Flushing and Westchester, p. 148.

a small portion of Flushing. It consists of 5,402 acres, with an estimated future population of 135,050. For the purposes of drainage it is further subdivided into three divisions.

Area No. 7 is a small section lying to the south of Flushing between the Mill Creek Valley above the 60-foot contour and the crest of Area No. 6. It consists of 476 acres, with an estimated future population of 11,900.

Area No. 8 lies on the east side of Flushing Creek Valley, extending to the confluence with Mill Creek. It consists of 893 acres, with an estimated future population of 22,325.

Area No. 9 includes the valley of Mill Creek below the 40-foot contour line on the east side and the 60-foot contour line on the west side, down to Lawrence street. It consists of 905 acres, with an estimated future population of 22,625.

Area No. 10 includes the small district between Flushing and Mill Creeks, and Lawrence and Myrtle avenues, below the 20-foot contour, having an area of 172 acres, with an estimated future population of 8,600.

Area No. 11 includes that portion of College Point between Myrtle and Whitestone avenues and the easterly crest of Area No. 2, which is below the 20-foot contour. It has 763 acres, with an estimated future population of 19,075.

Area No. 12 is on the west side of Flushing Creek Valley and Horse Creek Valley, all below the 20-foot contour. It has 1,734 acres, with an estimated future population of 43,350.

The acreage and population of these twelve areas are tabulated below. The total area of the drainage district is 14,923 acres and the estimated future population, 423,425.

Area.	Acres.	Population.
1	1,575	42,250
2	493	24,650
3	1,350	35,600
4	524	26,200
5	636	31,800
6	5,402	135,050
7	476	11,900
8	893	22,325
9	905	22,625
10	172	8,600
11	763	19,075
12	1,734	43,350
	14,923	423,425

General Scheme of Sewerage for the District.

The project which is here proposed for the collection of the sewage of the entire Flushing drainage area is briefly as follows:

The point of final discharge is located on the East River just to the east of Powells Cove and about twenty-five hundred feet to the west of Whitestone Point. To convey the sewage to this point we have provided two main systems which will be designated respectively as the "high level" and the "low level" intercepting systems. The high level system has three main branches. The first drains Area No. 1, above the 20-foot contour line; the small portion of this area which is below that line, consisting of a narrow strip along the shore, will drain directly to the waterfront. This branch meets the main interceptor at the point of discharge.

The second main branch of the high level system drains Area No. 2 above the 20-foot contour. It enters the main interceptor at the junction of Fourth avenue and Eighteenth street. The main interceptor itself may be considered to start at the point just south of the Flushing Cemetery, which is designated as Point "A." It follows Meadow road in a westerly direction, thence across country to Oak and Parsons, in Ingleside, along Oak to Colden, thence to Franklin, to Lawrence, to Washington, to Prince, to State, to Leavitt, to Whitestone, along Whitestone and Fourth avenue and on a continuation of Fourth avenue to the point of discharge. At a point in Whitestone, near Bayside avenue, suitable land is available for purification works if these be considered necessary. This point will be further discussed.

At the Point "A" previously mentioned the trunks from the Districts 6c and 6b will enter. The trunk from 6a joins the latter at a point shown on the map. The location of each of these trunks is sufficiently well indicated to make detailed description unnecessary. At the corner of Myrtle and Leavitt the force main from the low level interceptor enters this line. A short distance beyond at the proposed site for the sewage disposal works the trunk from Area No. 3 joins this line, and at the points already indicated the main trunks from Areas No. 1 and No. 2 enter. This high level system will therefore drain by gravity Areas Nos. 1 to 7, inclusive, a total area of 10,456 acres on which the estimated future population is 307,450.

The low level interceptor has its low point located at the pumping station near the corner of Lawrence and Myrtle avenues in Flushing. To this point a small line draining Area No. 11 is brought. To this point, also, is brought the main trunk from Area No. 12, this trunk crossing Flushing Creek at the foot of Myrtle avenue by means of an inverted syphon. A third line reaches this point by closely following Flushing Creek to its end, draining Area No. 8. This latter line branches at the confluence of Flushing and Mill Creeks, one branch extending to the upper end of the valley of Mill Creek, as shown. The total area tributary to the low level interceptor is therefore made up of Areas Nos. 8 to 12, inclusive, having 4,467 acres with an estimated future population of 115,975. The future discharge of this low level system is therefore seen to be approximately 28 per cent. of the total discharge from the Flushing drainage area.

From the pumping station to a point already indicated on the high level interceptor there will be a 30-inch cast-iron force main having a total length of approximately 3,000 feet.

Design of Main Trunk Lines From Each Area.

For the purposes of this investigation it has been deemed necessary to determine fully the route, grades and dimensions of the high level interceptor and the routes, points of entrance, and maximum sizes of the trunks of the various areas. It has not been considered advisable to make a more detailed study of these trunk lines. Such a study would involve a full investigation of all existing sewers, information as to which is meagre or altogether lacking. In estimating the maximum capacity of the trunk lines at their point of junction with the interceptor, or with another trunk, a water consumption of 125 gallons per capita per diem has been allowed, based upon the reports of the Chief Engineer of the Board of Estimate and Apportionment. In addition to this strictly sanitary flow an allowance of .003 cubic foot per second per acre has been made for ground water flow. This allowance is based upon the practice of the Borough Engineer of Brooklyn. No provision for storm water has been made further than the placing of storm water overflows at those points at which existing combined systems of sewerage will enter the interceptor. Upon this basis of estimate the flow is found to be .01023 and .01746 cubic feet per second per acre, for populations of twenty-five and fifty per acre respectively. It has further been assumed that of the total flow per 24 hours, half will pass in 8 hours, and upon this assumption the maximum discharge has been estimated. It is believed that this assumption is a conservative one in consideration of the size and length of the trunk sewers. Experience elsewhere has shown that in sewers of this size the ratio of maximum to average flow rarely reaches the value that we have assigned. Velocities and discharges have been computed for sewers flowing full, 0.8 full, 0.5 full and 0.2 full. Estimates of size are based upon the computation at 0.8 full. In the summary which follows it has been deemed sufficient to give this maximum velocity and discharge and the minimum velocity and discharge at 0.2 full. The dimensions, slopes, velocities and discharges of the various trunk lines are given in detail in the following tabulation:

Area No.	Maximum Discharge, Sec., Ft.	Slope 1 Foot in	Maximum Diameter, Feet.	Sewer 0.8 Full. Velocity, Sec., Ft.	Sewer 0.8 Full. Discharge, Sec., Ft.	Sewer 0.2 Full. Velocity, Sec., Ft.	Sewer 0.2 Full. Discharge, Sec., Ft.
1........	17.0	1,000	3.0	2.88	17.0	1.50	1.47
2........	8.6	600	2.0	3.22	8.6	1.68	0.75
3........	14.4	1,000	2.75	2.76	14.4	1.44	1.25
4........	9.15	500	2.0	3.45	9.15	1.80	0.80
5........	11.1	1,000	2.5	2.53	11.1	1.32	0.96
*6a.......	19.8	800	3.0	3.34	19.8	1.74	1.72
6b.......	18.8	900	3.0	3.22	18.8	1.68	16.30
6c.......	20.6	700	3.0	3.45	20.6	1.80	1.79
7........	4.87	600	2.0	2.88	4.87	1.50	0.43
8........	9.15	1,000	2.33	2.32	9.15	1.26	0.78
9........	0.25	800	2.25	2.64	0.25	1.38	0.80
**8-9.......	18.4	1,000	3.0	3.00	18.4	1.56	1.60
10........	3.0	400	1.33	2.53	3.0	1.32	0.26
**8-9-10....	21.4	700	3.0	3.56	21.4	1.86	1.90
11........	7.8	1,000	2.25	2.42	7.8	1.26	0.68
12........	17.75	1,000	3.0	3.0	17.75	1.56	1.54
Force Main.	47.0	....	2.5	9.68 full	47.0 full	.....	....

* Including No. 7.
** Below junction.

Design of the Intercepting Sewer.

The design of this sewer from point to point is determined by the available slopes and by the entrance of the various trunk lines. To facilitate reference the sewer will be divided into sections which are described as follows:

Section A—From point A on the map, south of Flushing Cemetery, to the Ingleside inlet, corner of Oak and Parsons.

Section B—From this point to the Flushing inlet on Broadway.

Section C—From the Flushing inlet to the force main junction on Myrtle.

Section D—From this junction to No. 3 inlet at or near the disposal works.

Section E—From No. 3 inlet to the purification works (No. 3 inlet may be at the disposal works, in which case Section E will not have to be considered).

Section F—Purification works to No. 2 inlet.

Section G—No. 2 inlet to No. 1 inlet.

Section H—Outfall sewer.

The dimensions, slopes, velocities and discharges of the high-level interceptor, subdivided into the above-described sections are given in the following table:

Section.	Maximum Discharge.	Slope 1 Foot in	Maximum Diameter, Feet.	Sewer 0.8 Full.		Sewer 0.2 Full.	
				Velocity, Sec., Ft.	Discharge, Sec., Ft.	Velocity, Sec., Ft.	Discharge, Sec., Ft.
A	59.2	1,500	5.0	3.45	59.2	1.80	5.13
B	70.3	1,700	5.5	3.45	70.3	1.80	6.10
C	79.5	2,100	6.0	3.22	79.5	1.68	6.90
D	127.0	1,800	7.0	3.80	127.0	1.98	11.10
E and F..	141.4	2,100	7.5	3.80	141.4	2.00	12.30
G	150.0	2,000	7.5	3.9	150.0	2.00	13.00
H	167.0	2,000	8.0	4.02	167.0	2.10	14.50

Details of Main Interceptor.

Section.	Length, Feet.	Total Fall, Feet.	Elevation of Invert, Upper End.	Elevation of Ground, Upper End.	Contributing Area, Acres.
A	6,000	4.0	22.1	33.1	5,878
B	12,000	7.1	18.1	27.6	6,514
C	3,500	1.7	11.0	21.0	7,038
D	3,500	2.0	9.3	20.3	11,505
F	3,600	1.7	7.3	18.8	12,855
G	3,200	1.6	5.6	17.1	13,348
H	1,000	0.5	4.0	16.0	14,923

In order to minimize the expenses to be incurred immediately, in view of the fact that the sewers recommended are of a size suitable to serve a population greatly in excess of that at present found in the drainage area, it is recommended that the interceptors and main trunk lines be constructed first of a less capacity, leaving to the future the installation of a duplicate set on the same lines.

Similarly, it is suggested that as a temporary expedient, while the sewage flow remains at its present volume a temporary outfall could be made into the channel near the head of the bay. This would be less unsanitary than the continuance of discharge through the existing outfalls into Flushing Creek, though not a condition which should be permitted to exist for any prolonged period.

Purification.

We are not prepared at the present time to report upon the degree of purification which we consider necessary in carrying out this drainage project. A site has been selected for purification works if they be found necessary. It was not feasible to determine upon a site nearer the outfall which would intercept all the sewage of the drainage area. It will be noticed that areas No. 1 and No. 2 drain into the interceptor below the purification works. Estimating upon the basis of future populations, these drainage areas will contribute about 15 per cent. of the total discharge. It is our opinion that if purification be necessary at all the remaining 85 per cent. of the discharge can be purified to such a degree that the average purification of the whole will be maintained at a point which is found desirable. In any event and as a minimum measure of purification, we are of the opinion that screening of all the sewage will be necessary. This will involve suitable screening plants on the two trunks indicated and on the main interceptor in addition to any purification which may be decided upon later.

It is recommended that an area of about three acres should be secured at once at the site recommended for the purification works. The value of property in that vicinity is increasing rapidly and should future advances in sewage purification methods make a less area necessary, the excess of land could be sold profitably.

The system, as laid out, is designed for purification by methods other than the form of sprinkling filters now in use. Should it prove necessary to adopt the method of purification by sprinkling filters, the works could be located in the existing marsh land between Flushing and College Point, and would require an area of about forty acres, and the purified effluent discharged into Flushing Bay. All of the flow entering the outfall can readily be brought to this point.

Storm Water Overflows.

The present sewerage system of Flushing is a combined system. This will be intercepted at some point on Broadway and a storm water overflow will be provided and so designed that the maximum dry weather discharge into the interceptor allowed for Area No. 4 cannot be exceeded in times of storm. This overflow will discharge into Flushing Creek at the foot of Broadway under the bridge. In our opinion this situation is an undesirable one and future construction should as far as practicable be made upon the separate system. We do not, however, advise the complete reconstruction of this Flushing system at present.

Very respectfully,

W. M. Black,
Earle B. Phelps.

SPECIAL REPORT

ON THE

Jamaica Drainage District

SUBMITTED TO THE

BOARD OF ESTIMATE AND APPORTIONMENT

JANUARY 12, 1911

CHIEF ENGINEER'S OFFICE,
BOARD OF ESTIMATE AND APPORTIONMENT,
CITY OF NEW YORK, December 12, 1910.

Hon. WILLIAM J. GAYNOR, *Mayor,*
Chairman of the Board of Estimate and Apportionment:

SIR—Herewith is transmitted the progress report of Colonel William M. Black and Professor Earle B. Phelps, bearing date of November 18, 1910, concerning the investigation made by them relative to the points suitable for use as sewer outlets for the territory comprising the southern slope of the Boroughs of Brooklyn and Queens, extending from the Narrows to the Nassau County line, and also for the section adjoining the north shore in the vicinity of Little Neck Bay, the entire area being designated by them as the Jamaica Drainage District.

The area comprises about 49,000 acres which is estimated to have a total future population of about 1,700,000. Following the method used in the investigation of the Corona and Flushing districts, both of which have been reported upon to the Board, a study has been made of the lines which could be followed for the main sewers of this territory in order to reach the points selected as outlets, and the entire area has been divided into 53 drainage districts, for each of which the trunk lines are indicated, the design being worked out in such a way as to intercept sewers already built and to conform with the plans heretofore adopted in so far as practicable.

Excluding the Little Neck, Coney Island and Rockaway Beach districts, together with the area for which plans have already been prepared with provision for an outlet into the Narrows, the sanitary flow of the entire district now reported upon is to be concentrated at three points, from which it will be discharged into the waters of Jamaica Bay. These concentration points are located, respectively, at Riches Point Meadow, at the site of the Twenty-sixth Ward disposal works, and at a point on the Three-Mile Mill Road, near the toe of the upland. The point first referred to is to be used as the outlet for the drainage areas heretofore laid out upon the drainage plan of the City with provision for concentration points at the existing Sheepshead Bay disposal plant and at the head of Paerdegat Basin, and also for all of the unplanned area west of the Rockaway Parkway.

The Twenty-sixth Ward disposal plant will be used for the collection of the flow from the remaining unplanned area within the limits of the Borough of Brooklyn, together with the flow from the marsh-land adjoining the Jamaica Bay located west of the Remsen Landing Road, and from all of the portion of the upland within the limits of the Borough of Queens south of the ridge, excepting the area lying east of the Bergen Landing Road and south of the Old Country Road.

The remaining area within the limits of the Borough of Queens, with the exception of the Rockaway Beach and Little Neck sections, is to be outletted from the third concentration point of reference.

Screening and aeration are to be ultimately provided at all of these points, the time of applying the latter and the extent of purification required depending upon the development of each of the areas.

Plans have already been adopted providing for the concentration of the sewage from the westerly end of Coney Island at the existing West Twelfth street station, where a chemical purification plant is in use. The investigators recommend that all of the sewage from the island be collected at this point and discharged either into the interceptor which is to extend from the pumping station located at the head of the proposed Bensonhurst Drainage Canal to the Narrows, or that it be discharged about 2,000 feet off-shore and south of the westerly end of the island; it is believed that the latter treatment can be resorted to without requiring purification and without causing nuisance.

It is proposed to provide an outlet for the Rockaway section at three points from which the sewage will be discharged about 1,000 feet off-shore at a depth of about 15 feet, no treatment being required other than the removal of the grosser suspended matter, following the method now in use along the New Jersey coast. It is stated that there is "little or no probability of the sewage reaching the beach without such dilution as to make it undistinguishable."

The sewage from the Little Neck Bay section is to be concentrated at a point near the head of the bay, whence it will be forced into tidal waters, after sedimentation, screening and a certain amount of aeration.

The report includes tables giving the elements necessary for the design of the various interceptors and their tributary trunks, together with the pumping capacity required at each of the power plants which will be needed. A plan is also presented showing the boundaries of each of the drainage areas and the route, size and grade of each of the sewers proposed, together with the locations of the pumping stations, concentration points, and points of final outlet.

The study is based entirely on the drainage needs in so far as the sanitary flow is concerned, but provision has been made for storm water overflows at all points where the sanitary trunks intercept existing or authorized combined sewers.

It is understood that the experimental work which has been carried on relative to the aeration process of purification will be made the subject of an independent report, but information is now given indicating the amount of oxygen required in order to accomplish the required degree of purification at each point of outfall. It is understood that owing to a lack of necessary data the map submitted with this report is of a general character and that more precise surveys may establish a need for radical revision of the design in many particulars.

I would suggest that a copy of this report and of the accompanying map be transmitted to the President of the Borough of Brooklyn and to the President of the Borough of Queens, with the recommendation that they be given careful consideration in the preparation of the drainage plans for the areas affected.

Respectfully,

NELSON P. LEWIS,
Chief Engineer.

November 18, 1910.

Mr. Nelson P. Lewis,
Chief Engineer, Board of Estimate and Apportionment,
New York City:

Sir—In connection with our general studies of the sewerage problems of certain portions of Greater New York, we beg to submit herewith a third report which deals with the main drainage problem of that portion of Queens Borough lying south of the ridge with a small area lying adjacent to the head of Little Neck Bay, which was not included in the Flushing District; also the southern portion of the Borough of Brooklyn, lying between the boundary of the Corona District already described and Jamaica Bay and including Coney Island, Bay Ridge and the territory directly tributary to Jamaica Bay. For purposes of convenience and identification we have designated this drainage district "The Jamaica Drainage District," and have further sub-divided it into four sections as follows:

The area south of the ridge including portions of both boroughs; the main portion of the Brooklyn area; the area adjacent to the head of Little Neck Bay, and the whole of Rockaway and Far Rockaway. These subdivisions will be known as the Queens, Brooklyn, Little Neck Bay and Rockaway Sections, respectively. Reference to the accompanying map* marked "The Jamaica Drainage District" will make more clear the discussion which follows.

Divisions of the Drainage District.

For the purposes of this study we have divided the above designated district into fifty-three drainage areas, numbered respectively 1 to 53. In the map the division lines between these areas are indicated by heavy dotted lines. Contour lines at 20-foot intervals are shown, but these are only approximate, by reason of the lack of detailed topographic surveys and of available time and funds for making such surveys, which has been commented upon in our first report. Our proposed sewer lines are indicated in red and other features are sufficiently described in the legend. Estimates of future populations have been made upon a basis of either twenty-five or fifty persons per acre, depending upon the location of the area in question and the character of the country. Those areas for which a population of fifty per acre has been assumed lie about Jamaica Bay and in the region of the proposed improvements. Owing to the probable character of the future population, laborers about the docks, a water consumption of 100 instead of 125 gallons per day has been allowed. This gives an "equivalent population" of forty per acre with a water consumption of 125 gallons. Our table of estimated future population is based upon this "equivalent population." The populations to be cared for in the Coney Island District and also in the Rockaway District are necessarily treated along somewhat unusual lines. In the case of Coney Island a maximum population of five hundred thousand persons, with an average water consumption of fifteen gallons per capita daily has been assumed, and the sewage has further been assumed to run off in twelve hours. This estimate reduced to our usual basis

*Omitted. See general map of Drainage Districts of Jamaica, Corona, Flushing and Westchester, p. 148.

of calculation is equivalent to a permanent population of seventy persons per acre, with a daily per capita water consumption of 125 gallons. Similar assumptions and calculations for the Rockaway District would give an equivalent permanent population of fifty persons, with a consumption of 125 gallons per capita per day. In other respects our assumptions as to population, water consumption, ground water run-off and ratio of maximum to average discharge are the same as were made in our Flushing report.

The areas will be sufficiently identified by reference to the map * and will be only briefly described:

Areas Nos. 1 to 10, inclusive, lie southeast of the crest line separating the Jamaica from the Flushing District, being numbered consecutively from the northeast corner. Area No. 6 is identical with the present Jamaica District, which already has a system of sewers installed. Area No. 8 is the Richmond Hill District for which sewer designs have been approved.

Areas Nos. 11, 12 and 13 comprise a small belt to the southeast of Areas Nos. 7 to 10.

Areas Nos. 14, 15, 16, 18, 19 and 20 constitute the northeastern corner of Brooklyn Borough, lying north of Rockaway Parkway.

Area No. 17 is entirely swamp land lying between Area No. 13 and Jamaica Bay.

Areas Nos. 21 to 27, inclusive, constitute a second belt lying to the southeast of the belt already described in Queens, extending from the northeastern boundary to Area No. 11, already described.

Areas Nos. 28 to 36, inclusive, constitute a third belt lying still lower and extending from the territory described to the Bay.

Area No. 20 is identical with Division "X" of the Sewer Department maps.

Areas Nos. 37 to 41, inclusive, constitute the eastern central portion of Brooklyn Borough, extending from the ridge on the west, which separates this section from the New York Bay drainage area, to Jamaica Bay on the east.

Area No. 42 comprises the whole of Coney Island.

Areas Nos. 43 to 46, inclusive, comprise the remainder of this Borough, which drains naturally to Gravesend Bay.

Area No. 39 is the District "Y."

Area No. 38 is the District "DD."

Area No. 46 is the District "W."

Area No. 45 is the District "Z."

Area No. 44 is the District "EE."

Areas Nos. 37 and 43 are the District "AA."

Area No. 42 includes the District "CC."

Areas Nos. 47 to 50, inclusive, are situated adjacent to and drain into Little Neck Bay.

Areas Nos. 51 to 53, inclusive, include the entire Rockaway and Far Rockaway Districts.

The acreage and future estimated populations of these various drainage areas are tabulated below.

The total area included in the district is 48,916 acres, and the total estimated future population is 1,661,495.

*Omitted. See general map of drainage districts of Jamaica, Corona, Flushing and Westchester, p. 148.

Area No.	Acres.	Assumed Future "Equivalent Population." Per Acre.	Total.
1	1,634	25	40,850
2	1,010	25	25,250
3	637	25	15,925
4	794	25	19,850
5	319	25	7,975
6	1,259	25	31,475
7	734	40	29,360
8	576	40	23,040
9	628	40	25,120
10	576	40	23,040
11	844	40	33,760
12	334	40	13,360
13	384	40	15,360
14	1,003	40	40,120
15	432	40	17,280
16	1,231	40	49,240
17	1,288	40	51,520
18	949	40	37,960
19	945	40	37,800
20	1,216	40	48,640
21	360	25	9,000
22	663	25	16,575
23	837	25	20,925
24	540	25	13,500
25	299	25	7,475
26	661	25	16,525
27	750	25	18,750
28	500	25	12,500
29	357	25	8,925
30	1,266	25	31,650
31	1,671	25	41,775
32	905	25	22,625
33	1,408	25	35,200
34	1,067	25	26,675
35	696	40	27,840
36	707	40	28,280
37	1,460	25	36,500
38	1,650	40	66,000
39	2,408	40	96,320
40	652	40	26,080
41	950	40	38,000
42	1,152	70	80,640
43	1,312	25	32,800
44	629	25	15,725
45	996	25	24,900
46	2,104	40	84,160
47	1,079	25	26,975
48	724	25	18,100
49	479	25	11,975
50	555	25	13,875
51	1,309	50	65,450
52	811	50	40,550
53	1,166	50	58,300
Total	48,916		1,661,495

General Scheme of Sewerage for the District.

Queens Section.

This section will have two main concentration points, one at the present Twenty-sixth Ward Pumping Station on Second Creek, the other at Three-Mile Mill on Cornell Creek. These concentration points are indicated on the map as "A" and "B," respectively. The sewage will be brought to point "A" by three gravity systems, one draining Areas 17 and 18, the second draining Areas 19 and 20, and the third draining the high-level district included in Areas 1 to 16, inclusive. This interceptor will be known as Interceptor No. 1 and a branch interceptor serving Areas 11, 12 and 13 will be known as Interceptor No. 2.

From point "A" the sewage will be forced through three four-foot cast-iron force mains to a point in Big Fishkill Channel. When the thirty-foot channel is excavated in front of the bulkhead line, the outfall sewers must be discharged into it, as the circulation in Fishkill and Broad Channels will then be markedly lessened, and the points of discharge shown will be in water of less depth. In this as in all cases, the most efficient means possible should be taken to insure diffusion of the sewage effluent in the sea water at the outlet so as to avoid a surface nuisance.

The remaining portions of Queens will drain to concentration point "B" by two main interceptors: Areas 21 to 27, inclusive, are served by high-level interceptors known as Interceptor No. 3; Areas 28 to 34, inclusive, by a low-lever interceptor known as Interceptor No. 4; and areas No. 35 and No. 36 by a trunk line with two branch lines leading directly to point B.

From point B the sewage will be forced through two four-foot cast-iron force mains to a point in Broad Channel shown on the map.

A discussion of the ability of the waters of Jamaica Bay to dispose successfully of the sewage from these two outlets, without the production of any nuisance, will be deferred to a later section of this report, under the head "Pollution of the Waters and Purification Necessary."

Brooklyn Section.

This section, with the exception of areas adjacent to the Queens boundary line, and which have been included in the Queens section, is already provided with sewer systems or with approved designs. Our proposed plans contemplate certain additions to the existing systems as follows: According to plans already approved, the flow from areas Nos. 43, 44 and 45 will be concentrated at point "E," from which it will be forced by pumping to the final outlet in the Narrows, just above Fort Hamilton. The flow from Coney Island concentrates at "CC," on West Twelfth street and Neptune avenue.

To dispose of the sewage concentrated at this point, we present two alternative projects: First, to lift the flow to a gravity line, leading through a siphon under Gravesend Canal, along Eleventh street and Avenue W to the concentration point "E." The objection to this plan lies in the pumping of the sewage cityward and discharging it into the Upper Bay, where conditions are not favorable for its reception. The second project contemplates pumping the flow from "CC" seaward, discharging about two thousand feet from shore. To permit this there must be found a point of discharge free from the danger of a return upon the beach. In this project a point has been selected well toward the western end of the Island, and the discharge will be in the path of the current around Nortons Point, so that no return of the sewage to the beach is anticipated.

The easterly section of the Brooklyn District, comprising drainage areas 37 to 41, inclusive, is, with the exception of areas 40 and 41, already provided with approved drainage plans. Areas 38 and 39, shown on the Sewer Department plans as "DD" and "Y," respectively, concentrate at point "N" on Flatlands avenue and Paerdegat Basin. Area 37, being the eastern part of the Sewer Department district "AA" concentrates at a point "P" at Knapp street and Avenue Y. The proposed plan contemplates the concentration of the flow from areas 40 and 41 at a point "M" on Ralph avenue and Avenue T.

A gravity interceptor will collect the sewage from these three points (N, P and M), and conduct it to the proposed disposal works in Riches Point Meadow for treatment. This line will be known as Interceptor No. 5. The sewage concentrated at "M" will be lifted directly to the interceptor at Ralph avenue and Avenue T; the flow of areas 38 and 39 will be lifted to a gravity line leading down Ralph avenue to the interceptor, and the flow concentrated at "P" will be lifted to a gravity line joining the interceptor at Avenue T and Flatbush avenue.

The extent and character of the treatment at the purification works will be discussed in a later section of this report. From these works the discharge will be by means of a 54-inch cast-iron pipe to a point in Rockaway Inlet, as indicated.

Little Neck Bay Section.

This section includes a small area with steep slopes and the design is simple. It is not considered advisable to attempt to carry the sewage from this section into the swifter waters of the Sound. Owing to the shallow character of the Bay and the absence of currents, purification works have been indicated near the point of discharge. The subject of purification will be dealt with in a later section of this report.

Rockaway Section—

The Rockaway section comprises low and flat land. The sewage will be collected at three concentration points with a low level trunk running the entire length of the section. From these points it will be discharged through three outfall sewers extending approximately one thousand feet from shore into water 15 feet deep, where there is little or no probability of the sewage reaching the beach without such dilution as to make it undistinguishable. The question of the degree of purification necessary in these cases will be discussed in a later section of this report.

Trunk sewers designated in general by the number of the area served will enter these interceptors and concentration points as follows:

Interceptor No. 1—

Trunk No. 1, from the 120-foot contour line on Little Neck road, following Little Neck road and Jericho turnpike to junction with Rocky Hill road.

Trunk No. 2, from near Marvin road, along Clinton avenue to Rocky Hill road, thence to junction point above.

Trunk No. 3, from Chestnut, along North Wertland to interceptor on Jericho turnpike.

Trunk No. 4a on Hillside avenue, from Vogel to Cornwall to Prospect to Palatina to interceptor on Hempstead and Jamaica Plank road.

Trunk No. 4b, from Kilbourn avenue and Old Country road along the latter to interceptor on Plank road.

Trunk No. 5, from Orchard and Hillside along latter to Columbus to interceptor on Fulton.

Trunk No. 6. This trunk is already constructed as a part of the Jamaica system. It runs along Lincoln avenue to the junction with the Hawtree Creek road. An 8-inch branch runs along Van Wyck avenue and Hawtree Creek road to this same junction. At its junction with the road to Bergens Landing its diameter is 2 feet 0 inches; its grade 1 in 750; and its elevation +15.85. A short branch from this point to the Interceptor on South street is designed. This design, in accordance with the general plan of these studies, is based upon estimated future population, and it is, therefore, larger than the existing trunk, which it serves. The latter will undoubtedly suffice for a considerable period in the future.

Trunk No. 7, from Metropolitan avenue along Gould street to Washington, to Chestnut, to Muh and Atfield avenue, to junction with interceptor on Van Sicklen avenue.

Trunk No. 8. This trunk is already designed as a part of the system of the Richmond Hill section, as shown on Map B-4755, on file in the office of the Chief Engineer, Board of Estimate and Apportionment. It is planned to intercept this trunk at its junction with the interceptor on Metropolis avenue.

Trunk No. 9, from Jamaica avenue to Napier, along the latter to Hatch, to interceptor on Liberty.

Trunk No. 10 (a), on Atlantic avenue from Thrall to interceptor on Rockaway Plank road.

Trunk No. 10 (b), from Jamaica avenue and Snedeker, along latter to interceptor on Atlantic avenue.

Trunk No. 14, from Hendrix and Belmont, along latter to Fountain to interceptor on Sutter.

Trunk No. 15, from Blake and Cleveland, along latter to New Lots, to Schenck, to interceptor on Wortman.

Trunk No. 16, from Belmont and Stone, along latter to Lott, to New Lots, to Pennsylvania, to Wortman, to interceptor on Hendrix.

Interceptor No. 2.

Trunk No. 11, on Hawtree Creek road, from the 40-foot contour line to Old South road, thence to head of Interceptor No. 2, at Centreville avenue.

Trunk No. 12, from Rockaway Plank road along Centreville avenue to the interceptor on Old South road.

Trunk No. 13 (a), from Ocean avenue and Park street, along Park to Woodhaven to Sutter to the cemetery to interceptor on Old South road.

Trunk No. 13 (b), from Atlantic avenue and Spruce along Spruce to Liberty to interceptor on Liberty.

Concentration Point A—

Trunk No. 17. This trunk is not definitely located, but will run through the central portion of Area No. 17 to Mill road.

Trunk No. 18, along Railroad avenue and Mill road, intercepting No. 17 on the latter.

Trunks Nos. 17-18, from above point of junction around head of Spring Creek Basin to concentration point A.

Trunk No. 19 will drain the southerly portion of Area No. 19 and will run along East One Hundred and Eighth street to Flatlands avenue, siphon under Fresh Creek Basin to discharge into Trunk No. 20, as shown.

Trunk No. 20. This is an intercepting trunk line draining Area No. 20, which is known as "X" on Sewer Department Maps of Brooklyn Borough. Flowing 0.8 full this trunk will amply provide for the future sanitary flow from Areas No. 19 and No. 20.

Interceptor No. 3—

Trunk No. 21 (a), from Long Island Railroad along Creed avenue to the upper end of the interceptor at Hollis.

Trunk No. 21 (b), from Claremont and Old Country road along the latter to the upper end of interceptor on Hollis.

Trunk No. 22 (a), on Old Country road to interceptor on Springfield.

Trunk No. 22 (b). This trunk will flow between the 45-foot and 55-foot contour lines through the northeastern section of Area No. 22. It is not definitely located. It will enter the interceptor at Central avenue and Springfield.

Trunk No. 23 (a), from a point on Bank avenue, near Springfield road, along Bank to Farmers to interceptor on Central.

Trunk No. 23 (b). This trunk is not definitely located, but will run from the northerly boundary of Area No. 23 in a southerly direction to Farmers avenue to the interceptor on Central.

Trunk No. 24, from Long Island Railroad and William street along latter across South street, thence through an unmapped territory to Canton avenue to interceptor on Central.

Trunk No. 25, from Farmers avenue and Merrick along latter to interceptor on Central.

Trunk No. 26 (a), from Cumberland and High View along prolongation of latter to interceptor on Anita.

Trunk No. 26 (b), from Cumberland and Brown along latter to Norris to interceptor on Meyer.

Trunk No. 27, along Rockaway Plank road, from point near Bergens Landing road to Birch to Central to interceptor on Three Mile Mill.

Interceptor No. 4—

Trunk No. 28, from Long Island Railroad and Rosedale avenue along latter to prolongation of Cherry avenue, thence to upper end of Interceptor No. 4 at Cherry and Old Fosters Meadow road.

Trunk No. 29. This trunk is not definitely located, but will run along the southwestern boundary of the area to the upper end of Interceptor No. 4.

Trunk No. 30, along Old Fosters Meadow road from City limits to upper end of Interceptor No. 4.

Trunk No. 31, along Rockaway turnpike, from Hook Creek to Country road, thence to interceptor on Cherry.

Trunk No. 32, along Springfield road, from Clifton avenue to interceptor on Cherry.

Trunk No. 33, along New York avenue, from Long Island Railroad to Nicholas to Rockaway turnpike to Garfield to interceptor on Eighth street, in Idlewild Park.

Trunk No. 34, along Marsh road, from near the waterfront to interceptor on Eighth street, Idlewild Park.

Concentration Point B—

Trunk No. 35. This trunk is not definitely located, but will run in a northeasterly direction through the central portion of Areas Nos. 35 and 36 around head of Bergen Basin to junction with Trunk No. 36.

Trunk No. 36 (a) and No. 36 (b). These trunks are not definitely located, but will drain the northerly and southerly halves, respectively, of Area No. 36, uniting with Trunk No. 35 at a common junction.

Trunks Nos. 35-36, from the above junction point to Concentration Point B.

Eastern Brooklyn District.

Trunk No. 37, from concentration point P along Avenue Y, Coyle street, Avenue U, Bragg street and Avenue T to interceptor at Flatbush.

Trunks Nos. 38-39, from existing concentration point N along Ralph avenue to interceptor on Avenue T.

Coney Island Section.

Trunk No. 42, from existing concentration point CC under Gravesend Bay Canal along West Eleventh street and Avenue W to existing concentration point E. To be used in case sewage is not discharged into sea directly.

Little Neck Bay Section.

Trunk No. 47, from City line following the valley in the centre of Area No. 47 in a southerly direction, thence still following valley in a northwesterly direction to Broadway, to Pine street, to Orient, to Willow, to Main at Junction with Trunk No. 48.

Trunk No. 48, from point at head of Alley Pond along Alley road, and thence following closely 40-foot contour line in a northwesterly direction to junction with Trunk No. 47 at Willow and Main.

Trunks Nos. 47-48, from the above junction point along Main to Cedar to purification works near head of Little Neck Bay.

Trunk No. 49, from West Alley road, near head of Alley Pond, following 40-foot contour line to junction with Trunk No. 50 on edge of swamp.

Trunk No. 50, from a point to the west of Oakland Lake following 30-foot contour line around Lake to junction with Trunk No. 49.

Trunks Nos. 49-50, from above junction point through meadow under creek to purification works. The kind and degree of purification to be given the sewage at this point will be discussed in a later section of this report.

Rockaway Section.

The three areas comprising the Rockaway section will be served by three separate systems with independent concentration points and outlets.

Trunks Nos. 51 (a) and 51 (b). These two trunks run parallel to the shore from the two ends of Area No. 51 to the concentration point X, located as shown.

Trunks Nos. 52 (a) and 52 (b). These two trunks drain Area No. 52 in a similar manner and concentrate at point Y, as shown.

Trunk No. 53. This trunk runs along the southern boundary of Area No. 53 from near the City limit to the concentration point Z, in the southern corner of the area.

Purification works are provided at each of these concentration points. The kind and degree of purification necessary will be discussed in a later section of this report.

Design of Trunk Lines from Each Area—

As in our previous report, it has been deemed sufficient for our present purposes to investigate fully the approximate routes, grades and maximum size of all trunk lines at the point of entrance into the interceptor. It has not been deemed advisable to make a more detailed study of these trunks. Such a study would involve the detailed investigation of all existing sewers, information as to which is often meagre or totally lacking. Estimates of capacity of trunk lines are based upon water consumption and ground water flow, as previously described in our Flushing report. Provision for storm-water overflows has been made at those points where these proposed lines intercept existing combined sewers, namely, at the intersection of Trunk No. 6, at Lincoln avenue and Hawtree Creek road; and of Trunk No. 8, on Metropolis avenue; and of Trunk No. 20, previous to its junction with No. 19. The first two overflows will continue in existing or approved sewers to the present Jamaica Disposal Plant; the third by a new overflow to Fresh Creek. While the sewers have been designed for sanitary and ground water flow only, until the population has been greatly increased, these provisions will suffice for storm water. Assumptions as to the relation between maximum flow and total mean flow for 24 hours have been made as described in our Flushing report. Velocities and discharges have been computed for sewers flowing full, 0.8 full, 0.5 full and 0.2 full. Sizes are based upon the normal flow, sewer 0.5 full. In the following table the principal items involved in the design of these trunks, including maximum discharge, available slope, maximum diameter and velocities and discharges at 0.8 and 0.2 full are given:

Design of Trunk Sewers.

Trunk No.	Length, Feet.	Total Fall, Feet.	Elevation of Invert, Upper End.	Contributing Area, Acres.	Maximum Discharge, Sec., Ft.	Slope 1 Foot in	Maximum Diameter, Feet.	Sewer 0.8 Full.		Sewer 0.2 Full.	
								Velocity, Sec., Ft.	Discharge, Sec., Ft.	Velocity, Sec., Ft.	Discharge, Sec., Ft.
1	10,200	34.00	112.55	1,634	16.72	300	3.00	5.52	32.80	2.88	2.84
2	5,300	29.45	108.50	1,010	10.33	180	2.33	5.75	20.23	3.00	1.76
3	4,200	21.00	88.92	637	6.52	200	2.00	4.83	12.78	2.52	1.11
4 (a)	6,350	52.92	91.27	529	5.42	120	1.67	5.64	10.62	2.94	0.92
4 (b)	6,350	21.17	51.95	265	2.71	300	1.50	3.34	5.31	1.74	0.46
5	5,700	45.60	73.11	319	3.26	125	1.50	4.95	6.39	2.58	0.55
6	875	1.65	15.85	1,259	12.88	500	3.00	4.26	....	2.22	....
7	4,850	38.80	54.00	734	10.69	125	2.17	6.67	19.99	3.48	1.73
8	*....	....	....	576	8.39	....	....	....	....	....	....
9	5,500	36.67	40.85	628	9.15	150	2.17	5.87	17.91	3.06	1.55
10 (a)	2,300	27.05	26.83	288	4.19	85	1.50	5.87	8.21	3.07	0.71
10 (b)	3,150	52.50	52.28	288	4.19	60	1.33	6.78	8.21	3.54	0.71
11	10,570	26.43	28.66	844	12.29	400	2.83	4.49	24.02	2.34	2.09
12	3,500	28.00	31.73	334	4.86	125	1.58	5.40	9.52	2.82	0.83
13 (a)	1,700	24.28	23.65	256	3.72	70	1.33	6.22	7.28	3.24	0.63
13 (b)	1,700	13.60	10.70	128	1.86	125	1.17	4.14	3.65	2.16	0.32
14	4,450	22.50	20.14	1,003	14.59	200	2.67	5.98	28.57	3.12	2.48
15	5,050	16.82	12.86	432	6.29	300	2.00	4.14	12.53	2.16	2.19
16	11,400	32.58	28.81	1,231	17.92	350	3.17	5.18	35.12	2.70	3.72
17	9,100	8.27	3.27	1,288	18.75	1,100	4.00	3.45	36.75	1.80	3.18
18	4,000	8.00	3.00	475	6.90	500	2.50	3.45	13.52	1.80	1.17
17-18	5,000	5.00	—5.00	2,237	32.55	1,000	3.67	3.45	32.55	1.80	2.82
19	7,350	8.17	—0.61	945	13.78	900	3.50	3.45	27.00	1.80	2.34
19-20	†....	....	....	2,161	30.03	....	3.50	....	....	....	....

*Already designed. †Constructed.

Trunk No.	Length, Feet.	Total Fall, Feet.	Elevation of Invert, Upper End.	Contributing Area, Acres.	Normal Discharge, Sec., Ft.	Slope 1 Foot in	Maximum Diameter, Feet.	Sewer 0.8 Full.		Sewer 0.2 Full.	
								Velocity, Sec., Ft.	Discharge, Sec., Ft.	Velocity, Sec., Ft.	Discharge, Sec., Ft.
21 (a)	2,300	11.50	68.89	180	1.84	200	1.25	3.45	3.61	1.80	0.31
21 (b)	3,400	5.67	63.06	180	1.84	600	1.50	2.30	3.61	1.20	0.31
22 (a)	3,800	19.00	57.39	331	3.39	200	1.67	4.26	6.64	2.22	0.58
22 (b)	4,750	13.58	46.46	332	3.39	350	1.75	3.45	6.64	1.80	0.58
23 (a)	6,350	10.59	31.28	418	4.28	600	2.00	3.10	8.38	1.62	0.73
23 (b)	6,350	35.28	56.31	419	4.28	180	1.67	4.60	8.38	2.40	0.73
24	6,750	15.00	33.82	540	5.52	450	2.17	3.45	10.82	1.80	0.94
25	6,150	6.83	22.11	299	3.06	900	2.00	2.30	5.99	1.20	0.52
26 (a)	2,650	6.63	19.56	220	2.29	400	1.50	2.88	4.49	1.50	0.39
26 (b)	3,150	7.88	18.55	441	4.47	400	2.00	3.45	8.76	1.80	0.76
27	6,300	10.50	14.00	750	7.67	600	2.50	3.45	15.03	1.80	1.30
28	9,950	9.95	12.27	500	5.11	1,000	2.50	2.53	10.01	1.32	0.87
29	4,000	4.00	6.32	357	3.65	1,000	2.17	2.30	7.16	1.20	0.62
30	10,550	21.10	23.42	1,266	12.95	500	3.00	4.26	25.38	2.22	2.20
31	9,700	9.70	6.39	1,671	17.10	1,000	3.75	3.45	33.75	1.80	2.91
32	9,300	14.31	13.00	905	9.26	650	2.75	3.45	18.14	1.80	1.57
33	12,000	13.33	6.50	1,408	14.40	900	3.50	3.45	28.22	1.80	2.45
34	6,600	9.44	2.44	1,067	10.90	700	3.00	3.45	21.38	1.80	1.85
35	7,000	10.00	3.93	696	10.13	700	3.00	3.45	20.02	1.80	1.74
36	3,170	7.46	1.39	354	5.15	425	2.17	3.45	10.09	1.80	0.87
35-36	2,750	3.93	—6.07	1,050	20.42	700	3.00	3.45	20.42	1.80	1.77

Trunk No.	Length, Feet.	Total Fall, Feet.	Elevation of Invert, Upper End.	Contributing Area, Acres.	Maximum Discharge, Sec., Ft.	Slope 1 Foot in	Maximum Diameter, Feet.	Sewer 0.8 Full. Velocity, Sec., Ft.	Sewer 0.8 Full. Discharge, Sec., Ft.	Sewer 0.2 Full. Velocity, Sec., Ft.	Sewer 0.2 Full. Discharge. Sec., Ft.
37	8,000	8.89	1.64	1,460	14.94	900	3.5	3.45	29.27	1.80	2.54
38-39	6,200	4.13	1.45	4,058	59.07	1,500	5.17	3.45	50.97	1.80	5.13
42	5,200	4.16	—6.47	1,152	26.62	1,250	4.83	3.45	54.35	1.80	4.62
47	19,850	172.50	177.09	1,079	11.06	115	1.67	5.75	11.06	3.00	0.96
48	8,050	44.70	49.29	724	7.41	180	1.67	4.37	7.41	2.28	0.64
47-48	2,750	4.59	4.59	1,803	18.47	600	2.75	3.45	18.47	1.80	1.61
49	4,450	29.65	36.65	479	4.81	150	1.25	4.14	4.81	2.16	0.42
50	5,050	29.70	36.70	555	5.68	170	1.50	4.14	5.68	2.16	0.49
49-50	3,150	7.00	7.00	1,034	10.49	450	2.17	3.45	10.49	1.80	0.91
51 (a)	9,000	10.00	0.00	827	14.44	900	3.50	3.45	28.32	1.80	2.46
51 (b)	7,400	12.33	2.33	482	8.41	600	2.67	3.45	16.50	1.80	1.43
52 (a)	9,500	10.56	0.56	390	6.81	900	2.67	2.88	13.36	1.50	1.17
52 (b)	11,600	11.60	1.60	421	7.35	1,000	2.75	2.88	14.40	1.50	1.25
53	6,300	5.25	0.25	1,166	20.37	1,200	4.17	3.45	39.90	1.80	3.46

Design of the Intercepting Sewers—

The design of these sewers is determined by the available slope and by the points of entrance of the various trunk lines. Sizes are based upon normal flow, sewers 0.8 full. To facilitate reference, the five interceptors have been subdivided into sections designated by letters and beginning at the upper end in each case. These sections are described as follows:

Interceptor No. 1—

Section A, from Rocky Hill road and North Jericho turnpike along latter to North Wertland avenue.

Section B, from last-named point along Jericho tunrpike and Hempstead and Jamaica Plank road to Palatina avenue.

Section C, from last-named point to Old Country road.

Section D, from last-named point along Fulton to Columbus avenue.

Section E, from last-named point along Fulton to Skidmore to Willow to Candace to Larch and South to Wells.

Section F, from last-named point along First street to Van Wyck to Wyoming to Van Sicklen.

Section G, from last-named point along Van Sicklen to Metropolis to Lefferts.

Section H, from last-named point along Metropolis to Hamilton to Liberty to Hatch.

Section I, from last-named point to Rockaway Plank road to Atlantic avenue.

Section J, from last-named point along Atlantic avenue to Elderts lane to Liberty.

Section K, from last-named point along Elderts lane to Glenmore to Railroad avenue to Sutter to Fountain.

Section L, from last-named point along Fountain to Vienna to Atkins to Stanley to Sheppard to Wortman to Schenck.

Section M, from last-named point along Wortman to Hendrix.

Section N, from last-named point to concentration point A.

Section O, outfall force mains from concentration point A to Big Fishkill Channel.

Interceptor No. 2—

Section A, from Centerville avenue and Old South road at junction of Trunks 11 and 12, thence along Old South road to Acacia Cemetery.

Section B, from last-named point around cemetery to Liberty.

Section C, from last-named point along Liberty to junction with Interceptor No. 1 on Elderts lane.

Interceptor No. 3—

Section A, from junction of Trunks 21 (a) and 21 (b) on Hollis and Springfield along latter to Old Country road.

Section B, from last-named point along Springfield to Central.

Section C, from last-named point along Central to Farmers avenue.

Section D, from last-named point along Central to Canton.

Section E, from last-named point along Central to Merrick road.

Section F, from last-named point along Merrick road to Anita, thence to Vine.

Section G, from last-named point along prolongation of Meyer avenue and Claude place to Norris.

Section H, from last-named point along Norris to Campbell to Rockaway turnpike to Rockaway Plank road to Three Mile Mill road to Central avenue.

Section I, from last-named point along Three Mile Mill to concentration point B.

Section J, from concentration point B by pressure force mains to point in Broad Channel.

Interceptor No. 4—

Section A, from junction of Trunks 28, 29 and 30 at Old Fosters Meadow road along Cherry avenue to Country road.

Section B, from last-named point along Cherry avenue and Eighth street to Garfield avenue.

Section C, from last-named point along Eighth street to concentration point B.

Interceptor No. 5—

Section A, from junction with Trunks 38-39 on Ralph avenue along Avenue T to junction with Trunk 37 on Flatbush avenue.

Section B, from Avenue T along Flatbush avenue in a southeasterly direction to purification works on Riches Point Meadow.

Section C, cast-iron force main from purification works to a point in Rockaway Inlet.

Design of the Outfall Sewers—

In addition to the three outfall sections of main interceptors, formerly described, there are five outfall sections contemplated in the proposed plans. Three of these are located on the shore front of the Rockaway District and one in Little Neck Bay, one in Coney Island (alternative project). These will be known as Rockaway Outfall Sewers No. 1, No. 2 and No. 3; Little Neck Bay Outfall Sewer; and Coney Island Outfall Sewer; serving Areas Nos. 51, 52 and 53, the Little Neck Bay District and Area No. 42, respectively.

The total length, total fall of each section, elevation of invert at upper end of section, area contributing to each section, dimensions, slopes, velocities and discharges at 0.8 and 0.2 full, of the above-described sections of these five interceptors, are given in the following tables:

Design of Interceptor.

Section.	Length. Feet.	Total Fall, Feet.	Elevation of Invert, Upper End.	Contributing Area, Acres.	Normal Discharge, Sec., Ft.	Slope 1 Foot in	Maximum Diameter, Feet.	Sewer 0.8 Full.		Sewer 0.2 Full.	
								Velocity, Sec., Ft.	Discharge, Sec., Ft.	Velocity, Sec., Ft.	Discharge, Sec., Ft.
					Interceptor No. 1.						
A	4,650	11.63	78.55	2,644	27.05	400	3.00	4.60	27.05	2.40	2.35
B	8,870	29.57	66.92	3,281	33.57	300	3.00	5.52	33.57	2.88	2.91
C	1,690	8.45	37.35	3,810	38.99	200	3.00	6.67	38.99	3.48	3.38
D	2,110	3.52	28.90	4,075	41.70	600	3.75	4.49	41.70	2.34	3.62
E	11,180	11.18	25.38	4,394	44.96	1,000	4.25	3.68	44.96	1.92	3.90
F	2,110	1.05	14.20	5,653	57.84	1,400	5.00	3.56	57.84	1.86	5.02
G	4,860	4.86	12.70	6,387	68.53	1,000	5.00	4.26	68.53	2.22	5.95
H	5,280	6.41	7.84	6,963	76.92	825	5.00	4.60	76.92	2.40	6.67
I	5,280	4.40	1.43	7,591	86.07	1.200	5.50	4.14	86.07	2.16	7.47
J	3,300	3.67	—2.97	8,167	94.45	900	5.50	4.71	94.45	2.46	8.18
K	4,860	1.22	—6.64	9,729	117.18	4,000	7.75	2.88	117.18	1.50	10.16
L	6,550	1.60	—7.86	10,732	131.77	4,100	8.25	2.88	131.77	1.50	11.43
M	260	0.06	—9.46	11,164	138.06	4,200	8.50	2.99	138.06	1.56	11.97
N	2,110	0.48	—9.52	12,395	155.98	4,400	9.00	2.99	155.98	1.56	13.53
O	14,800	13.50*	—10.00**	16,793	218.56		3 @ 4.00	Force Mains.			
					Interceptor No. 2.						
A	4,440	4.44	2.23	1,178	17.15	1,000	3.00	3.09	17.15	1.62	1.49
B	2,320	2.32	—2.21	1,434	20.87	1,000	3.17	3.22	20.87	1.68	1.81
C	2,110	2.11	—4.53	1,562	22.73	1,000	3.25	3.22	22.73	1.68	1.97

* Lift (Max. Value).
** El. of Surface in Pump Well.

Section.	Length, Feet.	Total Fall, Feet.	Elevation of Invert, Upper End.	Contributing Area, Acres.	Normal Discharge, Sec., Ft.	Slope 1 Foot in	Maximum Diameter, Feet.	Sewer 0.8 Full. Velocity, Sec., Ft.	Sewer 0.8 Full. Discharge, Sec., Ft.	Sewer 0.2 Full. Velocity, Sec., Ft.	Sewer 0.2 Full. Discharge, Sec., Ft.
		Interceptor No. 3.									
A	3,800	19.00	57.39	360	3.68	200	1.25	3.45	3.68	1.80	0.32
B	1,900	5.84	38.39	692	7.07	325	1.75	3.45	7.07	1.80	0.61
C	5,710	12.69	32.55	1,023	10.46	450	2.17	3.45	10.46	1.80	0.91
D	1,480	2.12	19.86	1,860	19.02	700	2.17	3.45	19.02	1.80	1.65
E	3,170	3.96	17.74	2,400	24.54	800	3.25	3.45	24.54	1.80	2.13
F	2,320	2.60	13.78	2,699	27.60	900	3.50	3.45	27.60	1.80	2.40
G	2,110	2.34	11.18	2,919	29.89	900	3.50	3.45	29.89	1.80	2.60
H	6,340	6.34	8.84	3,360	34.36	1,000	3.83	3.45	34.36	1.80	2.98
I	4,500	12.50	2.50	4,110	42.03	360	3.50	5.91	42.03	2.82	3.65
J	12,600	13.50*	—10.00**	12,687	135.82	....	2 @ 4.00	Force Mains.			
		Interceptor No. 4.									
A	4,500	5.63	2.32	2,123	21.71	800	3.00	3.45	21.71	1.80	1.88
B	7,400	5.69	—3.31	4,699	48.07	1,300	4.67	3.45	48.07	1.80	4.26
C	1,700	1.00	—9.00	7,174	73.37	1,700	5.67	3.45	73.37	1.80	6.36
		Interceptor No. 5.									
A	3,000	1.67	—5.58	5,660	82.41	1,800	6.00	3.45	82.41	1.80	7.14
B	10,000	4.75	—7.25	7,120	97.35	2,100	6.50	3.45	97.35	1.80	8.44
C	5,280	15.50*	—12.00**	7,120	97.35	....	4.50	Force Mains.			
	Additional Force Main Out Falls.										
1	1,200	13.00*	—10.00**	1,309	22.85	....	2.25	....	....	....	....
2	1,200	13.00*	—10.00**	811	14.16	....	1.67	....	....	....	....
3	2,000	8.00*	—5.00**	1,166	20.37	....	2.00	....	....	....	....
4	2,000	5.50*	0.00**	2,837	28.96	....	2.50	....	....	....	....
5	11,000	62.58	—9.78**	1,152	26.62	....	2.50	....	....	....	....

* Lift (Max. Value).
** El. of surface in Pump-well.

Pumping Stations.

These plans contemplate the establishment of eleven pumping stations, the ultimate maximum capacities and approximate locations of which are as follows: The capacities given are net horse power, without reference to efficiency, and refer to total lift between pump-well level and ordinary maximum high tide, in the case of out-fall works, or between the two fixed levels in case of subsidiary pumping stations. This power is also referred to the same maximum run-off for which our sewers are designed, namely, at the rate of half the total daily run-off of sewage in eight hours, plus the normal hourly rate of ground water flow.

In that section which we have described as the Queens Section, the drainage is entirely by gravity to the concentration point "A." At this point a pumping station having a capacity of 951 net horse power will be required.

At concentration point "B" the drainage is likewise collected by gravity systems. At this point a pumping station having a net capacity of 535 horse power will be required.

In the easterly Brooklyn Section five pumping stations have been designed. One located at concentration point "N" will lift the entire drainage from Areas 38 and 39 to gravity trunk designated 38-39. There will be required a capacity of 102 net horse power. A second station is located at concentration point "P," the capacity required being 29 net horse power. At concentration point "M" a pumping station will lift the discharge from Areas 40 and 41 into the gravity line running to the purification works. The capacity of this station will be 24 net horse power. At the purification works a fifth pumping station with a capacity of 258 net horse power will be provided.

In the Western Brooklyn Section the discharge in Trunk 42 will be lifted by a pumping station located at concentration point "CC" into a gravity line running to concentration point "E". A capacity of 15 net horse power will be required. A pumping station at "E" is already designed and it is not discussed in this report. In the alternative Coney Island project, a pumping station for the outfall at "CC" will be required, with a capacity of 190 net horse power.

In the Little Neck Bay Section a pumping station located at the purification works will lift the entire discharge of this area and force it through the outfall sewer. A capacity of 48 net horse power will be required.

In the Rockaway Section three small pumping stations, one at each outlet, are provided. That serving Area No. 51 will have a capacity of 49 net horse power, that serving Area No. 52, 34 net horse power, and that serving Area No. 53, 47 net horse power.

Pollution of the Waters and Purification Necessary.

In our previous reports matters relating to water pollution and the purification of sewage were left in abeyance until the completion of our experimental investigations into the condition of the waters of New York Harbor, and their ultimate capacity to receive sewage without giving rise to undesirable conditions. This present reports deals with the drainage area which is for the most part adjacent to waters which do not constitute a factor in the New York Bay problem. In the location of the seven outfall points which we have selected for this drainage area, therefore, we have given careful attention to the probable effect of such a plan of drainage upon the adjacent waters. The larger part of this entire drainage area, namely, the Queens and Brooklyn Districts, drains into the waters of Jamaica Bay. Careful investigation of the total amount of water entering this bay from the ocean, during each tidal period, has been made, and by a study of the relative cross sectional areas of the more important channels within the bay and of the tidal prisms tributary to these respective channels, the amount of water available for dilution purposes at each of our three outlets has been approximately estimated. For the purpose of these studies, United States Coast Survey Chart No. 542 and the records of the United States Engineer Office were used in estimating the effective dilution. The amount of partially polluted water remaining in each channel at the beginning of the flood was determined and was added to the total discharge during the next tidal period. This process of summation was continued for a series of tides until the residual correction became so small as to be negligible. In this manner the ultimate dilution of sewage discharged at each of the three outfalls and the ultimate dilution of the entire discharge with reference to the entire tidal flow in and out of Jamaica Bay was determined. The sewage discharged into Rockaway Inlet from Riches Point Meadow, if considered alone, would have an ultimate dilution, determined as indicated, of one part in 2,670, but when considered together with the discharges into other portions of the bay, the ultimate dilution is one in 209. The discharge from concentration point "A" into the Big Fishkill Channel will have a similar ultimate dilution of one part in 75. Sewage discharged from concentration point "B" into Broad Channel will have a similar ultimate dilution of one part in 95. The final dilution of the combined flow from these three discharges into the waters of Rockaway Inlet will be one part in 209, as stated above. These figures are based upon an assumption of thorough diffusion, and at such times as slack water the percentage of pollution will be much greater.

In the course of our experiments, which have been carried on during the past eight months, we have determined, among other things, the amount of oxygen which the sewage of Brooklyn as it now runs to the East New York Pumping Station will absorb from aerated water. The full details of these experiments will be reported upon in a special report. For our present purposes it may be stated that the oxidizability of the sewage in question, or its capacity for absorbing oxygen from the water with which it is mixed varies greatly during the season, being greatest in the summer time and least in the winter. One million gallons of the sewage, if diluted in 100 million gallons of sea water, will, in the course of twelve hours, absorb from the water about 1,950 pounds of oxygen, under conditions which exist during three months in the summer. During the remainder of the year the absorption averages about 500 pounds per million gallons. Obviously it is necessary to provide for the extreme conditions of summer. Under these same conditions the water of the outer bay may be assumed to have a temperature of about 17 degrees C., and a corresponding oxygen content of 66.8 pounds per million gallons. In this case it will be safe to allow a reduction of this oxygen to at least 75 per cent. of the full saturation value, giving us 25 per cent., or 16.7 pounds of oxygen per million gallons of water available for purposes of oxidation; a reduction in the oxygen value to less than 50 per cent. of saturation is almost sure to result in a nuisance, and as we are dealing here with average conditions, it is believed wise to base our calculations upon a reduction to about 75 per cent., thus allowing a margin of safety for fluctuating conditions of sewage flow and tide. Our fundamental data under extreme summer conditions are, therefore:

(1) One million gallons of crude sewage will absorb 1,950 pounds of oxygen in 12 hours, or one tidal period.

(2) One million gallons of sea water contain 16.7 pounds of oxygen which is available for purposes of oxidation.

With this data it is a simple matter to determine the limiting dilution of 1 in 117, above which it is not safe to go.

One other possible source of oxygen suggests itself, namely, absorption from the atmosphere. This phenomenon of absorption or reaeration undoubtedly exists, but a careful study of its quantitative aspects has convinced us that it has little practical value under the conditions with which we have to deal.

It is obvious, therefore, that with the full development of this drainage system some means will have to be utilized to reduce the oxidizability of the sewage before discharge.

The oxidizability referred to above was obtained from the crude sewage as it is now received at the pumping station. There can be little doubt but that some comparatively simple screening will reduce the figure somewhat, so that ultimate dilutions of 1 in 100 may be possible.

For a further reduction in oxidizability some form of purification will be found necessary. Our experiments have proceeded far enough to enable us to state at this time that by a simple and cheap process of aeration the oxygen requirements of the sewage can be reduced at least one-half, and probably, under summer conditions, two-thirds. In other words, this sewage which will now absorb 1,950 pounds of oxygen per million gallons in 12 hours, can by some such process as we shall fully describe later, be so altered that it will absorb not more than 975, and possibly not over 650 pounds. This will make dilution of 1 in 50, or less, permissible, and obviate entirely the necessity for further purification of sewage by filters.

We are prepared to recommend, therefore, that at Riches Point Meadow concentration point, and at both concentration points "A" and "B," provision be made for screening and aerating the sewage before discharge. Details of the aeration process will be given in a subsequent report. This treatment will probably not be necessary until the proposed drainage system has been developed to at least one-half of its ultimate capacity. After that time it will be necessary to employ the aeration process only during certain of the summer months, and at ultimate development such employment will probably not exceed four months of the year. These facts have an important bearing on the consideration of the ultimate cost of treatment.

The discharge into Little Neck Bay is necessarily into shoal water near the head of a land-locked bay in which practically the only circulation is that due to tidal flow. It is therefore impossible to make any accurate calculations of the dilution factor, but purification will evidently be required. We recommend at the start effective fine screening, a short period of sedimentation, and forced aeration. Our recommendation of the latter process is based upon experimental work which we have conducted during the summer at Brooklyn and at Boston. This work is not yet completed, but has gone far enough to enable us to state that in situations similar to the one under discussion an important reduction in the putrescibility of the sewage can be obtained in this manner and at reasonable costs.

The three outlets along the shore front of the Rockaway Section will each be carried about 1,000 feet off shore into water having a mean depth of 15 feet. Experience elsewhere, notably at Asbury Park and Ocean Grove, has indicated that with suitable provision for the removal of the grosser suspended matter, such a method of disposal may be used without any resulting nuisance. We recommend disposal works at these points, consisting of screening and a short period of detention in hydrolytic tanks, so designed as to clarify the sewage and give a maximum of liquefying action with a minimum of anaerobic putrefaction.

Very respectfully,

W. M. Black,
Earle B. Phelps.

Oversized Foldout

SPECIAL REPORT

ON THE

Richmond Drainage District

SUBMITTED TO THE

BOARD OF ESTIMATE AND APPORTIONMENT

MARCH 9, 1911

CHIEF ENGINEER'S OFFICE,
BOARD OF ESTIMATE AND APPORTIONMENT,
CITY OF NEW YORK,
March 4, 1911.

Hon. WILLIAM J. GAYNOR, *Mayor,*
Chairman of the Board of Estimate and Apportionment:

SIR—Herewith is transmitted the report of Colonel William M. Black, U. S. A., and Professor Earle B. Phelps, bearing date of February 15, 1911, in the matter of the locations which might properly be selected for the discharge of sewage from the entire Borough of Richmond.

This report has been prepared pursuant to the instructions given by the Board in 1909, under which Colonel Black was requested to advise concerning the method which, in his judgment, might properly be adopted in order to most advantageously use the harbor waters for the removal of sewage, and has been prepared along the same lines as were followed in investigating the Corona, Flushing, and Jamaica districts of the Borough of Queens, in each of which sections it was found necessary to outline a general plan for the drainage of the entire area affected in order to establish the practicability of using the points selected for outlet.

The report now submitted completes the investigation in so far as it relates to the portions of the City for which no complete drainage plan has yet been prepared.

The investigation was also made to include a study of the circulation of fresh and polluted water in the harbor, with a view of determining the amount of sewage which could properly be admitted in various sections, together with the results of experimental work concerning a new process of purification which it was believed might be employed with advantage. The results of the latter investigation are contained in another communication which will be made the subject of a separate report, this completing the entire work originally contemplated.

In this report it is pointed out that about 63 per cent. of the entire area of the Borough of Richmond is located on the northwesterly side of the backbone of the island and drains naturally into the Arthur Kill and the Kill von Kull, and that of the 36 miles of coast line about one-half borders upon the kills, neither of which can be considered as available for the discharge of crude sewage. It is also pointed out that the five miles of coast line bordering the upper bay are similarly unavailable for such use owing to the pollution to which they are already subjected, and that of the remaining thirteen miles having frontage upon the lower bay a considerable portion is unavailable for the discharge of sewage owing in part to the shallow depth, and in part to the tidal circulation which would result in the return of discharged sewage to the bathing beaches. These conditions leave only the upper portion of the lower bay in the vicinity of the Narrows and the southerly portion of the island as the only sections along the coast line suited for the use under consideration unless purification is resorted to. The plan which has been outlined is intended to meet these conditions in so far as practicable and provides for the collection and discharge of sewage at seven points.

Two of these points are located in the vicinity of Fort Wadsworth, here outletting into the deep waters of the Narrows. At these two points there will be concentrated more than one-half of the total sanitary flow for the Borough, this being accomplished by bringing a portion of the sewage from the westerly water-shed southwardly through the gap at Richmond, thence returning along the easterly slope of the island.

The five remaining points are located respectively at Great Kills, Seguine's Point and Red Bank on the southerly side of the island, and at Lake's Island and Bloomfield on the Arthur Kill. At the last two mentioned points purification by sedimentation and forced aeration will be required.

It has been assumed that the island will have a population representing a density of about 25 persons per acre and that the dry weather flow will be equivalent to a water consumption of 125 gallons per capita per day, of which one-half would be discharged into the sewers in eight hours. In determining the size of sewers for the sanitary flow an allowance has been made for a seepage of ground water at a uniform rate of 0.003 cubic feet per second per acre. It has been assumed that the flow in the sewers will have a velocity of three feet per second, and that a minimum of six feet of cover will be provided.

In the studies no provision has been made for the removal of the storm flow, it being understood that this study was in no way connected with the investigation desired by the Board.

Owing to the low elevation of many of the areas affected it has been deemed necessary to make provision for eleven pumping stations at which the sewage would be elevated through heights varying from 6 feet upwards to 42 feet, requiring an aggregate of 525 horse-power. Provision is also made for six force mains having an aggregate length of about 18,900 feet.

The report includes tables giving the essential elements of the system as planned, which is also shown upon a general map which accompanies the report.

It is understood that owing in part to the absence of data on which a complete plan could be prepared, and in part to the fact that this investigation was intended to be limited simply to such work as was involved in establishing the practicability of carrying the drainage to the points selected for outlet that the plan is not offered as of other than of a suggestive character and that a more or less radical revision may be necessary in many particulars.

I would recommend that a copy of this report and of the accompanying map be transmitted to the President of the Borough of Richmond with the suggestion that he be asked to give them careful consideration in the preparation of the drainage plans for this district.

Respectfully,

NELSON P. LEWIS,
Chief Engineer.

February 15, 1911.

Mr. Nelson P. Lewis,
Chief Engineer, Board of Estimate and Apportionment,
New York City, New York:

Sir—In connection with our general studies of the sewerage problem of certain portions of Greater New York, we submit herewith a report upon that portion of our work which deals with the Borough of Richmond, and which, in accordance with our previous practice, we will term "The Richmond Drainage District."

Physical Features.

Physically, the Borough of Richmond, or Staten Island, is not well suited for an economical design of a comprehensive drainage system. Although presenting bold slopes and favorable grades in many cases, in others, flat, marshy tracts render the collection of sewage by gravity extremely difficult. Again, the ridges and hills which produce the favorable slopes in some places, offer a most effective barrier to the outlet of the sewage when once collected, except by long detours and consequent loss of elevation, or by still more expensive processes of tunneling.

The island drains naturally in two directions; to the east, or towards the Lower Bay, where tidal circulation is excellent, the water is constantly renewed by influx from the unpolluted supply of the Atlantic Ocean, and the capacity for sewage reduction is almost unlimited; and to the west, or towards the Arthur Kill, where tidal circulation is poor, the water merely rising and falling without greatly changing on each tide, and where it is reported that in parts pollution from the various New Jersey rivers has already passed the stage of a nuisance.

The divide between these two watersheds consists of a pronounced ridge, running the entire length of and forming the backbone of the island. At the north end this ridge rises abruptly to a height of 200 feet and over, continuing south with steep slopes on either side, and increasing gradually in elevation to over 400 feet at a distance of about four miles from the upper end. Two miles farther south the ridge drops suddenly to the lowest point of its entire length, and rises again, but more gradually, forming a gap at an elevation of about 50 feet. From this gap, which plays an important part in the design hereinafter proposed, the ridge continues irregularly to the southern end of the island, averaging only about 100 feet in height, and nowhere rising above 150 feet.

The total length of the island is about thirteen miles, and its greatest width about eight miles. The area is over 57 square miles, or 36,623 acres, of which 13,584 acres, or 37 per cent., lie in the eastern watershed, and 23,039 acres, or 63 per cent., in the western watershed, which drains naturally into the already polluted kills. In the upper part of the island, and bordering upon the Arthur Kill, are extensive swamp areas, aggregating about 6,461 acres below the 10-foot contour.

The length of coast line is 36 miles, of which 18 miles, or 50 per cent., border upon the kills, and are not available for the discharge of untreated sewage, 5 miles upon the Upper Bay, which is already greatly burdened by the sewage from the East and Hudson Rivers and the Kill von Kull, and will soon feel the effects of the New Passaic Valley outlet, which leaves barely 13 miles, or 36 per cent. of the total perimeter, bordering upon the Lower Bay, where raw sewage may be safely discharged. Again, certain points only of this coast are available for discharge, as the water is shoal and prevents good tidal circulation in a number of places. At the Narrows, discharge is safe if carried out to deep water in the channel; below this, at the beaches, everything discharged returns upon the shore, so that no outfalls are permissible in this vicinity. The lower half of this coast, however, embracing the stretch between Great Kills and the southern extremity of the island, is shown by the United States Coast Survey charts to have a channel parallel to the shore, into which sewage may be discharged with a reasonable certainty of its being carried away by the tidal currents.

Division Into Drainage Areas.*

The island is divided into nine main divisions, lettered A to I, inclusive, as explained in the succeeding paragraphs, and each division is further divided into several drainage areas, numbered 1 to 85, inclusive, for the entire island. The locations of these areas are as follows:

Division A, Areas 1-9—

This comprises the area lying on the western slope of the ridge and tributary to the Kill von Kull, extending westward to the low land bordering upon the Arthur Kill.

Area 1 comprises Districts 17 (a), 18 (a), and 19 (a) of the Sewer Department.

Area 2 comprises the valley extending inland from Port Richmond.

Area 3 is composed of that section of the north shore extending from Snug Harbor westward to Port Richmond.

NOTE.—Areas 1-3 require a low-level system, the flow from which will be concentrated at the Shore road (Richmond terrace) and Columbia street, and pumped through a force-main along the latter to the gravity Interceptor at Post avenue.

Area 4 is a large tract lying upon the slope of the ridge, and extending from the crest down to the 50-foot contour.

Areas 5 and 6 occupy the head of the valley of Clove Brook, extending to the crest of the ridge.

Area 7 occupies the remaining portion of the valley around Richmond Lake and lying above the 40-foot contour.

Area 8 lies between Area 3 on the north and Area 6 on the south.

Area 9 lies at the junction of the line of the ridge with the shore.

Division B, Areas 10-17—

This comprises the area lying on the eastern slope of the ridge, above the Narrows, and tributary to the Upper Bay.

*See map of Richmond Drainage District following p. 182.

Areas 10, 11 and 12 occupy the extreme northeast corner of the island, 11 and 12 comprising Districts 1 (a) and 1 (D), respectively, of the Sewer Department.

Areas 13, 14 and 15 occupy the valley extending from Tompkinsville inland to the Fingerboard road.

Area 16 borders upon the Upper Bay, just above the Narrows.

Area 17 comprises the western shore of the Narrows, and includes the military reservation of Fort Wadsworth, which may at some future date connect with the sewerage system of the borough.

Division C, Areas 18-33—

This comprises the area lying on the western slope of the ridge, above the 50-foot contour, between Willow Brook on the north and Huguenot avenue on the south.

Areas 18, 19, 20 and 21 lie upon the western slope of the ridge, above the Gap, and in the order named from Willow Brook to Richmond Creek.

Areas 22 and 23 occupy the valley just west of the ridge and extending north from the Gap.

Areas 24 to 33 lie in an irregular semi-circle between the summit of the ridge and the low land bordering upon the Fresh Kills.

Area 24 lies at the western extremity of this semi-circle, near the Arthur Kill, and Area 33 at the eastern end, just south of the Gap.

Division D, Areas 34-46—

This comprises that area lying on the eastern slopes of the ridge, above the 40-foot contour, between the Narrows on the north and Great Kills on the south, including the low land back of South Beach.

Areas 34 and 35 occupy the eastern slope of the ridge, adjacent to the Gap, and between the summit and the low land around Great Kills.

Area 36 occupies the valley east of the ridge and north of the Gap.

Area 37 includes the village of New Dorp, lying at the mouth of the valley comprising Area 36.

Areas 38 and 39 lie upon the eastern slope of the ridge, back of Grant City.

Areas 40, 41 and 42 comprise the low land bordering upon the Lower Bay and extending from South Beach on the north to Elm Tree Beacon on the south.

Areas 43, 44, 45 and 46 lie, in the order named, upon the southern slope of the spur ridge extending from the main ridge to the Narrows.

Division E, Areas 47-51—

Areas 47 and 48 occupy the low land composing the western shore of Great Kills Bay.

Area 49 occupies the low ground extending from the head of Great Kills Bay back to the 50-foot contour.

Area 50 includes the low land north of Great Kills Bay and bordering upon the Lower Bay.

Area 51 constitutes the small peninsula which forms the eastern shore of Great Kills Bay.

Division F, Areas 52-58—

Areas 52, 53, 54 and 55 extend, in the order named, along the shore of the Lower Bay, from Great Kills on the north to Seguine's Point on the south.

Areas 56 and 57 occupy the head, and Area 58 the mouth, of the valley of Lemon Creek, which extends inland from the head of Princes Bay.

Division G, Areas 59-68—

This comprises the entire southern end of the island.

Areas 59, 60, 61, and 62 lie upon the shore of Arthur Kill, extending south from Smoking Point to Mill Creek.

Area 63 lies between the areas bordering upon Arthur Kill, and the summit of the ridge, north of Mill Creek.

Area 64 occupies the low land bordering upon the Arthur Kill, south of Mill Creek.

Area 65 lies south of Mill Creek, between the summit of the ridge and Area 64.

Area 66 lies upon the shore of Princes Bay.

Area 67 occupies the southern extremity of the island.

Area 68 lies upon the eastern slope of the ridge, about midway between Princes Bay and the southern extremity of the island.

Division H, Areas 69-79—

This comprises the low area tributary to the Fresh Kills and Arthur Kill.

Area 69 lies upon either side of Richmond Creek, just west of the Gap.

Areas 70, 71 and 73 occupy the south bank of Richmond Creek, extending, in the order named, from Area 69 towards the Arthur Kill, and Area 72 lies between Area 71 and the summit of the ridge.

Area 74 lies upon the shore of the Arthur Kill, south of Fresh Kills.

Areas 75, 76 and 77 occupy the low ground east of Fresh Kills Creek, lying below the 50-foot contour, extending, in the order named, from the head of the creek to the fork of Fresh Kills.

Area 78 lies on the coast of Arthur Kill, north of Fresh Kills.

Area 79 comprises Lakes Island, at the mouth of Fresh Kills.

Division I, Areas 80-85—

Areas 80 and 81 occupy the coast of Arthur Kill, opposite the mouth of the Rahway River, New Jersey, and Pralls Island, respectively.

Areas 82 and 83 occupy the valley of Old Place Creek.

Area 84 occupies the extreme northwestern corner of the island, at the opening of the Arthur Kill into Newark Bay.

Area 85 lies upon the shore of Arthur Kill, between the mouth of Old Place Creek on the north, and Pralls Island on the south.

The acreage and estimated future populations of these 85 drainage areas are tabulated below. The total area of the district is seen to be 36,623 acres and the total estimated future population 915,575.

Area	Acres	Assumed Future "Equivalent Population"	
		Per Acre	Total
1	336	25	8,400
2	1,085	25	27,125
3	339	25	8,475
4	1,235	25	30,875
5	555	25	13,875
6	311	25	7,775
7	474	25	11,850
8	603	25	15,075
9	411	25	10,275
10	277	25	6,925
11	108	25	2,700
12	95	25	2,375
13	298	25	7,450
14	430	25	10,750
15	592	25	14,800
16	453	25	11,325
17	411	25	10,275
18	736	25	18,400
19	644	25	16,100
20	215	25	5,375
21	408	25	10,200
22	615	25	15,375
23	458	25	11,450
24	261	25	6,525
25	265	25	6,625
26	157	25	3,925
27	365	25	9,125
28	711	25	17,775
29	312	25	7,800
30	341	25	8,525
31	405	25	10,125
32	107	25	2,675
33	180	25	4,500
34	250	25	6,250
35	294	25	7,350
36	482	25	12,050
37	307	25	7,675
38	98	25	2,450
39	71	25	1,775
40	642	25	16,050
41	499	25	12,475
42	681	25	17,025
43	398	25	9,950
44	301	25	7,525
45	238	25	5,950
46	133	25	3,325
47	279	25	6,975
48	302	25	7,550
49	511	25	12,775
50	739	25	18,475
51	161	25	4,025
52	440	25	11,000
53	342	25	8,550
54	498	25	12,450
55	695	25	17,375

Area	Acres	Assumed Future "Equivalent Population" Per Acre	Total
56	545	25	13,625
57	265	25	6,625
58	552	25	13.800
59	713	25	17,825
60	471	25	11,775
61	198	25	4,950
62	322	25	8,050
63	436	25	10,900
64	291	25	7,275
65	193	25	4,825
66	388	25	9,700
67	339	25	8,475
68	470	25	11.750
69	340	25	8,500
70	318	25	7,950
71	87	85	2,175
72	324	25	8,100
73	186	25	4.650
74	755	25	18,875
75	654	25	16,350
76	695	25	17,375
77	568	25	14,200
78	915	25	22.875
79	120	25	3,000
80	408	25	10,200
81	630	25	16,750
82	817	25	20,425
83	606	25	15.150
84	845	25	21.125
85	618	25	15,450
Total	36,623	......	915,575

General Scheme of Sewerage for the District.

The proposed design takes advantage of the most favorable physical features, and attempts to reduce to a minimum the cost of overcoming the difficulties.

Items which add greatly to the expense of a sewer system are: pumping, purification, detours involving great length of line, and tunneling. In order to concentrate at points allowing safe discharge, a certain amount of pumping is necessary, but this item has been kept as low as possible consistent with the avoidance of outfalls where purification would be required, and no lifts are here contemplated on the main lines, except where a force-main outfall must be installed, so that, generally, the amounts lifted, as well as the lifts themselves, are small, and may be served by automatic pumping stations.

Where pumping to a point of safe discharge would cost in excess of the cost of partial purification, small works are contemplated to purify to such extent as will render discharge into the Arthur Kill unobjectionable.

Only such degree of treatment is required as will produce an effluent of sufficient stability to delay putrefaction until the larger reservoir of the Lower Bay is reached.

At the main points of discharge, at the Narrows and in the Lower Bay, no purification is considered necessary.

Some long detours will have to be made, to secure favorable grades and to avoid the necessity of tunneling, which expedient will not be necessary in this design. The detours which are required to secure an outlet at the Gap will be less expensive than a tunnel through the ridge at any other point, as the distance between low ground on either side is considerable except at the Gap.

Divisions A and B, Areas 1-17—

The proposed design is as follows:

The area west of the ridge and tributary to the Kill von Kull, back to the low land bordering upon the Arthur Kill, is drained by a gravity interceptor, No. 1, along the north shore, the lower ground being served by a low-level system, whose flow is lifted by pumping to the level of Interceptor I. This interceptor encircles the northern point of the island, and serves also that area east of the ridge and above the Narrows which is tributary to the Upper Bay. The Outfall is just above Quarantine, at the foot of Pennsylvania avenue. The area tributary to this system is 8,013 acres, and the estimated maximum discharge at the outfall is 81.95 second-feet.

Divisions C and D, Areas 18-46—

The area lying on the western slope of the ridge, above the fifty-foot contour, and extending from about Willow Brook on the north to Huguenot avenue on the south, is served by two gravity interceptors, Nos. II and III, which unite at the Gap. Interceptor II serves the area north of the junction, and Interceptor III that to the south. After the junction, the interceptor, now known as No. IV, crosses the ridge at the Gap and serves that portion of the eastern slope between Great Kills and the Narrows which lies above about the forty-foot contour. The low-lying area back of and including South Beach is also served by this system, the flow being lifted through a force-main to Interceptor IV, in order to prevent the fouling of the beaches which would result were the outfall placed in this vicinity. The final discharge is located just below the Narrows, in deep water off shore.

The area tributary to this system is 10,574 acres, and the estimated maximum flow at the outfall is 108.18 second-feet.

Division E, Areas 47-51—

The low-lying area in the vicinity of Great Kills Bay is concentrated by gravity at a point near the head of the Bay, and pumped out to sea.

The tributary area is 1,992 acres, and the discharge 20.39 second-feet.

Division F, Areas 52-58—

The area on the eastern slopes of the ridge, lying between Great Kills on the north and Princes Bay on the south, most of which has a good elevation, is drained by Interceptor V to a concentration point at Seguine's Point, near the head of Princes Bay, and pumped seaward.

The tributary area is 3,337 acres, and the discharge 34.14 second-feet.

Division G, Areas 59-68—

The area on the western slopes of the ridge, lying between Smoking Point on the north and the southern extremity of the island, is concentrated by Interceptor VI, with one relay lift for that portion north of Kreischerville, at a pumping station on Mill Creek, whence it is pumped through a force-main to a continuation of the gravity interceptor at the summit of the ridge. From this point the discharge is by gravity into the deep water off shore.

The area tributary to the gravity system of this division is 2,624 acres, and the maximum discharge is 26.84 second-feet.

The low level portion of this Division consists of the area lying on the eastern slope of the ridge, between Princes Bay and the southern end of the island, whose flow is collected by gravity at Red Bank, and lifted to the gravity outfall, by pumping.

The area tributary to this low level system is 1,197 acres, and the discharge is 12.25 second-feet.

The total area of Division G is 3,821 acres, and the discharge is 39.09 second-feet.

Division H, Areas 69-79—

The low, marshy area adjacent to the Fresh Kills, and tributary to the Arthur Kill, is served by two interceptors, Nos. VII and VIII, draining, with one relay lift in each, the areas south and north, respectively, of Fresh Kills and Richmond Creek. Both interceptors concentrate at the same point on Lakes Island, at the mouth of Fresh Kills, where the sewage will be purified sufficiently to permit its discharge into Arthur Kill without nuisance.

The tributary area is 4,962 acres, the discharge 50.75 second-feet.

Division I, Areas 80-85.

The flow from the low area occupying the northwestern corner of the island, and tributary to the Arthur Kill, will be concentrated by a gravity interceptor, No. IX, at a point on the shore of the Arthur Kill, north of Pralls Island, where it will be partially purified and finally discharged into Arthur Kill.

The tributary area is 3,924 acres, and the discharge 40.13 second-feet.

Trunk sewers are designated in general by the number of the area served. Their locations are as given in the following summary a study of which will be facilitated by reference to the accompanying map. The division lines between areas are indicated by heavy dotted lines, the sewers in solid red lines. Other devices used are sufficiently explained in the legend. Contours are at 20-foot intervals.

Division A—

1. From 1,000 feet west of South avenue, east along Shore road (Richmond terrace), to junction with Trunk 2 at Lafayette avenue.

2. From near Richmond turnpike, north, nearly parallel to Port Richmond road and Richmond avenue, to junction with Trunk 1 at Shore road (Richmond terrace).

1-2. Along Shore road (Richmond terrace), from Lafayette avenue to Columbia Street Pumping Station.

3. From Bard avenue, west along Richmond terrace to Columbia Street Pumping Station.

1-2-3. Columbia Street Force-main. From Columbia Street Pumping Station, at Richmond terrace, south along Columbia street to Interceptor I. at Post avenue.

4. From near Ocean Terrace road, at summit of the ridge, west down valley of stream to about 50-foot contour; thence along latter to junction with Columbia Street Force-Main at Columbia street and Post avenue.

5. From near summit of ridge, north along valley of stream to junction with Trunk 6 at Schoenian Pond.

5-6. From Junction of Trunks 5 and 6, north along valley of Clove Brook to Richmond Lake.

7. No trunk has been designed for Area 7, the flow from which will be considered as entering Trunk 5-6 at Richmond Lake.

5-6-7. From Richmond Lake, north along valley of Clove Brook to Interceptor I at Post avenue and Columbia street.

8. From near summit of ridge, northwest along valley of stream, to Castleton avenue, along Castleton avenue, Rement avenue to Interceptor I at Henderson avenue.

9. From summit of ridge, north along Lafayette avenue to Interceptor I. at Richmond terrace.

Division B—

10. From near summit of ridge, north along Richmond turnpike and Jersey street to Interceptor I. at Richmond terrace.

11. No trunk has been designed for Area 11, as this area is already sewered, and its trunk will be intercepted at Church street and Richmond terrace.

12. No trunk has been designed for Area 12, as this area is already sewered, and its trunk will be intercepted at Arietta street and Central avenue.

13. From junction of Fingerboard and Richmond roads, north along valley of stream to De Kalb avenue.

14. No trunk has been designed for Area 14, the flow from which will be considered as entering Trunk 13 at De Kalb avenue.

13-14. From De Kalb avenue, north along Danube avenue, Simonson place and Targee street to Laurel avenue.

15. No trunk has been designed for Area 15, the flow from which will be considered as entering Trunk 13-14 at Targee street and Laurel avenue.

13-14-15. From Targee street, along Laurel avenue, Gordon, Broad and Canal streets to Interceptor I. at Riker street.

16. From Grasmere Lake, north and east to Interceptor I. on Willow avenue.

17. From high ground back of Fort Wadsworth, east and north along Fingerboard road and New York avenue to junction with Interceptor I. at Pennsylvania avenue.

Division C—

18. From about 300-foot contour, on Manor road, west down valley of Willow Brook to near Willow Brook road; thence southwest to Interceptor II. at Rockland avenue, on 50-foot contour.

19. From about 220-foot contour, at Manor road, west down valley of Springville Creek to junction with Trunk 18 at 50-foot contour.

20. From about 140-foot contour, near Forest Hill avenue, west and south to Interceptor II, south of Richmond Hill road.

21. From about 130-foot contour, near crest of small ridge, south along valley of stream to Interceptor II.

22. From 300-foot contour, near Egbert avenue, south down valley of Richmond Creek to 100-foot contour on Saw Mill road.

23. No trunk has been designed for Area 23, the flow from which will be considered as entering Trunk 22 at the 100-foot contour on Saw Mill road.

22-23. From 100-foot contour, on Saw Mill road, south along valley of Richmond Creek, to Interceptor II. at Richmond.

24. From about 100-foot contour, near Huguenot avenue, north and east to junction with Trunk 25 at 50-foot contour, north of Washington avenue.

25. From 120-foot contour, along Washington avenue and valley of small stream to Interceptor III. at 50-foot contour.

26. From near Fresh Kills road, south along Greenridge avenue to Interceptor III.

27. From about 140-foot contour, near Huguenot avenue, east and north along valley of small stream to junction with Trunk 27-28 at Washington avenue.

28. No trunk has been designed for Area 28, the flow from which will be considered as entering Trunk 27 at Washington avenue.

27-28. From junction of Trunks 27 and 28, east and north to Interceptor III.

29. From 80-foot contour, Woods of Arden, northeast, parallel to railroad to Wilson avenue; thence west along valley of stream to junction with Trunk 30 at about 50-foot contour.

30. From 60-foot contour, at Gifford's, south to Trunk 29.

29-30. From junction of Trunks 29 and 30, along valley of small stream to Interceptor III.

31. From 60-foot contour, north of Gifford's lane, west to Interceptor III.

32. From 80-foot contour, north along valley of small stream to Interceptor III.

33. From near summit of ridge, south of Gap, to Interceptor IV. at Gap.

Division D—

34. From Great Kills north, parallel to railroad, to junction with Trunk 35 at Clark avenue.

35. From 80-foot contour, east on Clark avenue to Trunk 34.

34-35. From junction of Trunks 34 and 35, north, parallel to railroad, to Interceptor IV. at Amboy road.

36. From 340-foot contour, on Todt Hill road, south along valley of creek to junction with Trunk 37 at Sixth street and Elm avenue, New Dorp.

37. From 140-foot contour, near New Dorp Beacon, east and south down valley of stream, along Grand avenue, Richmond road, Amboy road, Ocean avenue and Sixth street to Trunk 36 at Elm avenue.

36-37. From junction of Trunks 36 and 37 at Elm avenue, along prolongation of Elm avenue to Interceptor IV. on prolongation of Tenth street.

38. From Central avenue, along Richmond road and Barton avenue to Interceptor IV. at 30-foot contour.

39. From Jackson avenue, north along Richmond road, and east along Liberty avenue to Interceptor IV. at 30-foot contour.

40. From about 20-foot contour, near New Dorp lane, north and east to junction with Trunk 41 at New Creek.

41. From near railroad, Dongan Hills, east to Trunk 40.

40-41. From junction of Trunks 40 and 41, north to Sea View avenue Pumping Station.

42. From South Beach, south, parallel to shore, to Sea View Avenue Pumping Station.

40-41-42. Sea View Avenue Force-Main. From Sea View Avenue Pumping Station west along Sea View avenue to Interceptor IV. at 30-foot contour.

43. From 300-foot contour, near Ocean Terrace road, at summit of ridge, east down valley of stream to Interceptor IV. at 30-foot contour.

44. From 100-foot contour, near Grasmere, south along valley of stream and Parkinson avenue to Interceptor IV.

45. From 100-foot contour, on Fingerboard road, east and south along Fingerboard road and Sand Lane road to Interceptor IV.

46. From about 100-foot contour, south along Sea avenue to Interceptor IV. at Old Town avenue.

Division E—

47. From 60-foot contour, on Nelson avenue, southeast along Nelson avenue, nearly to shore of Great Kills Bay; thence following shore to junction with Trunk 48.

48. From 60-foot contour, along valley of small stream to Trunk 47, near shore of Great Kills Bay.

47-48. From junction of Trunks 47 and 48, northeast to junction with Trunk 49 at Mill Pond, near head of Great Kills Bay.

49. From 40-foot contour, near railroad at Courthouse, east and south along stream to Trunk 47-48 at Mill Pond.

47-48-49. From junction of Trunk 47-48 with Trunk 49, at Mill Pond, east to Great Kills Pumping Station.

50. South along shore from Elm Tree Beacon to Great Kills Pumping Station.

51. North along Great Kills Peninsula to Great Kills Pumping Station.

47-51. Outfall Section. From Great Kills Pumping Station, southeast to water 12 feet deep, 5,000 feet off shore.

Division F—

52. From 60-foot contour, opposite mouth of Great Kills Bay, south to shore, following shore southwest to junction with Trunk 53 at Barclay avenue.

53. From 60-foot contour, near Amboy road, south along small stream, parallel to Barclay avenue to junction with Trunk 52.

54. From 80-foot contour, near railroad, following valley of small stream south to junction with Interceptor V. at Latourette's Pond, near shore.

55. From 100-foot contour, south along valley of stream, to junction with Interceptor V. at Wolfs Pond, near shore.

56. From 120-foot contour, near Wood Row, west and south to junction with Trunk 57, at Maguire avenue, near fork of Lemon Creek.

57. From 100-foot contour, west and south to junction with Trunk 56, at Maguire avenue, near fork of Lemon Creek.

56-57. From junction of Trunks 56 and 57, south and east along valley of Lemon Creek, to a point nearly opposite Findlay avenue.

58. No trunk has been designed for Area 58, the flow from which will be considered as entering Trunk 56-57 at a point opposite Findlay avenue.

56-57-58. From bend in Lemon Creek, opposite Findlay avenue, along valley of Lemon Creek, to Seguine's Point Pumping Station.

Division G—

59. From Rossville, west and south along shore of Arthur Kill to Kreischerville Relay Pumping Station, at junction with Trunk 60, at mouth of stream opposite Boynton Beach, New Jersey.

60. From 100-foot contour, near Pleasant avenue, west along valley of stream to Kreischerville Relay Pumping Station, at junction with Trunk 59.

61. From 100-foot contour, west to south end of Kreischerville Force-main.

62. From 80-foot contour, south to Interceptor VI., near Mill Creek.

63. From about 100-foot contour, south of Sharrott's road, south and west to Interceptor VI., at junction with Trunk 62.

64. From near Hopkins avenue, Tottenville, north along shore of Arthur Kill to Mill Creek Pumping Station.

65. From 60-foot contour, near summit of ridge, along valley of Mill Creek to Mill Creek Pumping Station.

66. From 40-foot contour, near summit of ridge, south to shore of Prince's Bay; following shore southwest to Red Bank Pumping Station.

67. From near Bay Cliff Lake, at summit of ridge, south to shore, near southern extremity of island; northeast along shore to junction with Trunk 68 at Central avenue.

68. From summit of ridge, near 60-foot contour, south along Central avenue, to junction with Trunk 67 at shore.

67-68. From Central avenue, northeast along shore to Red Bank Pumping Station.

Division H—

69. From near Fresh Kills road, following line of Richmond Creek, to Richmond Creek Pumping Station, near Fresh Kills Bridge.

70. From 10-foot contour, near Eltingville road, east and north to Richmond Creek Pumping Station.

71. From 20-foot contour, near Greenridge avenue, and Fresh Kills road, northeast to west end of Richmond Creek Force-main, near bend in Richmond Creek.

72. From 40-foot contour, near Washington avenue, north along valley of small stream, to junction with Trunk 73, about 2,000 feet from Fresh Kills.

73. From spur of ridge, west of Trunk 72.

72-73. From junction of Trunks 72 and 73, north to Interceptor VII., near fork of Fresh Kills.

74. From 40-foot contour, near Fresh Kills road, and Huguenot avenue, north, parallel to shore of Arthur Kill, to junction with Interceptor VII. on Fresh Kills, opposite Lake's Island.

75. From about 40-foot contour, at Willow Brook, following the Brook and east shore of Fresh Kills Creek, west and south to junction with Trunk 76 at mouth of Springville Creek.

76. From near 40-foot contour, on Rockland avenue, following Springville Creek west to Fresh Kills Creek.

77. From 20-foot contour, near Old Turnpike, south along valley of stream, and west along Richmond Creek to Fresh Kills Pumping Station.

78. From Union avenue, southwest, generally parallel to Fresh Kills Creek, to west end of Fresh Kills Force-main.

79. No trunk has been designed for Area 79, but its flow will drain directly into the pump-well of the Lakes Island Pumping Station.

Division I—

80. From near Union avenue, west along valley of Neck Creek to shore, following shore north to junction with Trunk 81 at mouth of small creek, opposite Pralls Island.

81. From 10-foot contour, west along valley of creek to Trunk 80.

80-81. From junction of Trunks 80 and 81, north along shore of Arthur Kill to Bloomfield Purification Works, at a point north of Pralls Island.

82. From 10-foot contour, near Simonson avenue, west along valley of Old Place Creek to junction with Trunk 83.

83. From 10-foot contour, near Decker avenue, north to Trunk 82 at Old Place Creek.

84. From 10-foot contour, near South avenue, west along Bridge Creek to Western avenue, southwest to Old Place road, across Old Place Creek to Junction with Interceptor IX.

85. From near mouth of Old Place Creek, south along shore of Arthur Kill to Bloomfield Purification Works.

Design of Trunk Sewers from Each Area.

The daily flow of sewage has been assumed as equal to the water consumption, and for lack of more definite information, this latter figure has been taken at 125 gallons per capita per day.

Sewers are in all cases designed for maximum sanitary flow, as determined from the assumed future population and per capita water consumption. No allowance has been made for storm flow in this district. Ground water is taken uniformly at 0.003 second-feet per acre.

Future population has been assumed as suburban in character, with a density of 25 persons per acre, uniformly distributed over the entire district.

For the peak load upon the system, the maximum flow is assumed to be at a rate which would carry off half the daily flow in eight hours.

Trunks and branches, in which the flow is apt to vary greatly from the assumed maximum, owing to the comparatively small areas served, and liability to local influences, have been designed to carry the assumed maximum flow when only half full, in order to provide for contingencies, while the interceptors, in which the flow will equalize and be much more uniform, have been designed to carry the assumed maximum flow when eight-tenths full.

The design for size, grade, etc., has been made from the diagrams in Swan & Horton's "Hydraulic Diagrams," and from a diagram of hydraulic elements for circular sections, in the same book, the discharges and velocities for the sewers 0.8, 0.5, 0.2 and 0.1 full, have been computed.

Except in very few cases, the grades have been taken so as to insure a velocity of 3.0 feet per second or greater, which will give a velocity of 1.8 feet per second when flowing 0.2 full, or at only 0.085 full discharge. This velocity is thought to be sufficient for self-cleansing purposes.

In all siphons, force-mains and outfalls, an effort has been made to secure a uniform velocity of 3.0 feet per second, as nearly as commercial sizes of cast iron pipe will permit.

All designs contemplate circular sections only.

The datum plane for all elevations is the plane of Mean Sea Level at Sandy Hook, as established by the U. S. Coast and Geodetic Survey.

When elevations are given, they refer invariably to the invert of the sewer, unless otherwise specifically stated.

In all cases where the depth of a sewer is mentioned, the depth to the inner top is meant; i. e., the depth to the invert, less the diameter.

In all possible cases, an earth covering of six feet over the inner top of the sewers has been allowed. In no case has this covering been reduced to less than four feet.

Wherever possible, the grades have been taken so as to fit the slope of the ground, but where this would give velocities in excess of about 7.5 feet per second, or where a portion of the ground has a slope flatter than the remainder, a flat grade has been adopted, and the sewer left at a uniform depth of about four to six feet by drop manholes installed at convenient intervals.

At the low-lying portions of the Borough, it is assumed that the finished grade of the surface, behind the bulkhead wall, will be about 7.35 feet above the datum of Mean Sea Level, or 5.0 feet above Mean High Water (Dock Department).

Whenever possible, at the junction of a trunk with an interceptor the invert of the former is elevated above that of the latter by an amount equal to the difference of diameter, or by half the diameter of the interceptor, if the difference of diameters exceeds this. This is done in order to preserve an unbroken invert in the interceptor, and thus prevent eddies and consequent deposit of suspended solids, and to prevent backing up into small trunks.

This elevation is not given where two trunks unite to form an interceptor, nor, obviously, where the two sewers are of the same diameter.

Where an existing storm sewer is intercepted, the interceptor is designed to take only the dry weather flow, and the remaining length of the storm sewer will be maintained and utilized as a storm overflow, to prevent choking of the interceptor.

In the following table are summarized the principal elements involved in the design of these trunk sewers, namely, length, total fall, elevation of invert at upper end, tributary area, slope, maximum diameter, maximum discharge, and velocities and discharges at 0.8 and at 0.2 full.

Design of Trunk Sewers.

Trunk No.	Length, Feet.	Total Fall, Feet.	Elevation of Invert, Upper End.	Tributary Area, Acres.	Slope 1 Foot in	Maximum Diameter, Feet.	Maximum Discharge, Sec., Ft.	Sewer 0.8 Full. Velocity, Sec., Ft.	Sewer 0.8 Full. Discharge, Sec., Ft.	Sewer 0.2 Full. Velocity, Sec., Ft.	Sewer 0.2 Full. Discharge, Sec., Ft.
A—											
1											
Sec. 1	5,000	10.00	2.40	336	500	1.83	3.44	2.88	6.74	1.50	0.59
Sec. 2	4,770	9.54	7.04	336	500	1.83	3.44	2.88	6.74	1.50	0.59
2	12,800	32.00	24.40	1,085	400	2.75	11.10	4.37	21.75	2.28	1.89
1-2	3,960	4.40	—7.60	1,421	900	3.50	14.54	3.45	28.50	1.80	2.48
3	6,470	16.18	4.18	339	400	1.83	3.47	3.22	6.80	1.68	0.59
1-3	*....	....	....	....	....	....	....	....	....	....	....
4	13,850	198.00	229.65	1,235	70	2.17	12.63	8.51	24.77	4.44	2.15
5	5,280	52.80	187.85	555	100	1.67	5.68	6.10	11.11	3.18	0.97
6	4,360	87.40	222.45	311	50	1.25	3.18	6.67	6.24	3.48	0.54
5-6	4,220	21.10	135.05	866	200	1.75	8.86	4.60	8.86	2.40	0.77
7	†....	....	....	....	....	....	....	....	....	....	....
5-7	3,700	82.30	113.95	1,340	45	1.67	13.70	8.63	13.70	4.50	1.19
8	7,920	79.20	106.62	603	100	1.75	6.17	6.10	12.10	3.18	1.05
9	5,020	125.40	147.23	411	40	1.25	4.20	7.83	8.23	4.08	0.72
B—											
10	7,000	140.00	160.45	277	50	1.17	2.84	6.44	5.57	3.36	0.48
11	†....	....	....	....	....	....	....	....	....	....	....
12	†....	....	....	....	....	....	....	....	....	....	....
13	3,300	11.00	96.03	298	300	1.67	3.05	3.45	5.98	1.80	0.52
14	†....	....	....	....	....	....	....	....	....	....	....
13-14	4,480	42.60	85.03	728	105	1.50	7.45	5.40	7.45	2.82	0.65
15	†....	....	....	....	....	....	....	....	....	....	....
13-15	2,770	30.80	42.43	1,320	90	1.75	13.50	6.67	13.50	3.48	1.17
16	4,890	85.90	95.06	453	57	1.50	4.63	7.01	9.07	3.66	0.79
17	5,150	49.05	56.53	411	105	1.50	4.20	5.53	8.24	2.88	0.71
C—											
18	11,350	189.20	230.37	736	60	1.67	7.53	7.94	14.75	4.14	1.28
19	5,940	118.80	159.97	644	50	1.67	6.59	8.05	12.91	4.20	1.12
20	3,300	91.60	126.83	215	36	1.00	2.20	6.80	4.31	3.54	0.37
21	7,260	85.40	115.52	408	85	1.50	4.17	5.87	8.17	3.06	0.71
22	8,710	174.00	265.87	615	50	1.50	6.29	8.05	12.32	4.20	1.07

23	†....	....	....	....	....	....	....	....	....	....	....
22-23	5,670	37.80	59.87	1,073	150	2.33	10.98	6.10	21.50	3.18	1.87
24	4,360	62.30	103.89	261	70	1.17	2.67	5.75	5.23	3.00	0.45
25	2,240	64.00	105.59	265	35	1.17	2.71	7.25	5.30	3.78	0.46
26	2,110	11.40	46.78	157	185	1.17	1.61	3.45	3.16	1.80	0.27
27	7,000	63.70	122.77	365	110	1.50	3.74	5.18	7.33	2.70	0.64
28	†....	....	....	....	....	....	....	....	....	....	....
27-28	5,680	31.55	59.07	1,076	180	2.50	11.01	5.75	21.60	3.00	1.87
29	5,020	29.56	68.50	312	170	1.50	3.19	4.26	6.25	2.22	0.54
30	2,510	8.37	47.31	341	300	1.75	3.49	3.45	6.84	1.80	0.59
29-30	3,040	10.12	38.94	653	300	2.17	6.68	4.14	13.10	2.16	1.14
31	2,640	17.60	45.15	405	150	1.67	4.14	4.72	8.11	2.46	0.70
32	2,110	42.20	65.61	107	50	0.83	1.09	5.06	2.14	2.64	0.19
33	3,040	43.45	65.63	180	70	1.17	1.84	5.18	3.60	2.70	0.31
D—											
34	7,920	28.80	53.70	250	275	1.50	2.56	3.45	5.02	1.80	0.44
35	1,450	41.45	66.35	294	35	1.17	3.01	7.48	5.90	3.90	0.51
34-35	2,510	5.58	24.90	544	450	2.17	5.57	3.45	10.91	1.80	0.95
36	9,640	192.50	220.27	482	50	1.50	4.94	7.48	9.68	3.90	0.84
37	5,940	59.40	87.17	307	100	1.50	3.14	5.75	6.15	3.00	0.53
36-37	660	11.00	27.77	789	60	1.75	8.08	8.05	15.83	4.20	1.37
38	2,380	36.62	51.33	98	65	0.83	1.00	4.49	1.96	2.34	0.17
39	2,640	37.75	50.97	71	70	0.75	0.73	4.02	1.43	2.10	0.12
40	8,580	25.24	16.73	642	340	2.17	6.57	4.03	12.89	2.10	1.12
41	5,280	12.42	3.91	499	425	2.17	5.10	3.45	10.00	1.80	0.87
40-41	1,190	1.49	—8.51	1,141	800	3.17	11.67	3.45	22.85	1.80	1.98
42	6,600	11.00	1.00	681	600	2.50	6.97	3.45	13.67	1.80	1.19
40-42	*....	....	....	....	....	....	....	....	....	....	....
43	5,940	169.70	182.60	398	35	1.25	4.07	8.05	7.96	4.20	0.69
44	2,640	75.50	86.41	301	35	1.17	3.08	7.47	6.05	3.90	0.52
45	3,830	76.60	85.75	238	50	1.17	2.43	6.20	4.76	3.24	0.41
46	1,980	79.30	87.57	133	25	0.83	1.36	6.90	2.66	3.60	0.23
E—											
47	6,600	22.00	23.87	279	300	1.67	2.86	3.45	5.61	1.80	0.49
48	2,640	8.80	10.67	302	300	1.67	3.09	3.45	6.06	1.80	0.53
47-48	2,770	9.23	1.87	581	300	1.67	5.95	3.45	5.95	1.80	0.52
49	6,070	8.68	1.32	511	700	2.33	5.23	2.88	10.25	1.50	0.89
47-49	1,320	2.64	—7.36	1,092	500	2.25	11.18	3.45	11.18	1.80	0.97
50	8,580	14.30	4.30	739	600	2.67	7.56	3.45	14.81	1.80	1.29
51	5,940	14.86	4.86	161	400	1.50	1.65	2.53	3.24	1.32	0.28

* Force main. † No trunk designed.

Trunk No.	Length, Feet.	Total Fall, Feet.	Elevation of Invert, Upper End.	Tributary Area, Acres.	Slope 1 Foot in	Maximum Diameter, Feet.	Maximum Discharge, Sec., Ft.	Sewer 0.8 Full. Velocity, Sec., Ft.	Sewer 0.8 Full. Discharge, Sec., Ft.	Sewer 0.2 Full. Velocity, Sec., Ft.	Sewer 0.2 Full. Discharge, Sec., Ft.
F—											
52	8,840	47.75	55.89	440	185	1.75	4.50	4.60	8.82	2.40	0.77
53	5,540	50.40	58.54	342	110	1.50	3.50	5.18	6.86	2.70	0.59
54	7,390	54.75	57.32	498	135	1.67	5.09	5.30	9.98	2.76	0.87
55	9,640	48.20	40.92	695	200	2.17	7.11	4.84	13.94	2.52	1.21
56	7,660	95.90	107.75	545	80	1.67	5.58	6.55	10.93	3.42	0.95
57	5,020	77.25	89.10	265	65	1.17	2.71	5.75	5.30	3.00	0.46
56-57	3,430	17.15	11.85	810	200	2.17	8.29	5.18	16.24	2.70	1.41
58.	†....	....	....	....	....	....	....	....	....	....	....
56-58	4,220	4.70	—5.30	1,362	900	3.50	13.94	3.45	27.30	1.80	2.37
G—											
59	10,560	19.20	7.20	713	550	2.50	7.29	3.45	14.29	1.80	1.24
60	7,130	57.00	45.00	471	125	1.67	4.82	5.30	9.45	2.76	0.82
61	2,640	88.00	90.02	198	30	1.00	2.03	7.02	3.98	3.66	0.36
62	3,830	47.90	39.54	322	80	1.33	3.29	5.75	6.45	3.00	0.56
63	8,580	90.40	81.87	436	95	1.50	4.46	5.75	8.74	3.00	0.76
64	7,260	14.52	4.52	291	500	1.75	2.98	2.88	5.84	1.50	0.51
65	3,300	60.00	50.00	193	55	1.17	1.97	5.75	3.86	3.00	0.34
66	6,860	22.90	12.90	388	300	1.83	3.97	3.68	7.78	1.92	0.68
67	7,390	18.45	13.95	339	400	1.83	3.47	3.22	6.80	1.68	0.59
68	4,220	52.80	48.30	470	80	1.50	4.81	6.22	9.44	3.24	0.82
67-68	3,300	5.50	—4.50	809	600	2.67	8.28	3.45	16.22	1.80	1.41
H—											
69	6,070	12.13	2.13	340	500	2.00	3.48	2.88	6.82	1.50	0.59
70	3,830	11.95	1.95	318	320	1.67	3.25	3.45	6.37	1.80	0.55
71	1,580	13.73	17.09	87	115	1.00	0.89	3.45	1.74	1.80	0.15
72	6,730	13.45	10.95	324	500	1.83	3.31	2.88	6.48	1.50	0.56
73	1,980	9.90	7.40	186	200	1.33	1.90	3.45	3.72	1.80	0.32
72-73	1,450	3.22	—2.50	510	450	2.17	5.21	3.45	10.20	1.80	0.89
74	8,450	14.08	4.75	755	600	2.67	7.72	3.45	15.13	1.80	1.31
75	11,880	13.20	9.36	654	900	2.67	6.69	2.88	13.11	1.50	1.14
76	6,340	7.04	3.20	695	900	2.75	7.11	2.88	13.93	1.50	1.20
77	8,710	17.42	7.42	568	500	2.25	5.81	3.45	11.38	1.80	0.99

78	7,520	7.52	0.48	915	1,000	3.17	9.36	2.88	18.36	1.50	1.59
79	†....	....	....	....	....	....	....	....	....	....	....
I—											
80	8,700	14.50	5.47	408	600	2.17	4.17	2.88	8.17	1.50	0.71
81	5,680	11.34	2.31	630	500	2.33	6.44	3.45	12.61	1.80	1.09
80-81	3,560	2.97	—9.03	1,038	1,200	3.33	10.61	2.88	20.80	1.50	1.80
82	8,180	13.63	8.82	817	600	2.67	8.36	3.45	16.38	1.80	1.42
83	3,040	6.08	1.27	606	500	2.33	6.20	3.45	12.15	1.80	1.05
84	7,260	11.19	3.45	845	650	2.75	8.64	3.45	16.92	1.80	1.47
85	5,680	10.81	—1.19	618	525	2.33	6.32	3.45	12.38	1.80	1.07

† No trunk designed.

Design of Intercepting Sewers.

The design of these sewers is determined by the available slope and by the points of entrance of the various trunk sewers. Sizes are based upon normal flow with sewers .8 full. To facilitate reference, the nine interceptors have each been subdivided into sections designated by letters and beginning at the upper end in each case. These sections are described as follows:

Divisions A and B—

Interceptor I.:

a. From Columbia street along Post avenue, Elizabeth street, Castleton avenue, Broadway, two intervening streets and Henderson avenue to junction with Trunk 8 at Rement avenue.

b. From Rement avenue, east along Henderson avenue, along 30-foot contour and Richmond terrace to junction with Trunk 9 at Lafayette avenue.

c. From Lafayette avenue, along Richmond terrace to junction with Trunk 10 at Jersey street.

d. From Trunk 10 at Jersey street, along Richmond terrace to Church street.

e. From Church street, along Richmond terrace, Jay street, South street, Stuyvesant place, Central avenue to Arietta street.

f. From Central avenue, along Arietta street, Van Duser, Hanna street, St. Paul's avenue, Clinton, Van Duser, Wright and Boyd streets, across to junction with Trunk 13-14-15 at Canal street.

g. From Canal street, along Riker and Tompkins streets, and various other streets at about the 30-foot contour to Trunk 16 at Willow avenue.

h. From Willow avenue, south to Maple avenue; thence along Maple and New York avenues to junction with Trunk 17 at Pennsylvania avenue.

i. From junction with Trunk 17, east along Pennsylvania avenue to shore.

j. Outfall Section—From foot of Pennsylvania avenue, east to water 50 feet deep in channel.

Divisions C and D—

Interceptor II.:

a. From Rockland avenue, following 50-foot contour south to junction with Trunk 20, south of Richmond Hill road.

b. Following 50-foot contour south from Trunk 20 to junction with Trunk 21, near Old Mill road.

c. From Trunk 21, following 40-foot contour eastward around spur of ridge to junction with Trunk 22-23 at Richmond Creek.

d. Richmond Creek Siphon—From junction with Trunk 22-23, east under Richmond Creek to Interceptors III. and IV.

Interceptor III.:

a. From Trunk 25, following approximately the 50-foot contour to junction with Trunk 26 at Greenridge avenue.

b. From Greenridge avenue, following 50-foot contour east to junction with Trunk 27-28, near small creek.

c. Eltingville Road Siphon—From junction with Trunk 27-28, east under stream to Trunk 29-30.

d. From Trunk 29-30, following the 40-foot contour northeast to junction with Trunk 31, near fork of stream.

e. From Trunk 31, following 40-foot contour north to junction with Trunk 32, south of Clark avenue.

f. From Trunk 32, north to east end of Richmond Creek Siphon.

Interceptor IV.:

a. From east end of Richmond Creek Siphon, east to junction with Trunk 33, north of Clark avenue.

b. From Trunk 33, north and east to junction with Trunk 34-35 on Amboy road.

c. From Trunk 34-35, at Amboy road, east to Tenth street, New Dorp, following Tenth street to junction with Trunk 36-37 at prolongation of Elm avenue.

d. From Trunk 36-37, north along 30-foot contour, Lincoln avenue and Thompson street to junction with Trunk 38 at Barton avenue.

e. From Trunk 38, at Barton avenue, following 30-foot contour to junction with Trunk 39 at Liberty avenue, Dongan Hills.

f. From Trunk 39, at Liberty avenue, north along 30-foot contour to junction with Sea View Avenue Force-Main.

g. From Sea View Avenue Force-Main, north along 30-foot contour to Trunk 43, south of Burgner avenue.

h. From Trunk 43, north and east along 30-foot contour to Trunk 44 on Parkinson avenue.

i. Along 20-foot contour, from Trunk 44 at Parkinson avenue to Trunk 45 at Sand Lane road.

j. From Trunk 45, on Sand Lane road, east along 20-foot contour and Old Town avenue to junction with Trunk 46 on Sea avenue.

k. From Old Town avenue, south along prolongation of Sea avenue to shore.

l. Outfall Section—From foot of Sea avenue, prolonged to shore, east 3,500 feet to water 50 feet deep in channel.

Division E—

Division F—

Interceptor V.:

a. From junction of Trunks 52 and 53, at Barclay avenue, following shore south and west to junction with Trunk 54, at Latourette's Pond..

b. From Latourette's Pond, following shore southwest to junction with Trunk 55, near Wolf's Pond.

c. From Wolf's Pond, southwest along shore to Seguine's Point Pumping Station.

d. From Seguine's Point Pumping Station, southeast to water 21 feet deep, 800 feet off shore.

Division G—

Interceptor VI.:

a. Kreischerville Force-Main—From Kreischerville Relay Pumping Station, at south end of Trunk 59, south, parallel to shore of Arthur Kill to junction with Trunk 61, at Kreischer street, Kreischerville.

b. From south end of Kreischerville Force-Main, south along shore of Arthur Kill and east along Mill Creek to junction with Trunks 62 and 63, near Richmond Valley road.

c. Mill Creek Siphon—From junction of Trunks 62 and 63, south under Mill Creek to Mill Creek Pumping Station, on south bank of creek.

d. Mill Creek Force-Main—From Mill Creek Pumping Station, southeast to summit of ridge.

e. From Mill Creek Force-Main, at summit of ridge, southeast to Red Bank Pumping Station, at shore.

f. Gravity Outfall Section—From Red Bank Pumping Station, southeast to 21 feet of water, 1,600 feet off shore.

Division H—

Interceptor VII.:

a. Richmond Creek Force-Main—From Richmond Creek Pumping Station, near Fresh Kills Bridge, west under Mill Pond outlet to junction with Trunk 71, near bend in Richmond Creek.

b. From junction with Trunk 71, at west end of Richmond Creek Force-Main, west along Richmond Creek to junction with Trunk 72-73, near fork of Fresh Kills.

c. From junction with Trunk 72-73, west to junction with Trunk 74, at a point on Fresh Kills opposite Lake's Island.

d. Fresh Kills Siphon—From junction with Trunk 74, on east bank, west under Fresh Kills to Lake's Island.

e. From west end of Fresh Kills Siphon, west to Lake's Island Purification Works, on shore of Arthur Kill.

Interceptor VIII.:

a. From junction of Trunks 75 and 76, at Springville Creek, south to Fresh Kills Pumping Station.

b. Fresh Kills Force-Main—From Fresh Kills Pumping Station, northwest under Fresh Kills Creek to Trunk 78, north of Little Fresh Kills.

c. From west end of Fresh Kills Force-Main at junction with Trunk 78, southwest to north bank of Little Fresh Kills.

d. Little Fresh Kills Siphon—From north bank, southwest under Little Fresh Kills to Lake's Island.

e. From south end of Little Fresh Kills Siphon, southwest to Lake's Island Purification Works, on shore of Arthur Kill.

f. Outfall Section from Purification Works—From Lake's Island Purification Works west to 21 feet of water in Arthur Kill, 800 feet off shore.

Division I—

Interceptor IX.:

a. From junction of Trunks 82 and 83, west along Old Place Creek to junction with Trunk 84, near Old Place road.

b. From junction with Trunk 84, southwest to Bloomfield Purification Works, on shore of Arthur Kill, north of Prall's Island.

c. Outfall Section from Bloomfield Purification Works—From Bloomfield Purification Works west to 21 feet of water in Arthur Kill, 750 feet off shore.

The total length, total fall, in each section, elevation of invert at upper end, tributary area, slopes, maximum diameter, maximum discharge and discharges at .8 and .2 full for each section of these nine interceptors are summarized below:

Design of Interceptors.

Section.	Length, Feet.	Total Fall, Feet.	Elevation of Invert, Upper End.	Tributary Area, Acres.	Slope 1 Foot in	Maximum Diameter, Feet.	Maximum Discharge, Feet.	Sewer 0.8 Full. Velocity, Sec., Ft.	Sewer 0.8 Full. Discharge, Sec., Ft.	Sewer 0.2 Full. Velocity, Sec., Ft.	Sewer 0.2 Full. Discharge, Sec., Ft.
A-B—											
I.											
a	5,280	4.40	29.49	4,335	1,200	4.33	44.34	3.45	44.34	1.80	3.84
b	7,390	5.68	25.09	4,938	1,300	4.67	50.51	3.45	50.51	1.80	4.39
c	2,110	1.46	19.41	5,349	1,450	4.83	54.71	3.45	54.71	1.80	4.75
d	1,450	0.97	17.95	5,626	1,500	5.00	57.55	3.45	57.55	1.80	5.00
e	5,670	3.78	16.98	5,734	1,500	5.17	58.65	3.45	58.65	1.80	5.09
f	6,600	4.40	13.20	5,829	1,500	5.17	59.62	3.45	59.62	1.80	5.18
g	4,490	2.56	8.80	7,149	1,750	5.67	73.12	3.45	73.12	1.80	6.35
h	3,170	1.76	6.24	7,602	1,800	5.83	77.75	3.45	77.75	1.80	6.74
i	920	0.48	4.48	8,013	1,900	6.00	81.95	3.45	81.95	1.80	7.12
j	Outfall section.										
C-D—											
II.											
a	4,360	7.27	41.17	1,380	600	2.50	14.12	3.45	14.12	1.80	1.23
b	3,300	5.28	33.90	1,595	625	2.67	16.32	3.45	16.32	1.80	1.42
c	5,410	7.22	28.62	2,003	750	3.00	20.49	3.45	20.49	1.80	1.78
d	Richmond Creek siphon.										
III.											
a	3,160	7.04	41.59	526	450	1.67	5.38	2.88	5.38	1.50	0.47
b	4,220	7.03	34.55	683	600	2.00	6.99	2.88	6.99	1.50	0.61
c	Eltingville road siphon.										
d	2,380	1.77	27.32	2,412	1,350	3.67	24.68	2.88	24.68	1.50	2.14
e	6,200	4.14	25.55	2,817	1,500	4.00	28.82	2.88	28.82	1.50	2.50
f	1,060	0.71	21.41	2,924	1,500	4.00	29.91	2.99	29.91	1.56	2.60

Section.	Length, Feet.	Total Fall, Feet.	Elevation of Invert, Upper End.	Tributary Area, Acres.	Slope 1 Foot in	Maximum Diameter, Feet.	Maximum Discharge, Feet.	Sewer 0.8 Full. Velocity, Sec., Ft.	Sewer 0.8 Full. Discharge, Sec., Ft.	Sewer 0.2 Full. Velocity, Sec., Ft.	Sewer 0.2 Full. Discharge, Sec., Ft.
C-D—											
IV.											
a	1,720	1.15	20.70	6,000	1,500	5.17	61.38	3.45	61.38	1.80	5.32
b	4,620	2.98	19.55	6,180	1,550	5.25	63.22	3.45	63.22	1.80	5.49
c	4,620	2.72	16.57	6,724	1,700	5.50	68.79	3.45	68.79	1.80	5.97
d	3,700	2.06	13.85	7,513	1,800	5.83	76.87	3.45	76.87	1.80	6.66
e	2,900	1.57	11.79	7,611	1,850	5.83	77.87	3.45	77.87	1.80	6.75
f	260	0.14	10.22	7,682	1,850	6.00	78.60	3.45	78.60	1.80	6.82
g	1,060	0.51	10.08	9,504	2,100	6.50	97.24	3.45	97.24	1.80	8.45
h	4,480	2.04	9.57	9,902	2,200	6.67	101.31	3.45	101.31	1.80	8.80
i	3,960	1.80	7.53	10,203	2,200	6.75	104.39	3.45	104.39	1.80	9.05
j	2,110	0.88	5.73	10,441	2,400	6.83	106.82	3.45	106.82	1.80	9.25
k	790	0.35	4.85	10,574	2,400	6.83	108.18	3.45	108.18	1.80	9.39
l	Outfall section.										
E—											
F—											
V.											
a	2,240	6.40	8.14	782	350	2.00	8.00	3.45	8.00	1.80	0.69
b	5,410	9.85	1.74	1,280	550	2.50	13.09	3.45	13.09	1.80	1.13
c	1,320	1.89	—8.11	1,975	700	3.00	20.20	3.45	20.20	1.80	1.75
d	Outfall section.										
G—											
VI.											
a	Kreischerville force main.										
b	6,200	10.30	0.77	1,382	600	2.50	14.14	3.45	14.14	1.80	1.22
c	Mill Creek siphon.										
d	Mill Creek force main.										
e	3,700	24.68	28.68	2,624	150	2.50	26.84	6.68	26.84	3.48	2.34
f	Outfall section.										
H—											
VII.											
a	Richmond Creek force main.										
b	5,150	8.58	2.36	745	600	2.00	7.62	2.88	7.62	1.50	0.66

c	2,640	3.11	—6.22	1,255	850	2.67	12.83	2.88	12.83	1.50	1.11
d	Fresh Kills siphon.										
e	1,580	2.26	—9.74	2,010	700	3.00	20.55	3.45	20.55	1.80	1.78
VIII.											
a	5,540	6.16	—3.84	1,349	900	2.75	13.80	2.88	13.80	1.50	1.20
b	Little Fresh Kills force main.										
c	1,980	2.20	—7.37	2,832	900	3.50	28.97	3.45	28.97	1.80	2.51
d	Little Fresh Kills siphon.										
e	1,720	1.91	—10.09	2,832	900	3.50	28.97	3.45	28.97	1.80	2.51
f	Outfall section.										
I—											
IX.											
a	2,640	2.93	—4.81	1,423	900	2.75	14.56	2.88	14.56	1.50	1.26
b	5,540	4.26	—7.74	2,268	1,300	3.50	23.20	2.88	23.20	1.50	2.01
c	Outfall section.										

Pumping Stations and Force Mains.

These plans contemplate the establishment of eleven pumping stations, the ultimate maximum capacity and the approximate locations of which are tabulated below. The capacities given are net horse-power without reference to efficiency and refer to total lift between pump well level and elevation of upper flow-line or ordinary maximum high tide as the case may be and include estimated loss of head in force-mains.

Table of Pumping Stations.

Designation.	Serving.	Discharge, Sec., Ft.	Lift, Feet.	Power Developed, H. P.
Van Pelt avenue relay.	Trunk No. 1..................	3.44	5.82	2.40
Sea View avenue.....	Sea View avenue force main...	18.64	27.56	58.30
Great Kills	Outfall E	20.39	16.17	37.40
Seguine's Point.......	Outfall F	34.14	13.54	52.50
Red Bank	Outfall G, low level lift.......	12.25	14.13	22.30
Mill Creek	Mill Creek force main........	26.84	42.16	128.90
Kreischerville	Kreischerville force main......	12.11	16.48	22.65
Lake's Island	Lake's Island purification works	50.75	16.61	95.90
Richmond Creek	Richmond Creek force main...	6.73	17.70	13.53
Fresh Kills	Fresh Kills force main........	19.61	6.79	15.13
Bloomfield	Bloomfield purification works..	40.13	16.66	76.00
Total power required				525.01

There will be six force-mains in the ultimate development of this plan, the essential details of which are tabulated below:

Table of Force-Mains.

Designation	Length Feet	Max. Disch. Sec. Ft.	Vel. Ft. Per Sec.	Diam. Feet	Elev. Pump Well	*Lift Feet	Power Required H. P.
Columbia St., Trunk 1-2-3	2,240	18.01	2.55	3.0	—12.00	45.87	93.85
Sea View Ave., Trunk 40-41-42	5,280	18.64	2.64	3.0	—10.00	27.56	58.30
Kreischerville, Intercept. VI. a.........	2,640	12.11	2.84	2.33	—12.00	16.48	22.65
Mill Creek, Intercept. VI. d	3,560	26.84	2.79	3.5	—10.00	42.16	128.90
Richmond Creek, Intercept. VII. a......	2,100	6.73	3.09	1.67	—10.00	17.70	13.53
Fresh Kills, Intercept. VIII. b	3,040	19.61	2.77	3.0	—10.00	6.79	15.13

* Note—The lift as given includes the loss of head in the pipe.

Siphons.

Five inverted siphons will be required located as follows:

Richmond Creek Siphon (Interceptor II., section d)—From junction Trunk 22-23, east under Richmond Creek to Interceptors III. and IV.

Eltingville Road Siphon (Interceptor III., section c)—From junction with Trunk 27-28, east under stream to Trunk 29-30.

Mill Creek Siphon (Interceptor VI., section c)—From junction of Trunks 62 and 63, south under Mill Creek, to Mill Creek Pumping Station, on south bank of creek.

Fresh Kills Siphon (Interceptor VII., section d)—From junction with Trunk 74, on east bank, west under Fresh Kills to Lake's Island.

Little Fresh Kills Siphon (Interceptor VIII., section d)—From north bank, southwest under Little Fresh Kills to Lake's Island.

The essential details of these siphons are tabulated below:

Table of Siphons.

Designation.	Location.	Length, Feet.	Diameter, Feet.	Maximum Discharge.	Velocity, Feet, Per Second.	Loss of Head, Feet.
Richmond Creek Interceptor II. (d)...	Under Richmond Creek	920	3.5	31.47	3.27	0.70
Eltingville road Interceptor III. (c).....	Near Eltingville road..	260	3.0	18.00	2.55	0.20
Mill Creek Interceptor VI. (c)...........	Under Mill Creek.....	530	3.0	21.89	3.10	0.47
Fresh Kills Interceptor VII. (d)........	Under Fresh Kills....	530	3.0	20.55	2.90	0.41
Little Fresh Kills Interceptor VIII. (d).	Under Little Fresh Kills	790	3.5	28.97	3.01	0.52

Points of Discharge, Pollution of Waters, and Purification Necessary.

The seven outfall sewers have been described as the last section in each case of the seven interceptors. Their location is more definitely shown upon the accompanying map. The question of the effect of these discharges upon the surrounding waters and of the purification necessary for the prevention of nuisance, is discussed fully in our general report upon the pollution of the waters of New York Harbor and the purification of sewage entering these waters. For the reasons more fully discussed in that report, no purification is thought necessary for Outfalls A-B, C-D, E-F and G. Outfalls H and I both discharge into the Arthur Kill. Owing to the comparatively poor tidal circulation available at these points, the small volume of water in which the discharge takes place, and the relatively large amount of pollution at present existing in these waters, it is recommended that a partial purification of the sewage from both of these outfalls be undertaken. A process of short-time sedimentation and of forced aeration similar to that employed by us in our Brooklyn experiments will probably be found satisfactory and sufficient.

The further details of the design of these outfall sewers which was omitted from the table of interceptors is summarized below:

Table of Outfalls.

Number.	Maximum Discharge, Sec., Ft.	Discharge, Gallons, Per 24 Hours.	Discharge by.	Diameter, Feet.	Length, Feet.	Distance Off Shore, Feet.	Depth Discharge, Feet.
A-B	81.95	40,594,824	Gravity	2–4	600	600	50
C-D	108.18	53,586,000	Gravity	3–4	3,500	3,500	50
E	20.39	10,099,300	Force main	3.0	6,200	5,000	12
F	34.14	16,910,856	Force main	4.0	1,580	800	21
G	39.09	19,362,888	Gravity	4.0	1,720	1,600	21
H	50.75	25,139,376	Gravity	4.5	1,060	800	21
I	40.13	19,878,912	Gravity	4.0	1,060	750	21

Very respectfully,

W. M. Black,
Earle B. Phelps.

New York, February 15, 1911.

Oversized
Foldout

SPECIAL REPORT

ON THE

Oxygen Content of Sea Water as a Standard for Measuring Sewage Pollution

SUBMITTED TO THE

BOARD OF ESTIMATE AND APPORTIONMENT

JULY 1, 1910

Board of Estimate and Apportionment,
City of New York,
June 27, 1910.

Hon. William J. Gaynor, *Mayor,*
Chairman of the Board of Estimate and Apportionment:

Sir—Colonel William M. Black, who is making an investigation of the location of sewer outlets and of the disposal of sewage for the Board of Estimate and Apportionment, and Professor Phelps, who is associated with him in this work, have handed me a report dated June 7, in which they point out the important bearing which the amount of unpolluted water daily entering the harbor of New York has upon the sewerage problem, and the lack of definite information upon this subject.

There is no question but that the starting point of any investigation designed to offer a solution of this problem must be a determination of the capacity of the harbor to take care of the sewage discharged into it without permitting the water to become so polluted as to be offensive. While some data has been collected by the United States Coast and Geodetic Survey and by the New York Bay Pollution Commission, the information is very meagre. The report of the Metropolitan Sewerage Commission has not been published, but I understand that this Commission has not secured sufficient information along these lines to lead to a definite conclusion. This would seem to be an excellent line of investigation for this Commission to follow, and I would recommend that the report of Colonel Black and Professor Phelps be sent to the Metropolitan Sewerage Commission, with the request that the Commission follow the lines of investigation suggested in the report and furnish the Board with such information as it can secure.

Respectfully,

Nelson P. Lewis,
Chief Engineer.

NEW YORK CITY, June 7, 1910.

MR. NELSON P. LEWIS
Chief Engineer, Board of Estimate and Apportionment,
No. 277 Broadway, New York, N. Y.:

DEAR SIR—The question of the proper disposal of the sewage of New York embraces many problems interesting from an engineering and an economic standpoint. For the present and probably for many years to come water carriage is and will be the most economical method of conveying sewage from the points of production to common points of disposal. To-day, the sewage is discharged at many points into the waters bordering the city. These waters form the harbor of New York and are the source of its greatness and even of its life. Their preservation in a condition fit for commerce is essential and no expenditures necessary to that end can be considered too great. The practical business sense of the American citizen only requires that he be convinced of the necessity for a given work in order to induce him to provide the means for its execution.

To-day the condition of purity of these waters is a subject of controversy. Some eminent engineers declare that their capacity for receiving and disposing of sewage is so great as to suffice not only for the needs of the population now found in the drainage area, but also for the probable increase of that population during many years. Others, professing equal technical knowledge, claim that the waters are now overtaxed and that an inadmissible and dangerous degree of pollution already exists. The former cite in support of their opinions analyses of water taken from portions of the harbor which show practically a normal degree of purity. The latter show analyses of specimens taken from other parts which show septic conditions. Both are honest in their professions, but with the system now in use by which sewage is discharged without an attempt at general distribution and without regard to the volume of flow or the circulation of the water in the vicinity of the outlets, it is natural that different localities should show to-day entirely different conditions, and that it is only necessary to make a judicious choice of locality in order to obtain an apparently irrefutable argument in support of either side of the controversy.

In so far as known, no attempt has been made as yet to consider the subject as a whole and to determine whether the capacity of the entire body of water is adequate to the task of receiving and purifying continuously the sewage of the drainage area tributary to these waters.

It is evident that if the capacity be adequate, the problem resolves itself into a question of proper distribution, so that no part of this natural purification machine shall be overloaded. If it be insufficient for the work, then the load must be reduced by purifying all of the sewage partially, or by purifying a portion to a higher degree. It is quite conceivable that with improper distribution a part of the machine of limited capacity, such as Gowanus Basin, Newtown Creek or the Harlem River might be overloaded and break down, as evidenced by septic conditions, while another part does little or no work. It is further evident that with proper distribution, purification of a part to the necessary degree can be limited to and carried on at points where the physical conditions are such as to permit the work to be done with the greatest economy, thus making it possible for the sewage from other localities, under conditions less advantageous for this class of work, to be discharged safely without treatment.

It is economically unwise not to take the fullest advantage consistent with safety of the great purification machine provided by nature. To do this to the best advantage, the question should be treated from the standpoint of the interests and requirements of the population of the entire drainage area, irrespective of the artificial political boundary lines. If legal conditions make this impossible for the present, then minimum subdivision should be made by the corporate limits.

In other words, if the supply of oxygen provided daily to the waters of New York Harbor is sufficient to reduce a portion of the dose of sewage daily discharged into them without causing an undue reduction of their contained oxygen (and the consequent production of conditions of pollution), it is evident that artificial purification is required only for the remainder of the sewage, and that the purification of this excess volume can then be carried on to the extent required at those points of discharge where that work can be done most economically and advantageously to the entire community. It would then follow that, in certain districts of the city, sewage could be discharged with proper distribution into the waters without treatment, because of the treatment given elsewhere to other portions of the total daily discharge, and that the cost of the treatment wherever made should be borne by all citizens benefited, that is, by the inhabitants of all districts discharging sewage into the harbor waters. When this general treatment is made, it should not be a borough, or a ward, or a district question. Only by broad general treatment can the best and most economical results be obtained.

The ultimate disposal of sewage, the resolution into its primary elements, like that of all organic waste products, is reached by oxidation. This is true, whether the resolution take place in the air, under the earth or in the water. Water in its normal condition contains in solution a certain quantity of oxygen. About 30 per cent. of this dissolved oxygen can be removed without practical detriment to the limpidity of the water, or to its ability to support major fish life. When an unstable organic substance is discharged into water, oxidation begins at once and continues until the resolution of the substance into its elements has been made. During this process the water parts with its dissolved oxygen. If the circulation of the water be sufficient to divide the loss through a sufficient volume, no harm results, and the water gradually regains its normal oxygen contents from the atmosphere. Should the loss of oxygen be greater than 50 per cent., the water becomes offensive and major fish life disappears. Septic conditions are reached when the oxygen has been exhausted. In these conditions none but the lowest forms of life are possible and offensive gases are evolved.

As stated, the normal supply of dissolved oxygen is restored to exhausted water from the atmosphere. This process is slow in quiet waters. In streams, especially when the flow is swift, and where natural or artificial waterfalls exist, it is more rapid. For example, in 1900, the late Prof. Palmer found that the water of the Chicago Drainage Canal, above the Bear Trap Dam, at Lockport, Ill, contained 5.9 per cent. of dissolved oxygen, while 200 yards below the dam the aeration produced at the dam had increased the proportion of dissolved oxygen to 70 per cent. of saturation (Lederer, Treatment of Sewage).

In New York Harbor other sources than the reaeration from the atmosphere supply the greater part of the oxygen needed for the daily work of purification.

The sources of supply are as follows:

(*a*) The volume of normal sea water brought into the harbor daily by tidal action.

(*b*) The volume of fresh water discharged from streams emptying into the harbor.

(*c*) Rainfall reaching the harbor directly or from immediate surface drainage.

(*d*) A portion of the city water supplies.

(*e*) Reaeration by surface absorption of oxygen.

The data available from which to obtain a measure of the supply of normal sea water brought in by the tides are found in the publications of the United States Coast and Geodetic Survey relating to the circulation of the sea in New York Harbor. The investigations of the New York Bay Pollution Commission confirm and illustrate the conclusions reached by the United States Coast Survey measurements.

Gaugings of the flow through the Sandy Hook entrance, the Narrows and the North and East Rivers were made in 1886 and earlier years. From several sets of careful measurements made opposite 23d street, East River, Prof. Mitchell found that there was a preponderance of flow westward (south) through the East River of about 440,000,000 cubic feet per tide. This conclusion has since been questioned, but inasmuch as the doubt was raised as a result of a theoretical discussion, without further measurement, and since other direct measurements seem to show the preponderance of flow westward, the writers accept Prof. Mitchell's conclusions. At Sandy Hook the preponderant volume of flow is to the south (outward).

To determine an approximate solution of the problem of the amount of oxygen available daily in the East River, the following method is being followed by the writers:

The calculations of the United States Coast and Geodetic Survey show for an average tide the easterly flow through the East River, opposite Old Ferry Point. When this flow begins the water level is at 4.26 feet above the mean low water plane and falling. The mean velocity is given for each lunar hour. While the easterly flow continues, the tide falls from 4.26 feet above mean low water to mean low water, and then rises to 4.47 feet above mean low water. The probable effects to the east of Old Ferry Point are that at the end of the easterly flow the entire body of water in the channel east to Stepping Stone Light, plus the tidal prism of the bays at the side, to the elevation 4.47, is composed of water, more or less polluted, which had flowed out past Old Ferry Point.

When the westerly current sets in, the tide is rising, the flow is through the channel and into the bays. As the tide rises, the tidal prism of the bays is completed from the channel and the volume of water flowing back past Old Ferry Point consists of the water which had flowed out, admixed with a volume of normal sound water equal to the amount used in filling the tidal prisms of the side bays, plus the preponderance of westward over eastward flows in the East and Harlem Rivers. The volume of this normal sound water thus entering (about 1,000,000,000 cubic feet) gives the measure of the new supply of oxygen provided by one tide, and of this supply 30 per cent. can be used with safety in sewage purification. Before the tide turns again this water has been divided between the East and Harlem Rivers and has entered into its work in the harbor.

For the Sandy Hook entrance the problem is more complex. Since the preponderance of flow is southerly (outward), and since at any one flood tide the fresh sea water is carried but a limited distance into the upper bay, it would seem that, excepting in the lower bay, but a very limited admixture took place. Due, however, to a marked underrun of the northerly flow under the ebb current at the beginning of the flood and for some time before the change in current direction has occurred at the surface, the normal sea water is carried into and distributed through the upper bay and lower Hudson.

For the determination of the volumes of flow the only data available is that supplied by the United States Coast and Geodetic Survey and that obtained from the Engineer Department of the Army. In 1886 and prior years, the Coast Survey made a number of careful measurements of the flow at various sections in the Sandy Hook channels, in the Narrows, the Hudson and the East Rivers. The results were calculated and reported on by the late Prof. Henry Mitchell, whose wide experience made him a most competent investigator. The investigations were confessedly incomplete, for the problem is very complicated and difficult. A lack of funds has prevented their continuation. Other calculations based on the observations then made and on a theoretical discussion have since been made by Dr. Harris of the Coast and Geodetic Survey. Dr. Harris' conclusions as to the relative volumes of flow north and south through the East River differ from those of Prof. Mitchell, in that Dr. Harris believes that the preponderance of southerly flow is much less than that found by Prof. Mitchell. Dr. Harris' discussion assumes that the velocities of the tidal currents follow strictly the laws of variation through a section as do river current velocities. This assumption is not believed to be fully supported by the scanty records of observations available—and the writers believe that Prof. Mitchell's conclusions are probably more nearly correct. The records of surface velocities published in the Atlantic Coast tide tables, as well as the float observations made by the New York Bay Pollution Commission, in so far as reported, would seem to support this opinion. The question is so important to New York City that it is hoped that provision will be made for further study.

The investigations of the Engineer Department give the only data for the tidal conditions in the Harlem River. From them it would appear that there is a resultant flow in the Harlem toward the Hudson. The Department is now making a further study of the question in connection with work contemplated for Hell Gate and its neighboring channels, Little Hell Gate and the Bronx Kills, and more data will soon be available. New sets of observations and measurements are needed near Old Ferry Point, at the extremities of the Harlem River, in the East River, south of Hell

Gate, near the Battery, and in Buttermilk Channel, at the Narrows and in the Sandy Hook Bar Channels—sufficient to determine with greater accuracy the daily supply to and distribution in the harbor of the normal sea water.

The volume of fresh water discharge of the streams into the harbor is known approximately. Since the greater part of these streams must care for the sewage from a population along their basins, little or no help for the harbor can be expected from them. Care must be taken that they be not polluted to such a degree as to add to the work which the harbor waters properly may be expected to perform. To-day the Passaic flow is probably distinctly detrimental. If care be not taken that of the Hudson may soon be in the same condition. Newtown Creek and Gowanus Basin are notoriously septic and add to the harbor's burdens. Recent analyses of the Harlem waters show conditions at times nearly as bad. It is safe to say that the Passaic, Newtown Creek, Gowanus Basin and the Harlem are overloaded.

The oxygen supply from the rainfall can be calculated approximately. In a very large part of the drainage area the run off is collected in the sewers and this, with the excess of the drinking water supply, is available for useful work, excepting when the detention in the sewers is long enough to produce septic conditions and a waste of oxygen before discharge. These conditions undoubtedly exist in many of the older and badly designed sewers. In the City of Washington, for example, the character of the sewage effluent, collected at the disposal pumping station, is to-day remarkably fresh, due to the fact that in recent years, the older sewers of that city have been reconstructed and no long detention of sewage in them now exists. The contrast between the character of the Washington sewage and that of Boston, for example, is marked. In New York, the length of the sewers is generally short, and there is little or no reason why the time elapsing between collection and discharge should not be short. If it were, the work of the harbor waters would be diminished.

For convenience, what may be termed normal American sewage is assumed to be of a dilution equal to a consumption of 100 gallons of water per day per inhabitant. The absolute composition of sewage must vary for each locality and with the changing seasons, depending on the conditions of living, the proportion of manufacturing establishments per inhabitant, and other causes. But in the larger cities there is a degree of similarity in composition and, therefore, that what is termed normal American sewage, as described by Profs. Winslow and Phelps, can be taken as representative, for calculation, in the absence of exact information. It is evident that when water consumption is at the rate of more than 100 gallons per day per inhabitant, and when the rainfall is collected in the sewers the dilution is greater, and by that dilution is supplied oxygen which is available for sewage resolution. In New York to-day data is lacking. There is no record attainable of water consumption by districts; no record of the volume of sewer discharge, either per sewer outlet or per drainage area; no record of average sewage composition and little from which the population per drainage area can be computed. Such data is required for a satisfactory discussion of the problem of sewage disposal.

The determination of the supply of dissolved oxygen obtained by reaeration from the atmosphere is too difficult to admit of more than an approximation. Dr. W. E. Adeney, of England, has propounded a certain hypothesis of the rate of reaeration of harbor waters, based on a series of laboratory experiments. His work is valuable in starting investigations into this subject, but his conclusions seem erroneous.

We are now engaged in further experimentation and investigation on the same subject. At best, however, little more can be learned than the probable rate of surface absorption of oxygen by still water and its rate of diffusion to the depths below. The important effects of wind and of surface agitation by passing shipping can only be guessed. Fortunately, these effects are beneficial, and if not overestimated may be considered a valuable factor of safety. Direct observations in the harbor itself would be of much value.

It is universally admitted that the harbor must not be permitted to reach a condition of pollution which will be detrimental to human health, or which will deter shipping from using the port. The exact degree of purity to be required has never been agreed on, nor is there any uniformity of opinion to-day as to what is the general condition of the harbor as regards allowable pollution. Localities are admittedly bad and costly provisions are being taken toward improving the local conditions in at least one of these, Gowanus Basin.

It is the belief of the writers that the waters of the harbor should be maintained in such a condition as to support major fish life everywhere, and that this condition requires that in no part shall there be found less than probably about 70 per cent. of the saturation quantity of dissolved oxygen.

When the importance of the subject and the vast amount of capital involved in the proper solution of the question are considered, it would appear self-evident that ordinary business sense would require the same careful investigation into existing conditions, into the necessity for a change, and into the most economical method of attaining the desired results, as is made for proposed betterments in private business undertakings.

The writers are endeavoring to find partial solutions to the problems with the limited resources available to them. They send you this letter in the hope that further interest may be awakened in this important subject and that a presentation of the problem as it appears to them, of the methods of solution suggested, and of the difficulties encountered may lead to a further discussion and to such official action as may permit a full and careful investigation to be made and a more accurate determination of the facts to be attained.

Very respectfully,

W. M. Black,
Earle B. Phelps.

www.ingramcontent.com/pod-product-compliance
Lightning Source LLC
LaVergne TN
LVHW010604110826
845149LV00003B/762